MACROMEDIA

Flash MX 2004
Games Most Wanted

Kristian Besley
Sham Bhangal
Anthony Eden
Brad Ferguson
Brian Monnone
Keith Peters
Glen Rhodes
Steve Young

friendsof

DESIGNER TO DESIGNER™

an Apress® company

MACROMEDIA

Flash MX 2004
Games Most Wanted

Credits

	v
Glen Rhodes	3
Character Animation and Personality	Brad Ferguson	33
Friction and Collision Detection	Keith Peters	69
Gravity and Physics	Keith Peters	103
Control	Steve Young	131
Sound for Games	Brian Monnone	159
Retro Flash Gaming	Sham Bhangal	191
Racing Cars	Anthony Eden	225
Index		259

Introduction

Welcome to *Flash MX 2004 Games Most Wanted*! In this book, the latest title in our popular *Most Wanted* series, you'll find what we at friends of ED regard as the definitive selection of game design techniques using Macromedia Flash MX 2004.

Flash is the industry standard for many designers and developers for creating multimedia applications, websites, and online games, and it's now used by over 1 million professionals. With its latest exciting new releases, Flash MX 2004 and Flash MX Professional 2004, Macromedia has yet again upped the standard for integrating video, text, audio, and graphics into rich, immersive digital experiences.

Each chapter in this book covers a distinct area of online gaming, describing the design and development of a finished Flash game or application. From logic to character development, physics to control dynamics, the book delivers as many complete example games as possible and is packed full of the most wanted tips, tricks, and techniques to demonstrate exactly how to produce exciting and interactive games. This is an inspiring sample of all the very best techniques that professional Flash game designers are using today.

All of the examples in this book will work for both Flash MX 2004 and Flash MX Pro 2004, and are available for download from www.friendsofed.com.

friends of ED

For news, books, sample chapters, downloads, author interviews, and more, point your browser to www.friendsofed.com. You'll also find the bonus chapter "Online Gaming with PHP and MySQL" by Kristian Besley on the friends of ED website. Be sure to sign up for our monthly newsletter to get the latest gossip about upcoming books!

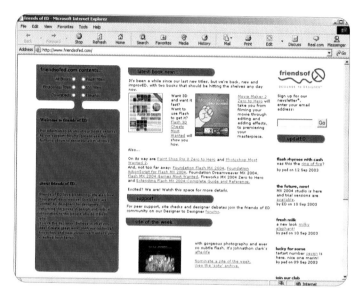

You can also visit our support forums at www.friendsofed.com/forums for help with any of the tutorials in this book or just to chat with like-minded designers and developers. Here, you'll find a variety of designers talking about all manner of tricks, tips, and techniques, and they might even provide you with ideas, insights, and inspiration.

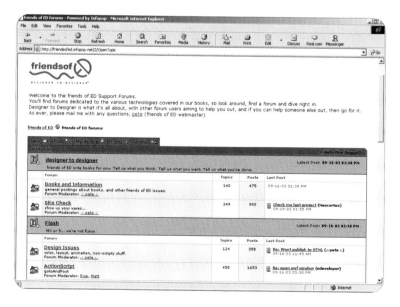

Even if you don't have problems, e-mail feedback@friendsofed.com to let us know what you think of this book—we'd love to hear from you! Whether you'd like to request future books, ask about friends of ED, or tell us about sites you've created after reading this book, drop us a line!

Styles Used in This Book

We use some simple layout conventions to make things clearer throughout the book:

■ We use this style to introduce **new terms** and this style to stress *important points* in the text.

■ We use this style for code that appears in text:

```
Blocks of code
Will appear in this style,
And we'll also use
This style to highlight new code,
Or code that deserves your attention
```

> *When we want to draw your attention to something really important, we put it in a bubble like this.*

■ File names appear in this style: HappyHappyJoyJoy.swf.

■ URLs are shown in this style: www.friendsofed.com.

■ Menu path descriptions appear like this: File ➤ Open ➤ Monkey ➤ Banana.

■ Keyboard stroke sequences are displayed in this style: *F4* and *CTRL+ALT+DEL*. Also, wherever possible and relevant, we suggest the Mac equivalents of all paths and keyboard shortcuts. For example, "Now press *CTRL/CMD+ENTER* to test your Flash movie."

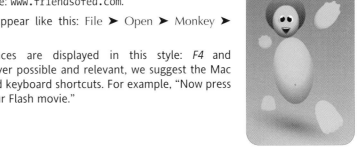

Glen Rhodes

Glen started his mind going early in life, when he was about 4 years old. At that age, he began playing the piano, which was sitting unused in his house, and he's been playing ever since. Later, in 1997, he cowrote a full-length musical called *Chrystanthia*. Somewhere along the way, Glen picked up game programming as a hobby, and he eventually ended up making games professionally for home console systems. Then, in 1998, he discovered how he could take all of his experiences and combine them when he found Flash. The rest is history. Glen shares his ideas on his website, www.glenrhodes.com.

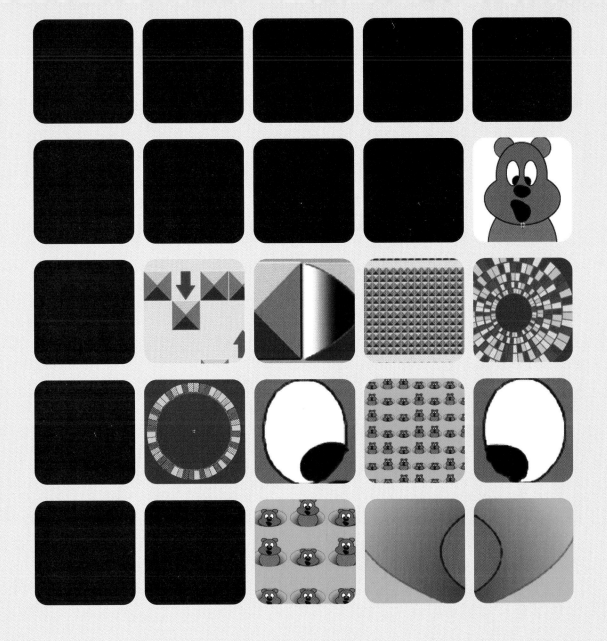

GAME LOGIC

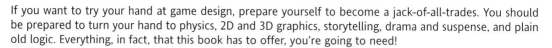

If you want to try your hand at game design, prepare yourself to become a jack-of-all-trades. You should be prepared to turn your hand to physics, 2D and 3D graphics, storytelling, drama and suspense, and plain old logic. Everything, in fact, that this book has to offer, you're going to need!

One of the key starting points in game design is *logic*. Logical rules form the basis of the decisions your program has to make. Logic comes into play at the crucial decision-making moments when the next step is decided on. Logic relies on taking external parameters and, from those, coming up with a decision for the next course of action.

Consider this real-life example. You're in an elevator, high above ground. You want to get to your car in the underground parking garage, so you press the Down button. As the descent begins, you *wait*. When the elevator stops, you check: *Is this the parking garage?* Maybe someone else is merely getting on the elevator at another floor. If this is the parking garage, you *exit* the elevator and go to your car; otherwise, you *wait*.

These rules are so important that you can actually construct complete games based on them. That's what this chapter's all about, and it's an excellent way to cut your gaming teeth. Simple rules, simply coded can make for an excellent gaming experience. Take, for example, checkers.

The rules are simple:

- You move your pieces in a diagonal fashion, always forward.
- If one of your pieces ends up diagonally adjacent to your opponent's piece, you may jump over his piece as long as your piece lands in an empty square. At this point, his piece is removed from the board.
- You may take more than one of your opponent's pieces at a time if your diagonal jumps make this possible.
- When your piece reaches the far end of the board, it is turned into a king, and it then earns the right to move diagonally forward and backward.
- The game is over when you've taken all of your opponent's pieces or he's taken all of your pieces.

Logical decisions (Has the piece gone forward? Has it gone diagonally? Has it reached the far end of the board?) form the skeleton of the game rules. By following these simple logical rules, an astronomical number of different games can be played, each fleshed out with its own unique moments of tension, excitement, and reward. Why do chess players see their game as an unequalled—even *mystical*—experience of battle-field strategy? It's just a game with uniquely refined logical rules. You can play it with ketchup bottles and pepper shakers if you like, but the logic remains devastating.

The advantage of logic is that it's relatively easy for a programmer to build, but the yield can be huge in terms of playability. These types of games rely on thought rather than speed and hand-eye coordination. The first game you're going to look at in this chapter took about 30 minutes to create (most of which was spent drawing the graphics), yet the first few times playing took us well past the 30-minute mark. That's a pretty good return!

On the other hand, other types of games, with levels, monsters, music, and storyline can take teams of people months to design, create, program, and polish. Frequently, upon completion, the programmer doesn't want to spend another minute playing it; by that point, she's usually done with it altogether!

> *It's no mistake that logical games tend to rely on a gridlike layout; it makes the decision-making process somewhat clearer. Grids tend to allow games to follow a set of rules that can be applied in two directions and also that are modular. For example, being that a checkerboard is a grid, isn't it technically possible to make the board twice the normal size with twice as many pieces? The game play rules remain the same, and it's the modularity of the grid structure that makes everything still hold soundly together.*

Mole Invasion

Let's take a look at our first example of a logic-based game. We call the game Mole Invasion. Essentially, we have an 11x8 grid on a screen of mole holes. The moles can exist in one of two states: in the hole or out of the hole. The object of the game is to get all the moles into their holes by clicking them to get them to descend.

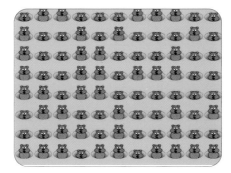

There's a catch, however. When you click a mole, all the other moles adjacent to him on the left, right, top, and bottom will toggle *their* positions. So, if you look at this group here:

and you click the middle mole, he and the mole below him will go into their holes, but the moles on top and on either side of him will pop up, like so:

With enough patience and strategy, it's possible to get all of the moles to descend into the ground. Take an advance look at the finished game, moleLogic.swf, and see how well you do!

The rules of this game are very, very simple. Looking at them logically, we can say this: If a mole is clicked, invert his position, and invert the position of the mole above him, below him, to the left of him, and to the right of him.

By *inverting position*, we simply mean *toggling* him: if he's up, he goes down, and if he's down, he goes up. It's this very simplicity that makes the game so fun and frustrating to play, and makes it so that the game takes 10 minutes to make and 20 minutes to play a round.

Making the Game

At the start of the game, the board is created and each mole is placed in a random state of up or down. This creates a virtually endless number of games as the moles and their states can lead to millions of board configurations.

1. Create a new Flash document in Macromedia Flash MX 2004. Click through Modify ➤ Document and make it 700x500 pixels and 62 frames per second (fps). If you check out the finished file (moleLogic.fla in this chapter's downloadable example files, which you can find at www.friendsofed.com), you can see there's not much to what you're going to do.

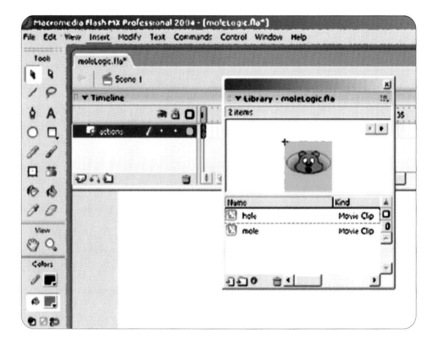

In fact, there's *nothing* on the stage at all, and all you have is one frame on a layer called actions. We'll come back to that. In the Library, there are only two movie clips, mole and hole. Let's set about creating them now.

2. Click through Insert ➤ New Symbol. Create a new movie clip and call it mole. Use your best drawing skills to do the game justice!

   Notice that we haven't included hands or feet on the mole in our movie clip, because these are never seen (being that they're always inside the hole).

   Feel the power: Whatever you put in this movie clip is going to dictate the flavor of the game. We've chosen a pesky, cute mole, which gives the finished game a pesky, cute feel. But imagine if we'd chosen to use a photograph of an unpopular political figure . . . we'd have a totally different kind of game right away! Such small decisions are important in these games.

3. When you're finished with mole, exit to the main timeline. Create another movie clip and call it hole. This clip will contain mole and its ascending/descending animation, along with the hole and the ground around the mole. Here's what you'll end up with:

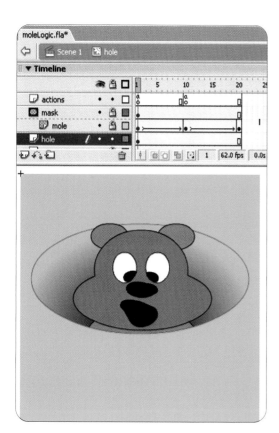

4. Rename the first layer grass, and create a flat green square, sized to 60x60 pixels. Note the registration point crosshair should be at the top left of the square, as you can see in our version.

5. Create a new layer and call it hole. Draw a nice hole on top of the green square. We've chosen a simple gradient to add a bit of depth.

6. Create a new layer and call it mole. From the Library, drag an instance of your mole movie clip onto this layer and place it as if it's down in the hole. One problem: of course it doesn't go *in* the hole—it simply hovers over it, so you'll have to apply a mask to complete the effect. Create a new layer called mask and scribble over where you want the mole to show.

   Then, right-click (or CMD+click) the mask layer and set it to Mask. You'll see what we mean!

7. Let's get the animation rolling. On the mole layer, go to frame 20 and click through Insert ➤ Timeline ➤ Keyframe. Right-click (CMD+click) the timeline and convert the mole's action into a Motion Tween. Then, click frame 10 and select Insert ➤ Timeline ➤ Keyframe. Move the mole into its raised position.

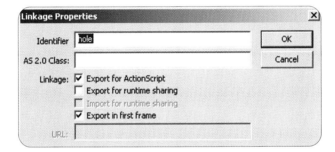

8. On frame 20 of the hole, mask, and grass layers, click through Insert ➤ Timeline ➤ Frame, just to make sure they remain visible throughout. You'll come back to this movie clip in a little while, to add a bit of code. For now, exit to the main root timeline.

9. In the Library, right-click the hole symbol. Click Linkage, set the identifier name to hole, and make sure that Export for ActionScript and Export in first frame are both selected (these will be selected by default):

10. OK, let's do some coding! Add the following code attached to frame 1 of the actions layer:

```
// grid variables to control number and spacing
COLUMNS = 11;
ROWS = 8;
TILE_X = 60;
TILE_Y = 60;
TILE_Y_OFFSET = 10;

init();

// draw molegrid
function init() {
  var moleCount = 0;
  for (var i = 0; i < COLUMNS; i++) {
    for (var j = 0; j < ROWS; j++) {
      var h = this.attachMovie("hole", ("hole_" + i + "_" + j), moleCount++);
      h._x = i * TILE_X;
```

```
        h._y = j * TILE_Y + TILE_Y_OFFSET;
        h.column = i;
        h.row = j;
        // send a random number of moles to up position
        if (Math.random() > .5) h.gotoAndPlay(10);
      }
    }
  }

  function moleClick() {
    this.play();
    this._parent["hole_" + (this.column - 1) + "_" + (this.row)].play();
    this._parent["hole_" + (this.column + 1) + "_" +(this.row)].play();
    this._parent["hole_" + (this.column) + "_" + (this.row - 1)].play();
    this._parent["hole_" + (this.column) + "_" + (this.row + 1)].play();
    delete this.onRelease;
  }
```

This code is 99% of the code you'll need for your game. What does it do? First, you set some constants to define your grid by specifying columns and rows and the spacing for each. Next, you call your initialization function, which runs through your grid and places your individual moles. In the attachMovie call, you construct the name of each instance of your hole movie clip as hole_i_j, so the upper-left instance will be called hole_0_0 and the lower-right instance will be called hole_10_7. You then set its position to be 60 times the column in _x and 60 times the row in _y (using the constants you defined up top). You're also adding an offset to _y so that the entire playing field is moved down 10 pixels—mainly to prevent the moles' heads from going offscreen at the top row. So, the columns will be 0, 60, 120, 180, 240, etc., and the rows will be 0, 60, 120, 180, 240, etc. This will create a nice clean grid of holes.

Next, you create two variables, column and row, in each movie clip. These will be used to tell each mole what his position is on the grid. Why do you do this? So that the mole knows the positions of the moles on either side of him when it comes time to adjust their state.

After this, you're using the Math.random statement to randomly set some of the moles to frame 10 of their animations:

```
    if (Math.random() > .5) h.gotoAndPlay(10);
```

Because Math.random() returns a number between 0 and 1, you test to see if the number is over .5 to have a 50% chance of setting the moles in their up position to begin. And with that, you're done with your loop and your initialization code.

After this, you see that there's a function called moleClick. What you're doing is creating a function that will be triggered whenever the mole is clicked (hence the name!). This function will soon be attached to the onRelease handler of the mole movie clip. When the mouse is pressed (and released), then you get the mole moving with the play() statement.

Following this are four lines of code that are responsible for altering the state of the four surrounding moles. You're using the column and row variables to determine the names of the adjacent mole movie clips on the parent timeline, and then you're telling those movie clips to play. This will cause all four moles to switch state because those on frame 10 (up) will play and come to frame 1 and stop, and those on frame 1 (down) will play until they reach this code on frame 10.

The last line of code in the function is where you delete the onRelease handler for the mole. It may seem strange to do this, but there is a good reason. If you're not careful, you can create a situation in which it's possible to click multiple times rapidly and get moles to change direction mid-ascent or -descent.

11. Earlier, you looked at the hole movie clip. Let's look in there again. First off, create a new layer and call it actions. In the first frame, add the following code:

```
this.onRelease = this._parent.moleClick;
stop();
```

12. Next, go to frame 10 and select Insert ➤ Timeline ➤ Keyframe. Add the same code again:

```
this.onRelease = this._parent.moleClick;
stop();
```

So here's what you're doing—you'll recall that when a mole is clicked, you delete his onRelease handler so he can't be clicked while he's animating. This is the point at which you assign that function to the onRelease handler (the function is located on the parent timeline), because reaching either frame 1 or frame 10 means that the animation is finished. If you didn't add this back, each mole could be clicked only once, which wouldn't leave much margin for error on the player's part. In the next line, you stop the timeline from playing further.

That's all the code. In fact, that's the whole game. It's very simple, yet if you run the game, you can spend a long time just trying to perfect the strategies required to get all the moles into their holes. How long will it take you?

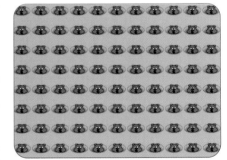

Be prepared to lose your mind while these nasty little moles go up and down, up and down. Sorry, do we sound bitter and frustrated? Let's just say we have yet to find the logical pattern that will allow us to solve this quickly—and painlessly.

Either way, you can see how easy it was to create a cool Flash game that has hours of replay value. All you need now to make the game complete are opening and game-over screens or graphics, and feedback for the user such as levels or score—all important aspects for games, but outside of our focus on games logic. There are also many ways that you could expand this game to include more variations. For example, what if every so often a mole randomly toggled his state? So, you could be just about to finish, when a mole at the other end of the board suddenly (frustratingly) pops his head up. Or, you could have the most frustrating configuration to clear, and suddenly the most awkwardly placed mole helpfully drops into the hole. Or perhaps you could have a few "freebie drops," in which you can click a mole and make him drop without making his neighbors drop. The choices are endless. . . .

Next, you're going to look at a different type of logical game, also based on a grid, that includes an enemy that follows its own logical rules, and in the process you'll create a rudimentary artificial intelligence.

Monstachase

In Monstachase, you play a character trying to escape from a room full of obstacles and one persistent monster that is after you. The floor plan is based on a grid, with open areas to move through and solid grid pieces to get in your way.

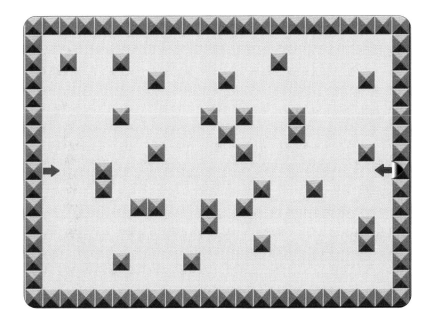

The object of the game is to get your character (the blue arrow on the left side of the screen) to the exit door on the right side of the screen without being captured by the monster (the red arrow). The control is simple: move the player left, right, up, and down with the arrow keys on your keyboard. All motion is turn based, and if you don't touch any keys, the monster stands still.

As you proceed, the monster will attempt to touch your player. If the monster succeeds in touching your player, the player is "captured" and the game starts again. Why don't you have a go at playing it before we give the game away (literally!) by getting into the logic? Open monstachase.swf from the example files.

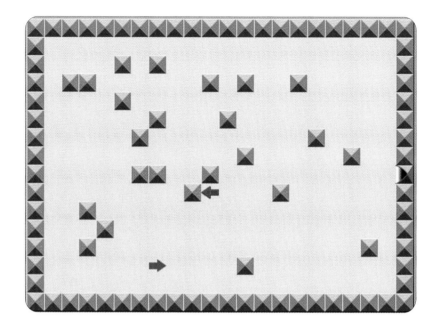

When you move your player, there are a few simple games rules that your logic tests will assess:

- You can move your player up, down, left, or right, but only *one* of those in a turn. So, you can't move the player diagonally—that would be two turns.
- Your player can't walk through a solid piece, but if you attempt to do so, that counts as a turn, and the monster will take its turn.
- When your player is on the same square as the monster, you've lost the round and your captures count will increase.
- When your player is on the same square as the exit tile, you've won the round and your escapes count will increase.

Now, every time you move your player, the monster is also given an opportunity to make one move. The monster follows a set of very simple logical rules:

1. If the monster is to the right of the player, and there's no block to the left, it will move left.

2. Otherwise, if the monster is to the left of the player, and there's no block to the right, it moves right.

3. Otherwise, if the monster is above the player, and there's no block below, it moves down.

4. Otherwise, if the monster is below the player, and there's no block above, it moves up.

The four rules are evaluated in that order, and if one rule is successfully completed, then the other rules aren't completed. In other words, the monster won't move left *and* down in the same move—it too can't move diagonally. If none of the rules is successfully completed, then the monster remains motionless—it's trapped!

This is where the logic and the strategy of playing the game comes in. You rely on trapping the monster—using its logic against it—to clear a path to the exit for your player. Trapping the monster looks something like this:

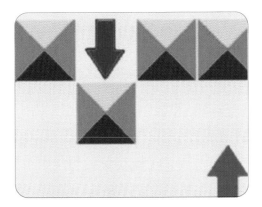

You can essentially move your player anywhere left and right as long as the player is below the monster, because the monster can't get to the player. As soon as your player goes higher than the monster, however, it will leave the nook and follow you once more. This arrangement is especially useful if it puts your player in line with the exit, like so:

Because the monster is trapped, your player is able to move straight up to the exit wall, and you can almost exit without the monster being able to move. However, when you move your player up two more times, the monster will step out of the nook because that will put your player *one* tile above it, like so:

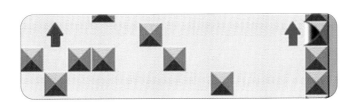

In this case, however, it's OK—with one keypress to the right, you've escaped successfully. This turn-based logic game forces you to use some strategy (and *logic*) to best get you past the enemy and to the exit.

Making the Game

Open monstachase.fla, and let's walk through the game to see what makes it tick.

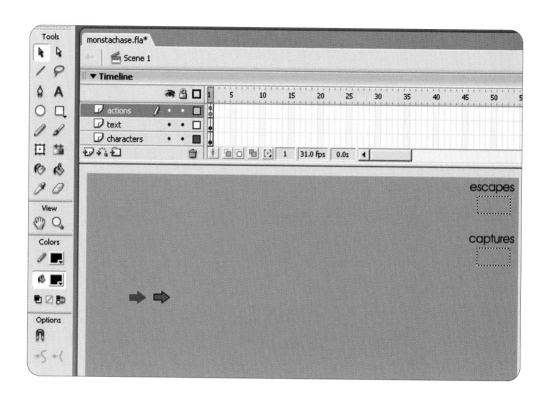

1. Start a new Flash movie with dimensions of 600x400 and a 31 fps frame rate. Name the bottom layer characters.

2. Create a new movie clip symbol and call it arrow. This clip symbol will form the basis of both the player and the monster. Draw a nice chunky-looking arrow on there, facing right. The dimensions of ours are around 22x15 pixels, with the registration point in the center. It's also bright red, which is important for step 4.

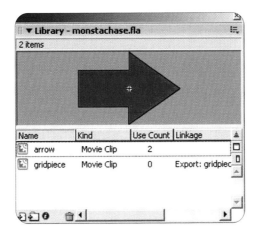

3. Back on the main timeline, drag two instances of arrow onto the stage. Name one instance player and the other instance monster.

4. You have to try and differentiate the instances, so go to the Property inspector and open the Color drop-down menu. Select Advanced and apply the following settings:

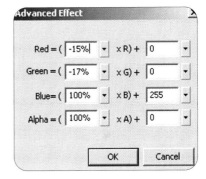

5. Next, create two text fields. Create a new layer called text. These fields are used to display the current Capture and Escape counts, and they have the instance names of escapeText and captureText, with the following settings:

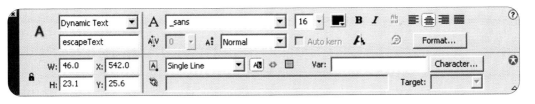

6. Finally (in terms of graphics), create one more movie clip and call it gridpiece. It should be 24x24 pixels, again with the registration point at the top left. Within this space, you should design the squares you're going to use to define your board. In actual fact, this should contain three square designs on the first three frames. On frame 1, draw the empty floor; on frame 2, draw the solid obstacle; and on frame 3, draw the exit tile. Our designs are shown here:

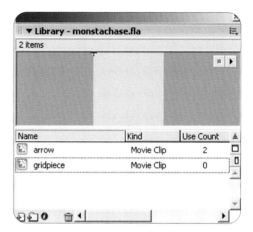

7. Now exit to the main root timeline and give gridpiece the linkage ID name gridpiece. This single tile will be duplicated many times to create your game board.

8. Create a new layer called actions. This is where the magic will take place. Type in the following code:

```
// constants for grid
ACROSS = 22;
DOWN = 16;
SQUAREWIDTH = 24;

// hold game data
gameboard = new Array();
escapes = 0;
captures = 0;
escapeText.text = escapes;
captureText.text = captures;
```

This code defines the grid dimensions, much like in the previous example, and sets up some variables you'll use in your game. This grid is 22x16 because the pieces are smaller and you can fit more onscreen. gameboard is an array you'll use to store the values of the tiles in your game board. You'll look at it more in a moment. Finally, you set your escape and capture counts to 0, and then place these two values in the escapeText and captureText text fields.

9. Now it's time to define a function called makeboard, which is responsible for creating a new board and repositioning the player and monster in their starting positions. Be assured that though this function looks long, it's really very simple:

```
function makeBoard() {
  var gridCount = 0;
  for (var i = 0; i < ACROSS; i++) {
   // two-dimensional array for two-dimensional grid
    gameboard[i] = new Array();
    for (var j = 0; j < DOWN; j++) {
      // set each gridpiece initially to 0
      gameboard[i][j] = 0;
      var s = this.attachMovie("gridpiece", "sq_" + i + "_" + j, gridCount++);
      s._x = i * SQUAREWIDTH;
      s._y = j * SQUAREWIDTH;
```

```
      // walls
      if (i == 0 | j == 0 || i == (ACROSS - 1) || j == (DOWN - 1)) {
        gameboard[i][j] = 1;
      }
      // random blocks in the center
      if (i > 1 && i < (ACROSS - 2) && j > 1 && j < (DOWN - 2)) {
        gameboard[i][j] = (Math.random() < .125);
      }
      // the exit
      if (i == (ACROSS - 1) && j == Math.floor(DOWN/2)) {
        gameboard[i][j] = 2;
      }
      s.gotoAndStop(gameboard[i][j] + 1);
    }
  }

  player.swapDepths(gridCount++);
  monster.swapDepths(gridCount);

  player.x = 1; // left of grid
  player.y = Math.floor(DOWN/2); // vertical center
  player._rotation = 0;
  player._x = player.x * SQUAREWIDTH + SQUAREWIDTH/2;
  player._y = player.y * SQUAREWIDTH + SQUAREWIDTH/2;

  monster.x = ACROSS - 2; // right of grid
  monster.y = Math.floor(DOWN/2); // vertical center
  monster._rotation = 180;
  monster._x = monster.x * SQUAREWIDTH + SQUAREWIDTH/2;
  monster._y = monster.y * SQUAREWIDTH + SQUAREWIDTH/2;
}
```

Just as in the previous example, you're creating a grid of ACROSS x DOWN pieces onscreen. Earlier you created an array called gameboard. Now you're taking that array and at each index creating another array, like so:

```
gameboard[i] = new Array();
```

This is how you create a two-dimensional array, which is merely an array or arrays stored within another, larger array. You see, an array by itself is a linear (or one-dimensional) list of information. This doesn't serve you too well for a two-dimensional construct such as your grid (with both x and y dimensions). To store information in two dimensions, you take a single array, such as gameboard, and in each index of gameboard you store *another* array. Now gameboard[0] can hold a list of information, as can gameboard[1], gameboard[2], and so on. In this way, you store your information for the game board in two dimensions.

Next, you create instances of the gridpiece movie clip:

```
// set each gridpiece initially to 0
gameboard[i][j] = 0;
var s = this.attachMovie("gridpiece", "sq_" + i + "_" + j, XgridCount++);
s._x = i * SQUAREWIDTH;
s._y = j * SQUAREWIDTH;
```

Before you do anything, you set the corresponding index in gameboard for your gridpiece to 0. You do this because each point in your grid, by default, needs an initial value of 0, which will represent an "open" area of your game board. In Flash MX, you didn't need to assign this value, because an undefined value (one not assigned) would evaluate to 0. It doesn't work that way in MX 2004, though, so you need to explicitly set that value. As for the movie clip itself, each new instance is called sq_i_j, where i and j are going to be the row and column (sq_0_0 to sq_21_15), and they're being placed at 24-pixel intervals, which is the value of your SQUAREWIDTH constant.

Now, these movie clips are purely for visual reference, because the state of the grid is going to be held in the game-board array. Remember that in the previous example it was the frame number of the moles' movie clips that determined the status of the game. In Monstachase, you're going to draw the board and then forget about it.

After the piece has been positioned, you have several if statements that are responsible for deciding which tiles will be solid and which will be open floor. The first if statement is responsible for drawing the solid border around the outside of the board:

```
if (i == 0 | j == 0 || i == (ACROSS - 1) || j == (DOWN - 1))
    gameboard[i][j] = 1;
```

As you're stepping through your loops, you're looking at the row and the column. If i is zero, then you're looking at a piece of the left edge; if j is zero, then you're looking at a piece of the top edge. Conversely, if i is equal to ACROSS - 1 or j is equal to DOWN - 1 (minus 1 because arrays start counting at 0, so the game board holds values from 0 to 21 for columns and from 0 to 15 for rows), then you're looking at the right and bottom edges, respectively. In all of these cases, you're going to be setting gameboard[i][j] to 1, which means solid.

The next if statement checks to make sure that this particular piece in your loop exists within the range that is two squares from each edge. You don't want to touch the outer edge because you don't want to destroy the outer wall, but you also don't want to touch the ring inside the outer edge (the next tile inward) because you want at least to have a clear track along which the player can run.

Because boards are randomly created, it would theoretically be possible for your computer to make a board that has blocked exits. By making sure you don't place any obstacles on this inside track, you keep at least one clear path to the exit. Here, for example, would be the worst-case scenario:

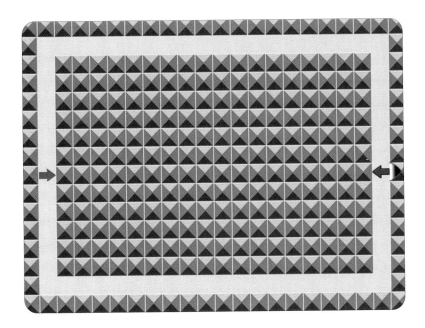

Notice the nice untouched inner ring. At least you have a path. This board would be very difficult to have occur naturally and would be a statistical anomaly (but still possible, because the boards are random).

Once you've determined that the piece you're contemplating in your loop is within this game-play region, then you run a simple random statement to decide what to place:

```
gameboard[i][j] = (Math.random() < .125);
```

If the random number generated by Math.random() (which will produce a number between 0 and 1) is less than .125, then the statement will evaluate to TRUE or 1. If the number is greater than .125, then the statement will evaluate to FALSE or 0. This means that one out of every eight times (on average), this statement will equal 1. When it does, you set gameboard[i][j] to 1 (solid); otherwise, it's set to 0 (open floor).

You have one more if statement after this:

```
if (i == (ACROSS - 1) && j == Math.floor(DOWN/2)) {
  gameboard[i][j] = 2;
}
```

This statement simply checks if you're at a specific tile in your loop, which is the right edge, vertical center. If you're at this point, then this is where you'd like to place your exit, so you set gameboard to 2.

So far, you've been filling up gameboard with numbers. What do you do with them? Well, you're going to use them for collision detection later, but for now you're going to use them to set the frame of the grid piece from the gridpiece movie clip.

```
s.gotoAndStop(gameboard[i][j] + 1);
```

This will set the piece to gameboard plus 1, which will be 1, 2, or 3, which happens to correspond to the three frames in the gridpiece movie clip. Simple, huh?

After this, you're setting the player and monster's movie clips to have a depth level greater than each clip in the entire grid by using the gridCount depth counter, and then you're setting the starting positions of the player and monster. The player will be situated on the left edge, and the monster will be on the right edge, in front of the door. You're also rotating them both to face each other.

When you set the player and monster's positions, you're using variables called x and y, which are not to be confused with the movie clip properties _x and _y. In movie clips, x and y refer to tile positions. Once the tile positions have been set, you can translate them to screen positions like this:

```
player._x = player.x * SQUAREWIDTH + SQUAREWIDTH/2;
player._y = player.y * SQUAREWIDTH + SQUAREWIDTH/2;
```

You multiply x and y times 24 (SQUAREWIDTH) so they'll be lined up with the tiles, and then you add 12 (SQUAREWIDTH/2) to x and y so they'll be centered in the actual tile.

That's the entire makeboard function. Once this function is run, your entire board will be built and drawn, and the player and monster will be in position, ready to begin.

10. OK, let's move along! Next, you have a function called movePlayer, which controls the player's movements.

```
function movePlayer(code) {
  // holds current values
  this.ox = this.x;
  this.oy = this.y;
  // checks which key was pressed
  switch (code) {
    case Key.RIGHT:
      this.x++;
      this._rotation = 0;
      break;
    case Key.LEFT:
      this.x-;
      this._rotation = 180;
      break;
    case Key.DOWN:
      this.y++;
      this._rotation = 90;
      break;
```

```
      case Key.UP:
        this.y—;
        this._rotation = -90;
    }
    // if blocked by a wall...
    if (gameboard[this.x][this.y] == 1) {
      this.x = this.ox;
      this.y = this.oy;
    // else if exit is reached
    } else if (gameboard[this.x][this.y] == 2) {
      makeBoard();
      escapeText.text = ++escapes;
      return;
    }
    this._x = this.x * SQUAREWIDTH + SQUAREWIDTH/2;
    this._y = this.y * SQUAREWIDTH + SQUAREWIDTH/2;
    // moves monster if player has moved
    if (code == Key.LEFT || code == Key.RIGHT || code == Key.UP || code == Key.DOWN) {
      monster.move();
    }
  }
```

This function is going to be called every time the player presses a key (you'll capture this event using the onKeyDown handler in a moment). The first thing you do is store the player's current position in variables called ox and oy, for "old x" and "old y."

This function takes one parameter, code, which is going to be passed in by the Key object later. This corresponds simply to the code of the key that was pressed. You look at each code of Key.RIGHT, Key.LEFT, Key.UP, and Key.DOWN using a switch statement. Each case looks for the key that was pressed and performs the corresponding adjustment to the x or y value and the player's rotation.

Next, you check to see if the value of the gameboard array at the player's position is 1. If it is, you know the player has hit a solid tile, and you move the player back to the player's old position at this.ox and this.oy. If not, you check to see if the player has hit the exit. If the player did hit the exit, you call makeboard again (thus rearranging the game board, and moving the player and the monster back to their starting positions), and then you increase the number of escapes, displaying the new value onscreen. You want to exit the function at this time, so you use return to accomplish this.

After this, you set the position of the player's movie clip onscreen to this:

```
this._x = this.x * SQUAREWIDTH + SQUAREWIDTH/2;
this._y = this.y * SQUAREWIDTH + SQUAREWIDTH/2;
```

This causes the arrow to be displayed in the actual position onscreen.

You have one more line of code in the function:

```
if (code == Key.LEFT || code == Key.RIGHT || code == Key.UP || Xcode == Key.DOWN) {
monster.move();
}
```

If the player pressed an arrow key, then you call the "move" function of the monster movie clip (we'll get to that function shortly). You need to make sure that the player did indeed press an arrow key and not just any key. You don't want someone to accidentally press the space bar, for example, a key that has no bearing on the game, and yet cause the monster to move one step closer. And that's the function!

11. Next, type in the code to control the monster's movement. This is where the monster's logic comes into play. The function is called moveMonster, and it goes like this:

```
// moves monster based on player's position
function moveMonster() {
  if (this.x < player.x && !gameboard[this.x+1][this.y]) {
    this.x++;
    this._rotation = 0;
  } else if (this.x > player.x && !gameboard[this.x- 1][this.y]){
    this.x–;
    this._rotation = 180;
  } else if (this.y < player.y && X !gameboard[this.x][this.y+1]) {
    this.y++;
    this._rotation = 90;
  } else if (this.y > player.y && !gameboard[this.x][this.y- 1]){
    this.y–;
    this._rotation = -90;
  }
  // if monster reaches player
  if (this.x == player.x && this.y == player.y) {
    makeBoard();
    captureText.text = ++captures;
    return;
  }
  this._x = this.x * SQUAREWIDTH + SQUAREWIDTH/2;
  this._y = this.y * SQUAREWIDTH + SQUAREWIDTH/2;
}
```

The first four if/else if statements are where you determine the direction of motion, and it's the ActionScript version of the four basic monster logic rules from earlier. First, you see if the monster is to the left of the player, and if there's no block to its right, you move it right. Otherwise, you check to see if it's to the right of the player, and if there's no block to its left, then you move it left. This continues as described earlier.

On each move, the monster movie clip is also rotated to make it clear that the monster is traveling in that specific direction.

After this, you check to see if the monster is on the same tile as the player:

```
if (this.x == player.x && this.y == player.y) {
```

If it is, then you know that the monster has captured the player, and so you rebuild the board with makeBoard, and then increase the number of captures and display that number onscreen. That's the moveMonster code.

12. Now that you've defined your game functions, jump back to the top of the code where you declare your variables. Type the following new statements (in bold):

```
// hold game data
gameboard = new Array();
escapes = 0;
captures = 0;
escapeText.text = escapes;
captureText.text = captures;

// reference to function that moves sprites
player.move = movePlayer;
monster.move = moveMonster;
```

You're giving the player movie clip and monster movie clip the variable move, which holds the movePlayer function. That way, any references inside the movePlayer function to this are actually references to player.

13. Next, it's time to create your key listener. Add these bold lines:

```
// reference to function that moves sprites
player.move = movePlayer;
monster.move = moveMonster;

this.onKeyDown = function() {
  player.move(Key.getCode());
};
Key.addListener(this);
```

The onKeyDown handler will be called whenever a keyDown event is fired in your movie. It's here that you determine the key that was pressed with Key.getCode and pass that code to the movePlayer function via player.move. To allow your movie to hear keypresses, you add it as a listener to the Key object.

14. Finally, the last thing you do is add this code, which you can place right after your onKeyDown handler:

```
// initializes gameboard and game
makeBoard();
```

You make a call to the makeBoard function to make the game start off with a new board and put the player and monster in place. Otherwise, the game will start in a nonfunctioning state.

Improving the Game

There are many ways that you can improve the game. Of course, a few feedback screens for the user would be a welcome enhancement, as would an option for quitting. In addition, there are a number of ways you can make the game more challenging and increase the complexity of the logical flow. You could, for example, introduce another monster into the equation:

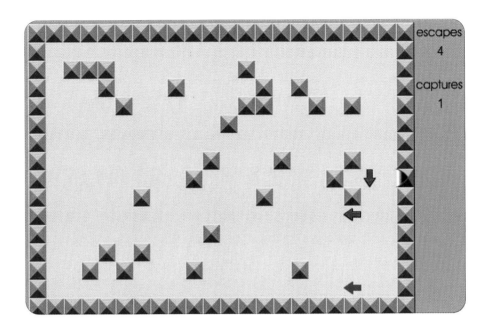

This adds a whole new dimension of challenge in that you now have to try to trap and evade two monsters instead of one. An example of this is saved in monstachase_doublePeril.fla.

Or perhaps you could try a variable level of difficulty that uses a single variable, say diff, to determine a few things:

- Number of squares on the board
- Speed at which the monsters move (perhaps they take two steps for every one of the player's?)

If you look at monstachase2.fla, you can see this in action. There are a few modifications to the code. When you begin, you set a variable called diff to 1.

```
// hold game data
gameboard = new Array();
diff = 1;
escapes = 0;
captures = 0;
escapeText.text = escapes;
captureText.text = captures;
```

Then later at your random statement, you've modified it to look like this:

```
if (i > 1 && i < (ACROSS - 2) && j > 1 && j < (DOWN - 2)) {
gameboard[i][j] = (Math.random() < .5/diff);
}
```

Rather than having a solid piece be placed at a random chance of 1 in 8 (a number between 0 and 1 that's less than .125), now you check for a number between 0 and 1 that's less than .5/diff. This means that at first each piece will have a 1 in 2 chance of being solid, then as the game progresses and you increase the diff variable, the likelihood of an interior grid piece being solid will decrease. So initially, the board will be dense, like so:

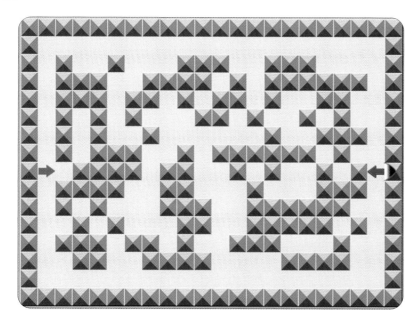

On the second level, however, things look a little sparser:

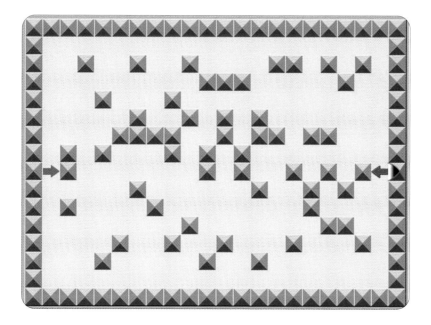

In addition, as `diff` increases, you'll allow the monster to take more moves for every one of the player's. To do this, you alter the `monster.move` call to look like this:

```
if (code == Key.LEFT || code == Key.RIGHT || code == Key.UP || Xcode == Key.DOWN) {
  for (i = 0; i < diff; i++) {
monster.move();
}
 }
```

You have the same `if` statement, but you also have a `for` loop within it that calls `monster.move`, `diff` number of times. Also, when the exit is successfully reached, you change the code slightly to look like this:

```
else if (gameboard[this.x][this.y] == 2) {
  diff++;
  makeboard();
```

Just before calling `makeboard`, you increase `diff` by one. Those are all the required changes to make a different and more interesting iteration of Monstachase (though adding another text field to display the current level would be nice, as would adding some color code to alter the color scheme of your tiles as you increase levels). There are even other ways you could make the game more interesting. Perhaps the blocks could be moveable, so it would be possible to completely block a monster in on all four sides. Or maybe some blocks could be "deadly"—rather than a block being simply an obstacle, there could be a block that acts as a hole in the ground, and if the player or monster moves over it, the player or monster would fall in and die. There are lots of options.

Ring Puzzle

We have one more logic game to cover called Ring Puzzle, which you can find in `ringpuzzle.fla`. Whereas the previous logic games were rooted in pure deduction, this logic game is based on the type of logic that revolves around geometry. In Ring Puzzle, there are five rings, four inner rings and one outer ring, like so:

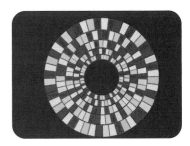

Each ring is divided into 48 segments of red, blue, green, orange, or gray. The object of the game is to make all of the *red* segments line up from inside to outside. In other words, the red segments are the same in each ring, but the other colors aren't. The color arrangement is random except for red, so it's difficult to know what lines up with what, and it takes trial and error to get it right.

Play is simple: when the game begins, the rings are randomly rotated and adjusted so that all colors are misaligned. When you click a ring and drag, the ring will rotate. When you solve a puzzle (that is, when you line up all segments of a particular color), you've won the game:

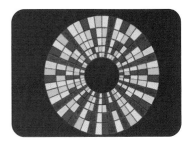

Making the Game

The design of this game is very simple. You have the five ring movie clips on the stage to start, with instance names of r0, r1, r2, r3, and r4:

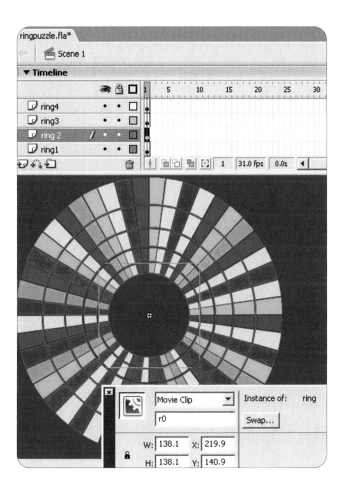

At the beginning, all the rings are rotated to an angle of 0 degrees, and they all look the same. If you look inside the movie clip, you can see how the rings are differentiated:

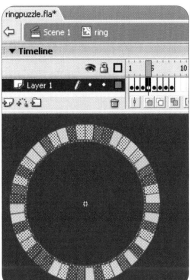

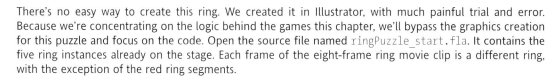

There's no easy way to create this ring. We created it in Illustrator, with much painful trial and error. Because we're concentrating on the logic behind the games this chapter, we'll bypass the graphics creation for this puzzle and focus on the code. Open the source file named ringPuzzle_start.fla. It contains the five ring instances already on the stage. Each frame of the eight-frame ring movie clip is a different ring, with the exception of the red ring segments.

1. We'll begin this tutorial with the code. Back on the main timeline, the following code is attached to frame 1 of the actions layer:

```
// total of rings in game
NUM_RINGS = 5;
// number of segments in rings
NUM_SEGMENTS = 48;
// amount out of 360 for each segment
SNAP_ANGLE = 360/NUM_SEGMENTS;
// number of frames in ring clip
NUM_FRAMES = 8;
```

As always, you declare your variables and constants at the top of your code, so you're able to make modifications easily in the future. These should all be fairly self-explanatory, and if they're not, that's what the comments are for.

2. Let's set up the rings next:

```
for (var i = 0; i < NUM_RINGS; i++) {
  var ring = this["r" + i];
  ring.onPress = startTurn;
  ring.onRelease = ring.onReleaseOutside = stopTurn;
  / random 7.5 degrees out of possible 48
  ring._rotation = Math.floor(Math.random() * NUM_SEGMENTS) * SNAP_ANGLE;
  // random frame between 1 and 8
  ring.gotoAndStop(Math.floor(Math.random() * NUM_FRAMES) + 1);
};
```

Here you run through the number of rings in the game and give them functions (which you'll write in a moment) for the press and release events. This is to allow the player to click and spin the rings during game play. You also give each ring a random rotation at the start based on your SNAP_ANGLE constant and a random frame to go to.

3. Because you've already assigned your onPress, onRelease, and onReleaseOutside handlers, you'd better write the functions. Place this code after the previous for loop:

```
function startTurn() {
  // mouse position in relation to center of clip
  var x = this._parent._xmouse - this._x;
  var y = this._parent._ymouse - this._y;
  // angle of mouse in relation to center
  this.startAngle = Math.atan2(y, x);
  this.onMouseMove = function() { turnRing.apply(this) };
}
```

```
function stopTurn() {
  delete this.onMouseMove;
  // snaps rotation to nearest 7.5 degrees
  var snap = this._rotation % SNAP_ANGLE;
  if (snap > SNAP_ANGLE/2) snap = -(SNAP_ANGLE - snap);
  this._rotation -= snap;
  // checks for end game
  checkRot();
}
```

In the startTurn function, which is called when the player first clicks a ring, you need to find out the angle at which the ring begins its turn. You do this through some basic trigonometry (well, *Flash* does this through some basic trigonometry—you just type a function name!). After determining the x and y distance from the mouse to the center of the ring clip being clicked, you can find the angle of the mouse in relation to the ring by calling Flash's Math.atan2() method. This gives you an angle in radians that you place into your startAngle variable for the ring. You then assign a function to the ring's onMouseMove handler, which will be called each time the mouse is moved until the player releases the mouse button. Inside this function, you call another function named turnRing, which you'll write in a moment. Notice that you use apply in this instance. You use this so that whenever turnRing is called, any reference to this inside the function will refer to whichever clip the function is applied to. In this way, you can apply one function to any of your rings whenever you need to.

Next, in the stopTurn function, you first get rid of the onMouseDown handler so that the ring can no longer be turned by the player. Because the end of the game will be determined by checking whether the rotation of each ring is equal, you need to ensure that you snap the rings into exact positions when they're released by the player. This is what these next few lines take care of. Using the modulo operator (%), you find the difference between the current rotation and the nearest SNAP_ANGLE. The if statement that follows just checks to see if you should add or subtract from the rotation to get to the nearest SNAP_ANGLE. For instance, if the player releases a ring with a rotation of 5, then the modulo would return 5 (5 divided by 7.5 leaves a remainder of 5). Because 5 is greater than 3.75 (SNAP_ANGLE/2), snap would be recalculated to be –2.5 (-(7.5 – 5)). This means the nearest angle to snap to would be 7.5. If the player releases the ring at 11 degrees, then snap would evaluate to –3.5, snapping the rotation to 7.5 degrees as well.

After the rotation is snapped, you call a new function called checkRot. This function will run through all of your rings to see if they have equal rotations, which will mean the player has won. You'll write that function next.

4. Add the following function after stopTurn:

```
function checkRot() {
  // runs through each ring to see if all rotations are equal
  for (var i = 0; i < NUM_RINGS - 1; i++) {
    if (this["r" + i]._rotation != this["r" + (i + 1)]._rotation) return false;
  }
  trace("complete!");
}
```

This function simply runs through each ring and tests it with the next. If at any time the rotations are not equal, you return out of the function. If, however, you make it through all of the rings, you know that the player has succeeded and you trace a "complete!" message to the output window. Of course, for a finished game you would want something more elaborate such as a success screen and an option to play again.

5. The final function you need to address is the turnRing function you assign to a ring when it's clicked. It is this function that allows for the rings to spin around at the user's behest.

```
function turnRing(axis) {
    // mouse position in relation to center of clip
    var x = this._parent._xmouse - this._x;
    var y = this._parent._ymouse - this._y;
    // angle of mouse in relation to center
    var angle = Math.atan2(y, x);
    // difference in degrees between startAngle and current angle
    var difAngle = (angle - this.startAngle) * 180/Math.PI;
    // adjust rotation to match difference
    this._rotation += difAngle;
    // new start angle equals current angle
    this.startAngle = angle;
    updateAfterEvent();
}
```

The first few lines of code are exactly the same as in your startTurn function and, if you recall, are used to determine the current angle of the mouse in relation to the ring. Using this value, you can find the difference between the current angle and the previous angle, and turn the ring accordingly. Once you've done that, you set the new startAngle to equal the mouse's current angle to start the process all over again. updateAfterEvent() is used to refresh the screen at this point.

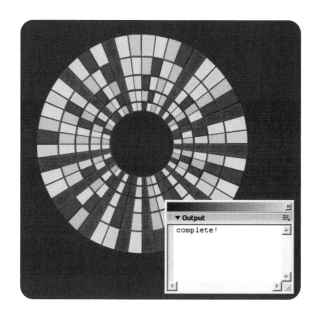

That's all there is to this game. It's very simple, but it forms the foundation for something that could be made much more complex. For example, what about making it so that instead of red always being the lining-up color, you don't *know* which color is the lining-up color? So not only do you have to line things up, but also you first have to look at the puzzle and determine which color it is that you *should* line up. That would add an extraordinary level of complexity, but it would also require some more programming to create the wheels dynamically with ActionScript rather than prebuilding all the rings in the Flash editing environment.

Or perhaps the rings could have a tendency to move or rotate on their own—the longer you go without clicking them, the more likely that they'll begin to rotate away from position. This means that you have to hurry or you'll lose your place, and that makes things confusing and difficult.

Summary

We've looked at logic in this chapter—the logic of games from the perspectives of both the programmer and the player. You've seen how very simple rules can create a game that has an endless variety of outcomes and game play. You've also seen how these simple rules can force the user to do her best to *understand* the logic and *conquer* the game. Learning how the monsters move is what allows the player to beat Monstachase—the logic is predictable, and that's part of the challenge.

You've also looked at geometric logic—where you use your eyes to play the game. Such a game has been produced in real life many times, with Rubik's Cube being an obvious example.

Logical games are probably the fastest to program, but they often require greater depth of planning and thinking. As a game designer, you might ask yourself, "How can I design this logic so that it will be smart and fun?" You don't, for example, want to create a logic system in which the game is easily beatable—a "loophole" through which the monster runs offscreen and disappears. The logic should be simple but strong, pure, and effective.

Brad Ferguson

Ever since Brad could hold a crayon, he's been fascinated with story-telling through the mediums of art and animation. He found the thought of breathing life into characters and entire worlds using a blank sheet of paper amazing. Brad feels fortunate to have extensive experience in entertaining people by communicating his ideas and concepts for a living. From his classical animation and design background he entered the realms of Flash animation, gaming, design, and television with the intent to entertain and perhaps even inspire people. He always challenges himself to create the most original, innovative, and entertaining ideas possible. Feel free to look through Brad's online portfolio at www.canvasobrad.com.

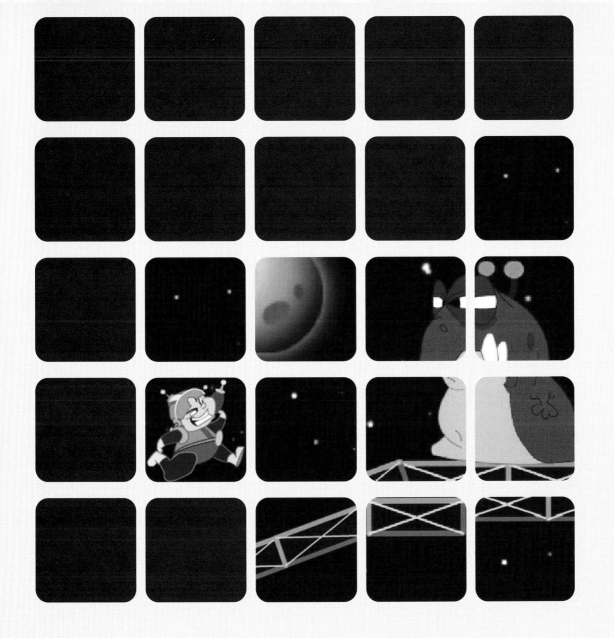

CHARACTER ANIMATION AND PERSONALITY

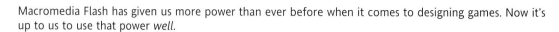

Macromedia Flash has given us more power than ever before when it comes to designing games. Now it's up to us to use that power *well*.

One largely overlooked aspect of home-game design is character animation and personality. Far too often we see well-intended ideas crumble into a heap when it comes to animation and character development.

Proper planning and development is critical to creating great projects in any line of work. This is especially true in such a visual medium. Concept and development is the evolution of an idea, whether it's a story, a character, or any type of design. It's the foundation of an appealing and strong product. It's the beautiful stage where we see our ideas take form and mold them into what they will become. If we skip this step, it will be obvious and the projects—more often than not—will fail.

In this chapter we're going to look at what it is that gives characters personality. Although we're fully aware these products of imagination are purely fictional, there's an unexplainable attachment to them. It's this phenomenon we have to tap into in the early stages of character development. We must decide which emotions we wish our characters to provoke and think deeply on how to succeed. The same questions should be asked when we're developing a story idea. Nobody will enjoy a story that doesn't mean something to him or entertain him in some way. There must be some type of connection and it's up to us to create it.

Coming from a classical animation background, I've dedicated a great deal of time to translating those methods to the world of Flash. It's our hope your characters will spring to life in your next game like never before!

We'll begin this chapter by covering some technical basics to help you explore the foundations of successful Flash animation. From there, we'll get into the guts of it—the part we affectionately call the "hands-on, creative, touchy-feely aspects of design, animation, and personality."

The Importance of Optimization

One of the fundamental aspects of creating successful Flash animation is knowing the performance limitations and how to work around them. Performance is, of course, a very important aspect of creating Flash animation for games. It's a constant balancing act—having the most beautiful animation means very little if it plays at 3 frames per second!

Some things you should avoid to help keep performance up are animated gradients, alphas, and an excessive numbers of vector points. By simplifying your graphics through reducing vector points, you make calculations easier on the computer and thus improve performance. You've got to balance maximum appeal with minimum processor power: *that's* the trick.

> *Here's a tip for you if you're serious about doing any type of computer graphics, animation, or design. We strongly recommend you make use of a Wacom tablet. It makes your graphics much more professional and controlled. The pressure-sensitive pen makes it easy to give your designs a "thick-and-thin" line quality. This is useful for roughing out your animation and designing characters almost as though they're on paper. It truly is an artist's best friend and pays for itself many times over. No matter how much practice you have, you simply won't get the same results out of a mouse. Another benefit, of course, is no more raging cases of repetitive strain injury!*

Drawing in Flash

We'll begin by taking a look at an effective process for minimizing the number of vector points in an image. This method will help keep file size down and performance up. This is the crosshair theory behind optimizing vector points.

The important factors to remember are

- ■ Every line is defined with a vector point on each end.
- ■ Every time two lines intersect, it creates yet another vector point.

Imagine a grid drawn on a single layer in Flash.

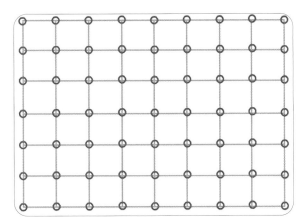

Every red circle represents a vector point. There are 63 vector points that define this image.

Now let's look at the optimized method:

1. On the first layer draw the main shape.

2. Create a second layer and draw the horizontal lines on it.

3. Create a third layer and draw the vertical lines on it.

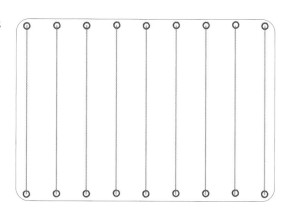

Now compare the original with your optimized version:

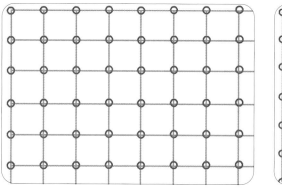
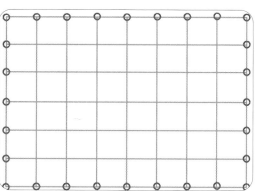

You've eliminated all intersecting lines, and in doing so, you've brought the number of vector points down from 64 to 32. Now, for the sake of organization, you can take each individual layer and convert it into a separate movie clip. Once the objects are individual movie clips, other lines won't intersect them. You can now cut and Edit ➤ Paste in place so the separate objects are now on one layer.

As foreign from drawing characters as this may seem, it's actually very relevant. A grid was used for this example for simplicity, but the same rules apply to all objects and images. You're forced to adapt your way of thinking. No longer can you create a single, flat image. You must think ahead and plan to separate. Let's get started with a character.

Drawing a Character

To begin, open a new Flash project.

1. Select the Brush tool and roughly draw a character as though you were sketching on paper. This is where the pressure-sensitive pen with the Wacom tablet proves very useful. The figure on the left is the rough sketch the way we see it. The figure on the right is how Flash sees it. Every tiny blue square is a vector point.

Note the high number of vector points in the second figure. Every point is responsible for increased file size and is an enemy of performance. If this image was in color and was animated with other objects on the screen, the results would be painful to watch.

2. Lock the first layer with the rough character by clicking the little padlock in the timeline. Create a new layer over the top of it.

Be sure the Snap to Objects tool is selected by selecting View ➤ Snapping ➤ Snap to Objects. At times, you may need to deselect this tool to draw certain curves or lines, but it's very useful for joining vector points.

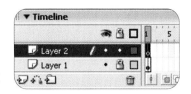

3. Select the Line tool and assign it a bright color that stands out from the rough character. This is done temporarily for clear visibility and will be changed later. Zoom in, and on layer 2 begin tracing the character with a series of straight lines.

Begin by drawing only the cranium, so other features such as the cheeks, eyes, brows, and mouth can sit on individual layers above it. You want to avoid intersecting lines—this is the crosshair theory applied to a character.

4. Select the Arrow tool and use it to join lines and bend them around the rough image.

5. Lock the layer with the new, vector-friendly cranium. Create a new layer and use the same methods to draw the cheek mass. Draw the character from back to front in this way. Continue this process until the drawing is complete. Check your progress by making the layer with the original sketch invisible from time to time.

6. Once the line drawing is complete, you should have an image that resembles the following. Notice how the image is not only traced, but also altered where it needs to look its best. Notice the foot placement, for example—it has been changed to present a stronger pose and better proportions.

Once you have your one-color character sorted out, the next thing to do is to apply the correct line colors and fills, as per your chosen style. You might want to copy our style for simplicity or move off in your own direction.

7. Delete the layer with the rough drawing on it. Select the Paint Bucket tool and color your character in.

8. Select the Arrow tool and click a line to select it. Hold down the Shift key to select multiple lines at once. Another handy trick is to double-click a line to select every line that intersects it and is the same color. Once the lines are selected, you can assign each one an appropriate color and thickness in the Property inspector.

As a general rule, it's a good idea to have the outline of a character be slightly thicker than the inside lines. Not only does this give the character a more appealing look, but it also separates the character from the background—that is, it "pops" the character forward. Of course, this rule is entirely dependant on the style of design and may not always be necessary.

After you've appropriately altered the line thickness and colors, these are the cleaned-up body parts. They aren't drawn spread out as shown; this is done only to represent the separated layers. The body on the left represents the bottom layer and shows the layer order in progression to the right.

This is what the character looks like put together. Note the insane vector point comparison between the original rough sketch and the cleaned-up version. This method also reduced the file size from 6KB in the original rough sketch to 1KB in the cleaned-up version.

So what is it that makes the file size of the original sketch so much larger? When you use the Brush tool, it isn't drawing the same, simple two-vector-point line the Line tool does. Instead of drawing the line simply from one point to another, the Brush tool draws the outer edge of the line. Basically, this means the Brush tool is drawing twice as much as the Line tool, which draws one vector point on each end. This combined with the fact that every time your hand jiggles slightly while you use the brush adds a bump to the line. Every subtle bump in the world of vectors increases the amount of information used to define it, hence the increased file size.

The Principles of Animation

The art of successful animation derives from two things: strong drawing skills and an even stronger desire to know how everything around us works. Animators are masters of motion and creative problem solvers. If we can't see a solution, we simply make one up. We're actors with pencils. We must study and under-stand performance, emotions, and physics. A successful animator sees the world around her as if it were in slow motion. Studies show this may be the reason animators are often left alone by the punch bowl at school dances. We're truly a rare breed, so enjoy it!

There are many principles that are applied when creating successful animation. We'll now explore some of the methods that help make characters and movements entertaining and believable. These techniques help bring life to animation, and as you progress, the connections between them will become more seamless. The techniques and principles we discuss in this section of the chapter are

- Keyframes
- Squash and stretch
- Timing
- Anticipation, action, reaction, and overlapping action
- Arcs
- Character animation, and character posing in particular

Keyframes

Keyframes in Flash are the equivalent of a classical animator's keys. *Keys* are the most extreme or subtle poses of movement drawn by the lead animator. Any successful animation is created with well-drawn and expressive key poses. Once the animator has created these poses and worked out the timing from key drawing to key drawing, the work is handed to the inbetweener.

The *inbetweener* is responsible for creating all the drawings between the keys to give the animation its strong timing and smooth movement. It's easy to see that animation is like one large jigsaw puzzle.

Luckily for us lazy folks, Flash assists us in skipping the inbetweening process with *motion tween*. Flash creates the in-between drawings when you tell it where and when you want the object to start and to stop (or change) by setting the keyframes. Many times, you'll have to fine-tune your motion tweens by adding more keyframes to create the movement you desire.

Squash and Stretch

Squash and stretch is what makes your characters look as though they're made of flesh. It gives a sense of softness and weight to your subject. Without squash and stretch, your characters would look very stiff, as though they were made of rock. The fundamental theory behind it is that the shape of the subject reacts to the speed and forces of movement. It's important to always keep the volumes of the object solid throughout the animation, no matter how much you may skew or distort it. You can use squash and stretch in either a subtle manner to make things appear alive or in an extreme manner to give a more exaggerated style of movement.

Timing

There are two realms of timing an animator must be conscious of: the timing of movement and the timing of performance. These are crucial elements, as they give animation its believability and appeal. The timing of movement gives animation a sense of weight and gravity.

Slowing in and *slowing out* are important aspects of believable timing. Also known as "hang time," these aspects are used to cushion the end points or high points of a movement to avoid a robotic, stiff movement. They also give an object that moment of weightlessness as it reaches the high point of an arc.

So much of performance depends on timing—just ask any stand-up comedian! The rules of performance are no different when you're dealing with animation.

You'll now create an animation that relies strongly on the principles of movement and performance timing. In this exercise, you'll animate a looped ball bouncing in place.

Open the file `ballbounce.swf` to view a final example of what you're about to create. This file is available for download from www.friendsofed.com, along with all the other examples in this book. To begin your own version, start a new Flash project and set the frame rate to 24 fps.

> *All animation for this chapter will be done at 24 fps.*

Bouncing Ball

1. Rename the existing layer Ball. Select the Oval tool. Hold down the Shift key as you make a circle. (Pressing *SHIFT* locks the tool to draw a perfect circle, rather than an oval.)

2. Select the circle (double-click it to select both stroke and fill) and press *F8* to convert it to a movie clip. Name the movie clip Ball.

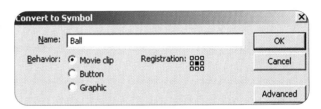

3. Create a new layer and call it Background. Place it below the layer the ball is on. On this layer draw a simple background with a horizon line for orientation of where the ground plane is. Lock the background layer.

4. In the timeline, go to frame 14 and insert a frame for both layers by selecting Insert ➤ Timeline ➤ Frame or by pressing *F5*. Because you're animating at 24 fps, 14 frames is theoretically just over half of 1 second. We judge this to be good timing for a ball bounce in this cartoon world!

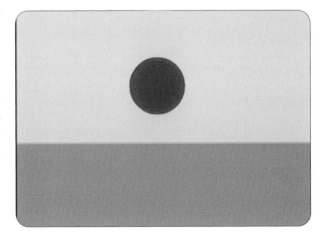

> *Be sure to make the height and scale of your ball bounce similar to ours; otherwise, your timing will be different than the timing intended for this example.*

This exercise is what's called a *loop animation*. This means it won't have a starting or an ending—the ball will continuously bounce forever. Therefore, your last frame must "hook up" to your first frame. When the last frame of the animation plays, you want the ball to be in a position that will meet seamlessly with frame 1. If it doesn't, the animation will appear to skip every time it loops back to frame 1. To achieve this continuity, continue to the next step.

5. Select the ball in frame 1 and notice the hollow circle in the center of the movie clip (the hollow circle may be on top of the movie clip's registration point if that's in the movie clip's center as well). You now can move this circle, called the center point, using the Selection tool and so change the point from which an instance is scaled, rotated, skewed, and so on. Because your ball will hit the ground at the bottom, it will serve you well to move your hollow circle to that point before you begin animating (if you don't and you create keyframes first, the circles in each keyframe might not match up on the instance, which can cause some quirky results).

6. On frame 14 of the Ball layer, create a keyframe (Insert ➤ Timeline ➤ Keyframe or F6). Select any of the Ball layer's first 14 frames and create a motion tween either in the Property inspector through the context menu that appears on right-click or with the menu command Insert ➤ Timeline ➤ Create Motion Tween. Because frame 14 is now set as a keyframe that's identical to frame 1, your animation will now loop. No matter where you move the ball from frames 2 to 13, it will always end up at this point to hook up with the first frame. This is how you make your animation loop.

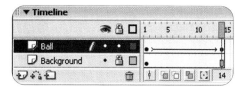

7. When the ball is bouncing up, it's fighting the force of gravity and will therefore move slower than when it falls (because it's being pulled down by gravity).

   On frame 4 create a keyframe on the Ball layer and move the ball to its "squash" position, which is the point of impact with the ground.

8. Select the Free Transform tool on frame 4 and use it to squash and stretch the ball. Always work with the height and width when squashing and stretching. The flatter you make the ball, the wider you need to compensate it. It's important to compensate in this way to maintain the believability of the ball's volume. Notice how moving the center point helps to maintain the ball's position as it hits the ground.

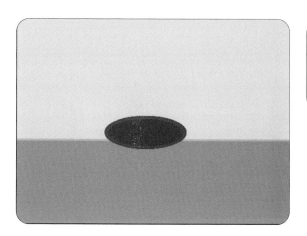

If you now scroll through the timeline, you'll see the ball start and stop in the same position, which roughly creates your "loop animation." (Don't relax yet, you aren't done!)

On both the fall and rise of the ball, you want to stretch it to give the illusion it's traveling quickly. This effect will be slightly more extreme on the fall because the ball is moving faster.

9. Select frame 2 and create another keyframe. On the keyframe, stretch the ball vertically and squash it horizontally.

   You want the ball to return to its original proportions after the stretch you just created and before the impact with the ground.

10. Select and copy frame 1. Paste this frame into frame 3. If you don't place this keyframe, the motion tweening may cause the ball to morph into the squash position before it hits the ground, and that's just horribly wrong.

    Duplicating frame 1 to frame 3 will re-create your original proportions after the ball

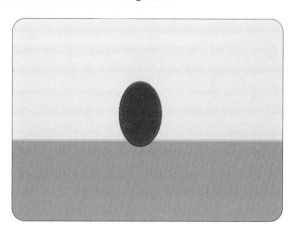

stretches and the instant before it squashes on the ground. However, because you've copied and pasted the first frame, the ball on frame 3 is in the wrong position.

11. Activate the *Onion Skin* tool and click the Ball layer to wireframe mode to make viewing much easier. Move the ball on frame 3 down so it's slightly below the stretch position on frame 2 and slightly above the squash position on frame 4.

    You'll now animate the ball bouncing up and into the high point of the arc. Remember, the rise will be slightly slower because the ball is fighting gravity. Therefore, your keyframes will not be as close to one another as in the fall; there will be more time between keyframes. Again, you'll want the ball to obtain its original, circular proportions before and after the stretch of the bouncing up animation.

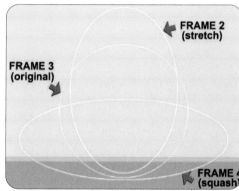

Your timeline should now look something like this:

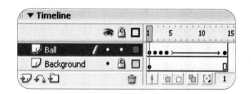

12. Now you must stretch the ball before it reaches the high point of the arc. Create a keyframe on frame 8. Stretch the ball vertically.

13. Copy frame 3. Paste frame 3 into frame 6. This will make the ball retain its original proportions *after* it squashes on the ground and *before* it stretches up.

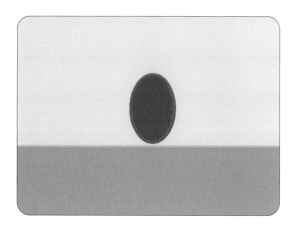

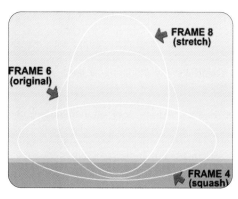

Now you must add the hang time. Because frame 1 and frame 14 are identical, the ball will appear to hit an invisible wall. It will freeze abruptly for a moment, which is something you want to avoid. You must soften the movement in and out of the high point. You do this by creating another keyframe that makes the ball go slightly higher than frames 1 and 14.

14. Copy and paste frame 14 to frame 10. On frame 10, set the Ease Out slider in the Properties palette to 100.

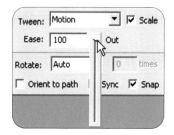

Flash will automatically time the animation between keyframes evenly, unless you use the Ease In and Ease Out features. This means that if you select a keyframe and drag the slider down to –100, the animation will be slower from that keyframe and speed up to the next keyframe. The opposite applies for setting the slider at +100: the animation will start fast and slow down as it reaches the next keyframe.

15. On frame 12 create another keyframe and move the ball up very slightly. This will now be the highest point the ball reaches. The high point will no longer be frames 1 and 14.

Imagine the feeling in your stomach when you drive over a hill too fast. This is the feeling you want the ball to have—that momentary sense of weightlessness. By creating more time in less physical space at the high point, you achieve this.

16. On frame 12, set the Ease In slider to –100. This will make the ball start slower into the animation to frame 14.

The final timeline should look something like this:

Your ball is now alive! Play around with the animation in your movie, and notice that the example, `ballbounce.fla`, has a drop shadow animating underneath it. Have fun with it and experiment.

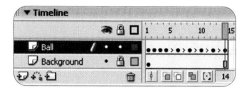

Take note of how you took an inanimate object and gave it life and personality. Suddenly this ball feels alive. This is what applying the foundations of classical animation does. This ball could just as easily be rabbit or a character's plump body bouncing up and down. Understanding the fundamental animation rules and how to apply them in Flash will bring your characters to life.

Anticipation, Action, Reaction, and Overlapping Action

It's important to know that unless you're animating stiff machinery, very few objects produce an action without first anticipating and then reacting.

Anticipation is used to demonstrate the buildup of energy before an action takes place. The idea is to make it very clear to the audience what is about to happen. A very important part of animation is clarity—pay close attention to how a street mime moves, for example. A mime always makes every action as clear as possible by displaying anticipation, action, and reaction.

Reaction is a result of the speed and forces of the action. Reaction is when the movement stops, but the object briefly continues moving and then comes back into the settled pose. Imagine swiping your entire arm as quickly as you can through the air, for example. No matter how hard you try, it's impossible to just *stop*. There's a moment when your arm must go too far and snap back. Not unlike squash and stretch, this method can also be used as extremely or as subtly as the animator wishes. Either one will have a great impact on the style of your animation.

If you pay careful attention when you swipe your arm through the air, you'll also notice that your hand is dragging even further behind this force. Your hand takes more time to come to a complete stop. This is called *overlapping action*. This is a hierarchy you must always be conscious of. If you imagine you're wearing a baggy-sleeved silk shirt, for example (as we always do when we're animating . . . or pretending to be a pirate . . .), it would take even longer for the sleeve to stop because of its light weight and how much material is trailing behind the rest of the action. Overlapping action refers to the fact that not everything will stop moving exactly at once—some things are being dragged and are lighter, so they need extra time to catch up and settle to a stop position.

Arcs

To create the result of smooth animation, every object should follow an arc of movement. This is also known as the "path of action." Think of it as an invisible, smooth curve that trails through each object's movement. If you animate a hand picking up a kitten, you don't want your movement to be a straight, rigid line. You want a nice, smooth arc to give your animation a flowing feel.

Now you'll begin an exercise that applies both of these principles, as well as the last two from the bouncing ball exercise.

> *From this point onward in the book, you'll take a much more independent approach to animating. It's now up to you to remember what you've learned so far and employ your own talents, timing, research, and ideas as much as possible.*

Jumping Slime Ball

Remember how an object must anticipate before it moves? In this section, you'll begin to practice this theory. First you must convince yourself that you have a ball made of goopy, slime. Imagine how much it weighs, what it would feel like to hold it in your hands, and how little force it would take to distort it. You must really know what this ball feels like before you move it.

Imagine how long it would take to get from keyframe to keyframe if you were the object. This is where timing comes in. You must get up out of your chair and act out the movement. Use a stopwatch and time out how long it takes to get from pose to pose. Do this many times and, as a general rule, go with the quickest time you have. It may feel silly at first, but it will begin to eventually feel more natural. This step is critical.

Begin a new Flash project. Once again, make sure the frame rate is 24 fps.

> *You must get a firm grasp in your head of the movement you want before you begin. Remember, you want the path to be a series of smooth arcs for fluidity, not straight, jagged lines. A good idea is to draw a path of motion on a layer, lock it, and use it as a temporary guide. Then simply delete the layer when you're done with the animation.*
>
> *Because timing and spacing are so closely related in animation, the keyframes used in this example serve as guides only. If, for example, the jump you create is higher, that takes more time and the keyframes assigned in the example may not be as accurate to create a successful animation. Use you own judgment and have fun.*

1. Select the Oval tool and draw an oval standing vertically. You must imagine this oval is made of slime, so keep this in mind while you select your colors. Convert the ball into a movie clip named slimeBall. As before, on a separate layer draw a simple background for reference of the ground plane and lock it.

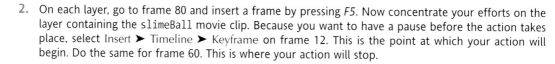

2. On each layer, go to frame 80 and insert a frame by pressing *F5*. Now concentrate your efforts on the layer containing the `slimeBall` movie clip. Because you want to have a pause before the action takes place, select Insert ➤ Timeline ➤ Keyframe on frame 12. This is the point at which your action will begin. Do the same for frame 60. This is where your action will stop.

Because you want the ball to leap forward, it must first anticipate backward to build the appropriate energy. Prior to that, it's sometimes necessary to "anticipate the anticipation," which means the ball will anticipate forward before it anticipates backward and then jumps. Doing this will build the momentum even more.

3. On frame 15 create a keyframe that will begin the ball's movement. On this frame stretch and skew `slimeBall` using the Free Transform tool so it's leaning forward.

> *Use the Onion Skin tool often when animating. Remember, you don't want your objects to be shifting from side to side on the floor every time they move. The Onion Skin tool will also help you keep your objects on the same path of action.*

4. Create a keyframe on frame 16. You do this so you can ease the slime ball in and out of the high point of the anticipation once you've added the motion tween (remember the bouncing ball?). Doing this will give the slime ball a smooth, quick hold at the top of the action before it squashes down.

5. Copy and paste frame 12 to frame 18. Like in the bouncing ball exercise, you do this to restore the ball's original proportions and position. Now anticipate the `slimeBall` back to show the shift of weight and buildup of forces.

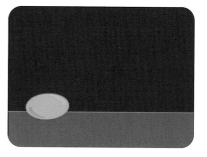

6. On frame 20 squash the ball down even further to show the buildup of energy before the leap.

> *Notice the short amount of time between frames. This is all happening very quickly*

7. Stretch the ball up and remember to follow the path of action. This movement will be fairly quick because the ball must thrust to fight the pull of gravity. Here's frame 23:

8. At the high point of the arc, create a sense of hang time and rotate the ball so it's changing directions. The animation in and out of this pose should be slower. Keep in mind this is the moment when the weight of the ball catches up with itself temporarily and is then pulled back down. We've done this in frame 31:

9. Stretch the ball down toward its resting position. Because the ball is being pulled by gravity, this fall will be fast.

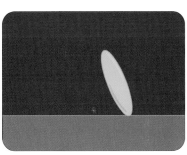

10. Squash the ball on impact.

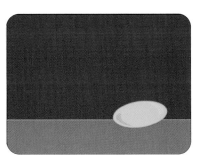

11. Make the ball react until it has settled into its final pose. Look at the next set of images in sequence to see the reaction and wobble-to-a-stop effect. The movements get less extreme and slower as the energy dissipates. This subtlety of movement is why it's important to view these images side by side.

Frame 41

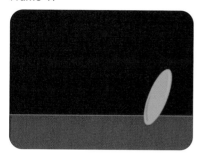

Frame 45

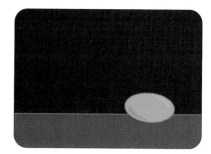

Frame 49

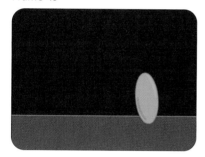

Frame 53

Frame 56

12. Select frames 12 through 56 and create a motion tween. Now you can watch your little slime ball leap smoothly through the air. Chances are very good that the animation will need some tweaking. Look through it frame by frame and make any changes needed. Don't be afraid to add in more keyframes to get the effect you want.

13. Use the Ease In and Ease Out sliders on the appropriate keyframes to help give the slime ball a sense of weight.

Now that you have the main movement, you can go back and fine-tune the paths of action and the timing, and add any details you want. Experiment away! Remember, if this wasn't a ball of slime, the way it moves, anticipates, reacts, and stops would be different. This is why it's important to understand the attributes of the object you're moving before you begin.

To view the final animation, open up slimeBall.swf from this chapter's downloadable source files.

Looking back, it's important to notice how all the principles of animation we've discussed are coming into play. If all these principles are this important just to make two simple balls bounce, think of how important they are to apply in more complex animations and characters.

Character Animation

Even the words "character animation" can sound intimidating, but realize if you remember the principles you've learned so far, it will make the job much easier and the results much more successful. When you animate characters, you must get in touch with the performer buried deep down inside yourself. It really is the best part of the job.

Posing

Yet another important part of creating successful character animation is strong *posing*. What this means is that if you were to take an image of your character and color it in completely black, it would still be obvious what that character was doing. This is called *silhouette* and it's strongly related to the clarity aspect we touched on when we discussed anticipation.

Jumping Character

Begin a new Flash project, and again be sure your settings are at 24 fps.

You'll begin by roughly *keying out* your animation. This stage involves deciding where all of your keyframes will lie on the timeline by using quick sketches of your character (for example, see characterJump-Ruff.fla). Because of the simple, straightforward nature of the bouncing ball and the slime ball, roughing out those objects first wasn't as essential.

1. Use the Brush tool to roughly draw a character standing close to the bottom-left side of the screen. Don't draw anything too detailed to begin with—this is just to get the movement and timing down. This will be your start position and first key pose.

Don't draw the character too far to the left so if the character was to raise its arm it would be offscreen. Give the character room to breathe and act.

2. Create a new keyframe on the same layer. This is where you draw the second rough pose of the animation. Use the Onion Skin tool to help place the poses in the same position on the screen. Continue adding more and more keyframes and roughing out the animation in this way. Scroll through the timeline periodically to see the movement progress. Think of all the principles you've learned and apply them to the animation.

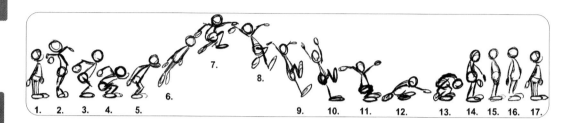

> *Notice the smooth paths of action here. Although this is only a rough sketch, you could draw a smooth curve through the series of hands, through the pelvis, through the head, and so on. There are no static movements—it all flows and everything works together. In these rough key drawings, see if you can find the applied principles of animation we've discussed.*

3. Once the entire jump is roughed out, play with the timing and stretch the duration of certain poses through the timeline for the slower parts and shorten them through the faster parts. This is a rough animation guide, and it won't be smooth animation because you still need to create the motion tween once you've cleaned up the character and body parts.

   To view an example, open the file `characterJump-Ruff.swf` from your source files directory.

   Let's continue to clean up the character.

4. Clean up the first pose of the character using the same methods discussed earlier, with each major body part on its own layer. Now you'll see this isn't only for optimizing but also so you can animate each separate layer individually. It's also important for organizational purposes to accurately name each layer.

5. Once you've completed cleaning up the first pose of the character, convert each body part into a movie clip. Because you may have more than one hand, for instance, name them in sequence (for example, frontHand01, Hips01, etc).

6. Start a new layer and lock the others. Scroll through the animation and decide where it may be necessary to create other symbols of each body part. Create a new layer and on it draw any of the other body parts needed for the animation. Now is a good time to get this process out of the way, before you start animating. For example, if you look at pose 2 in the rough character animation, you'll notice the hands are in more of a head-on view. Also, in pose 4, the hands are fists. Once you've drawn all the symbols you think you'll need, convert each one to its own movie clip and delete the layer. (Don't worry about deleting the layer—the important thing is that you can grab the symbols out of the library.)

These are the extra body parts needed throughout the rest of the animation. The head can have simple expressions, but don't worry about tweening into each facial expression for this exercise. The action is too fast here to notice it.

For a quick note on duplicating symbols, consider the head shown previously. The head you see here is a movie clip. If you go into this movie clip, you'll see the cranium on the bottom layer, and the mouth, eyes, brows, and hair on layers above. If you want to make changes to create a new head symbol, you can't simply edit the contents in the original head. If you did, whatever changes you made would affect all the originals wherever they may appear throughout your animation.

7. Open the library and right-click the head symbol you want to edit. Select Duplicate. Give the new copy a relevant name. Now you can edit this new copy of the symbol without affecting the original in any way.

8. Once you think you've built the Library, it's time to start animating. Create a keyframe on every layer on the last frame of each rough pose. You do this so you can almost "trace off" the rough animation with your cleaned-up body parts. By doing this, you'll have the same timing as your roughed-out animation. Create a motion tween on all the layers of cleaned-up body parts. Your timeline should begin to look something like this:

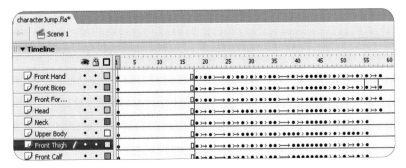

> Don't worry if this looks confusing. It will make much more sense when you're doing it for your own animation.

Notice where the keyframes sit in relation to the rough animation frames. There's a keyframe at the end of each rough pose. Also notice that there's no motion tween at the beginning and end of the animation—it's not necessary because you just want the character to stand still at those times.

9. Now you can begin literally moving the character over your rough poses on each keyframe to give you the same timing. This process feels a lot like tracing. Generally, it's best to first animate where the force is coming from. Everything else falls into place from there. In this case, the force is coming from the legs and hips.

Some Useful Tips While Animating

- *Be sure the Snapping options are off* (View ➤ Snapping *); you don't want it affecting your positioning when you animate. You should use the Snapping options only for drawing.*

- *Don't be afraid to turn certain layers invisible or wireframe for clearer viewing.*

- *Export the SWF file often to check the progress.*

- *Copy and paste frames wherever necessary.*

- *Create extra keyframes whenever necessary to get the proper movement.*

- *Notice that as you start animating, every time you move an object and scroll through the timeline the object returns to its original position of pose 1. This is fine, and it's actually good because no matter how much you stretch, squash, or distort the symbol, you know it will obtain its original proportions by the next keyframe.*

- *The* Swap *button is very useful for allowing you to replace one movie clip with another during the animation. For example, if you want to change the symbol hand01 to hand02 in order to create a sense of rotation, click the symbol on the keyframe it should be changed on. Then click the* Swap *button from the Property inspector. This will enable you to select hand02 from a list of all the symbols in the library and "swap" it with hand01. It will replace hand01 with hand02 in the same scale and position by lining up the crosshairs (this is very handy!).*

---

10. Once you have the main movement complete, scroll through the timeline frame by frame. If there are any problems of body parts disconnecting, correct them now. Try to see if the keyframes before and after the problem can be adjusted so the objects join properly during the tween. If not, create keyframes wherever necessary and nudge them into place manually.

11. Fine-tune the animation by scrolling through it again to find poses in which you may be able to add more squash and stretch, create stronger poses, or slow in and slow out.

12. If some movements seem too fast or too slow, go through and adjust the timing by adding frames or taking some away. (Be very careful not to delete keyframes, though—you just want to delete tweened frames.)

13. Delete the layer that contains the rough animation.

Open `characterJump.swf` from this chapter's accompanying source files to view a sample of the final animation.

Creating a Story and a Hero

Let's talk video games. First of all, you need a story, a situation, and a hero! So gather 'round, my friends, and we'll tell you a tale. . . .

> The sound of the screaming alarms aboard the space cruiser abruptly awoke Space Kid, our ultimate hero of the futuristic universe, from his cryogenic nap. When our hero investigated, it was obvious his worst fears were now true. His loyal sidekick, Teddy, had been bear-napped from the comfort of his own sleep chamber.
>
> Immediately Space Kid knew there could only be one ruthless and vile enemy capable of committing such an atrocity: his longtime arch nemesis, Lord Notaniceguy.
>
> Armed only with his trusty ray gun, Super Kid changes course for Quexxon Sector-G. Although our brave hero is fully aware he's falling for the bait in a trap, he must save Teddy.

So there you have it—the storyline for a Flash game. It's simple at the core, yet it still has a lot of potential. It has the typical elements of good versus evil as its motivation, with a slapstick twist. Here you have a child who wants his teddy bear back from aliens in the future with a ray gun. OK, so it's not *that* typical. This could be the story of a real hero in space or perhaps a dream a child is having while he sleeps.

To begin designing the characters, you want to have a firm grasp of the style you're aiming for. This is obviously a silly story and will most likely have a style to reflect that as much as possible. Grab your sketchbook and begin with some brainstorming. This is the best part—you can draw anything that comes into your head. At first you don't need to be too concerned with how it looks or how weird it seems; it's ideas and feelings you're trying to find.

Many times an entire personality of a character will appear from a single rough sketch. It may be the key that leads you down a path you never expected. You want to find the personality, style, and design of the character in this process. Every time you draw an image, you must look at it and decide which elements you like about it. You then apply these elements to the next drawing. As you draw, you must ask yourself which features you want the character to have and why. Do you want the character to be short or tall? Thin or plump? Brave or cowardly? You can never draw too many ideas. Most important, you must have fun with it. Here's how our thought processes went:

- Drawing 1: Pretty good character, but he looks like a wimp.
- Drawing 2: Nice drawing, and he would be fun to animate, but we may want to eliminate a tall, thin character as our hero in favor of a short, stocky character because it better portrays the feeling of comedic irony we want to achieve. Sure, a tall, thin hero may work, but is it as funny as it could be? Making the hero short will also exaggerate the dangers because everything is so much larger and menacing to a small hero.
- Drawing 3: This character is far too big. He looks much older than we want.

> *It is this thought process you must learn to develop. You must think of development as a chain and consider how everything relates to all aspects of the game.*

- Drawing 4: This character has a flat, graphic feel, which is good in some cases, but in this case the character is too dopey.
- Drawing 5: This version is far too innocent and good. We just want to take his lunch money.
- Drawing 6: What if he wears a space helmet? Although the visor must be up because the eyes are the most essential part of the face to express emotion—we don't want them to be covered.

- Drawing 7: Nice, but too nice. Who wants to watch this kid save the world?
- Drawing 8: This one is way too wacky and funny. He looks more like a clown.
- Drawing 9: Now we're on to something! The attitude behind this face may be just what this game needs. This character has the slightly "on edge" personality of someone who would enjoy blowing up aliens. The more, the better! He also has a sense of sneakiness to him, he's energetic, and he's not to be trusted 100 percent.

- Drawing 10: Oops—we went back a few steps to cute with this one.
- Drawing 11: There's the personality again, with the attitude we want.
- Drawing 12: Lots of energy—we know what this character's personality is like just by looking at him.
- Drawing 13: And here we have the hero that we'll use for the game!

The creative development process we've just briefly covered is essential for designing everything from characters to layouts and props. It's the best way to develop the strongest possible ideas. It really is an evolutionary process. We aren't only designing the way our character looks, we're also designing the way he thinks and acts.

Now you must make a list of all the movie clips you'll need to make to have a fully functional game character. The basic animations we must create for our hero are

- Run
- Jump
- Shoot
- Idle

Obviously, there could be no end to the number of animations you create, but for this example you'll focus on the basics. You want the animation for your game to be great; however, you must be careful not to make your animations too long. When the player presses the shoot key, you don't want her waiting for a long period of time before the character actually shoots because of all the extra animation beforehand. Your animation must be good and to the point.

Where to begin? After you have your main character designed, it's a good idea to start animating and designing the main run cycle. This will give you a sense of how your character will move, which is important because the way a character moves displays his or her personality. Animating the run will also build a library of body parts, which you can easily reuse in other animations you create. Because the player will control all of the animations, you must create the animation to be stationary, meaning everything will appear as though the character is on a treadmill until it's applied to the game.

The Running Man

You want to create a run that displays a lot of energy to help portray your hero's confidence and ability. Using the same methods you applied to the character jump exercise, you can rough out the run animation. Because you want the animation to loop seamlessly, it's a good idea to copy and paste your first frame temporarily after your last drawing. This way, you can use the Onion Skin tool to compare your last drawing with your first to be sure they hook up to one another.

> The animation process may point out problems in your design and may force you to make the appropriate changes. For example, once the animation process began for this example, it became obvious the character's arms were too short and were blocked by his large chest mass. Because the arms are such an important part of the run, you'll want to be sure they're as clear as possible. You must always allow room for this kind of testing and correction.

Open the file roughRun.swf from your downloaded example files to view a sample of this animation.

When the player isn't moving the character anywhere, the hero will be in the "idle" animation. Because of this, it's important that all your other animations can start relatively smoothly from the idle animation pose. If the character were standing idle and then ran, starting with the midair pose, it would look odd. You want each animation to look as though it's coming out of the idle animation.

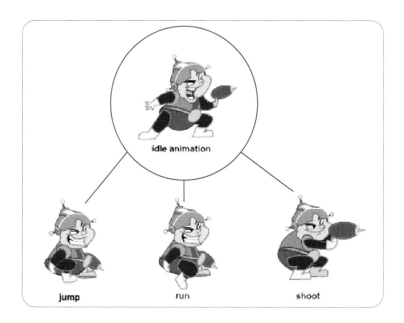

The villains your hero will be fighting for this sample are Lord Notaniceguy's goopy, brainless army of space slugs:

Now, what's the point in having a big, goopy enemy unless it makes a mess when it's shot? Here are the essential keyframes from the alien exploding:

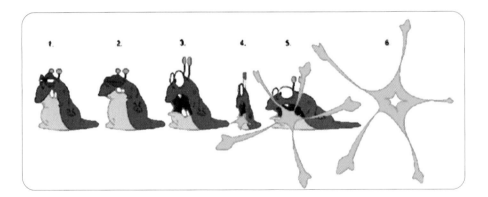

- ■ Frame 1: The enemy, looking as dumb as ever.
- ■ Frame 2: The quick anticipation.
- ■ Frame 3: The brief moment of fear.
- ■ Frame 4: A hit and a quick implosion to contrast what follows.
- ■ Frame 5: The alien quickly expands.
- ■ Frame 6: The slime wipe gets larger and larger, until it wipes the entire screen and reveals the alien is no more.

Remember that these images are running past the viewer's eyes at 1/24 of a second. Don't be afraid to distort and skew things to get the appropriate quick effect.

Now that we've discussed the development and processes of animation, personality, and game design, it's time to get technical.

The Game

OK, so let's run the proof of concept and sew up all this careful animation into a game. Introducing our demo game, which you can view by playing thegame.swf:

At start-up, you're presented with an instructions screen and a Play button. Click the Play button to start the game.

It's incredible how professional the game looks when all the elements are mixed together, along with the ActionScript code to control the game logic and physics. You could just as easily be looking at a professional console game!

The player can make the hero run around using the left and right arrow keys, jump with the up arrow key, and fire a projectile with the space bar.

We're not going into a lot of detail about the code here, because the focus of this chapter is animation and personality. You can, however, dig into the file `thegame.fla`, which is nicely commented, and see what you can learn. Right now, let's look briefly at some of the key concepts you should be aware of.

The Physics Is Controlled with Code, Not Animation

Although in the earlier examples, animation of a character's jump was designed with an arc to it, you must modify it to work properly in the game. The problem with having an arced jump in the context of the game is that the arc is a fixed height, and you can't allow for players bumping into things and cutting the jump short. So you must modify the animation and bring all frames vertically to the same level:

It's difficult to illustrate the animation here, but it's as if the character is performing the actions of a jump without leaving the ground. Now, when the jump key (the up arrow key) is actually pressed, you can move this entire jump animation up and back down, creating your code-controlled jump.

All of this is done with a simple gravitational effect. (Hint: Look at the code in the FLA file around lines 20 and 28.)

Collision with the Ground

Once the character brought into the game world, he must interact with the ground (or platforms, in this case). Now, one of the really nice things about this particular collision-detection technique is that it's based on arbitrarily shaped platforms. This means that the character isn't left colliding with merely square-shaped tiles—you can include nonuniform ramps, curves, hills, and bumps that the collision engine will intelligently allow the character to interact with.

Here's an example:

In this image, the character is running up a sloped ramp. To do this, your character must interact with and collide with the actual image or sometimes a hidden, invisible region of collision. You do this with several hitTests, as you can see in the FLA file.

Parallax/Multiplane Backgrounds

In traditional game programming, it's called parallax, and in animation it's called mulitplane—either way, we're referring to the cool effect of having the background scroll at a different rate than the foreground, which creates a fantastic sense of depth.

In the preceding images, although the platforms have moved dramatically, the background planets have not moved much. Notice the upper level of platforms on the left side. In the first image, the rightmost floor piece (the one that the character is almost touching with his gun) isn't over the small moon at all. In the second image, however, the rightmost floor piece is now on top of the small moon. The only way this is possible is if the background moves at a different rate than the foreground.

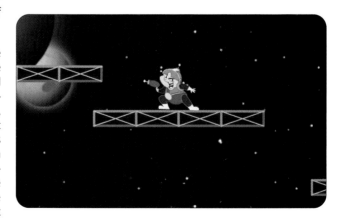

To keep game performance at a maximum, you use a large bitmap image for the distant space background. Because you have so many stars, a vector background will end up containing more pieces of information (and require more computations) than a straightforward bitmap image.

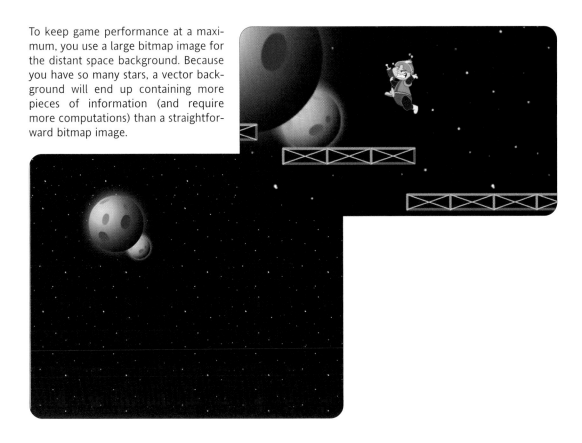

Hierarchical Arrangement of Character Animations

To smoothly switch between different animations, you arrange your characters so that each character is only one movie clip that contains several frames, with each frame corresponding to an action. On each frame is a movie clip containing the animation for the action.

Take a look at the main hero movie clip:

This movie clip consists of four frames:

Frame 1: The idle animation movie clip

Frame 2: The run animation movie clip

Frame 3: The jump animation movie clip

Frame 4: The shoot animation movie clip

So you can see, for example, that the run animation movie clip is contained within the hero movie clip.

This means that you have a common collision point for the character, no matter what animation he's displaying. In the hero's case, the collision point is the bottom middle of the movie clip, because this is where his "feet" are—this is where he's anchored to the ground and it's at this point that you'll check to see if he has "landed" from a fall or a jump.

In some cases, we've had to add frame ActionScript code to the animations because events are supposed to occur on those frames. For example, look at the jump:

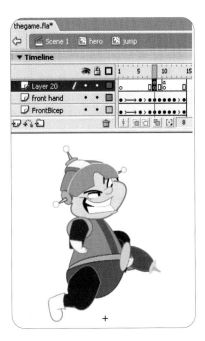

Frames 1 to 7 are all the "wind up" for the jump, during which time the character shouldn't actually leave the ground. On frame 8 of the animation, the physical jump is meant to begin, so you need code there to cause the hero to launch himself vertically. In this case, the code is simply this:

```
_parent.dy = -9;
```

He has a vertical velocity of –9, which causes him to leap into the air.

Also, you can try the special DirectX version of the EXE projector created with the program swfXXL (www.swfxxl.com). You see, if you take an ordinary SWF and then maximize it to become full screen by clicking the maximize window button or pressing *CTRL+F*, you'll experience some substantial performance degradation. That's because, even though the stage is 320x240, you're forcing Flash to render the vector details at whatever your screen resolution is.

Not so with swfXXL. This program creates a projector EXE file that causes the screen resolution to *become* 320x240. To Flash's rendering engine, it's still drawing at a mere 320x240, but because of the screen resolution shift, the game visually takes up the full screen. The advantage? The game becomes full screen, yet it remains as fast and smooth as though it's still in its original 320x240 form. It looks like a "real" game. The swfXXL projector is called game.exe.

Summary

In this chapter, you began by exploring methods to optimize the number of vector points in an image to greatly improve the performance of your Flash animations. In doing so, you learned a helpful trick to keep file sizes at an absolute minimum.

You then briefly experimented with the in-depth and amazing world of animation. You learned some of the basic principles of animation and how to apply them to Flash animation and gaming.

You then moved on to discover how a single sketch can create an entire personality. One mood or one subtle look may be all that's necessary to find exactly what you're looking for or perhaps to lead you down a path that never occurred to you before. You can use this same method for creating anything from characters and layouts to storylines and situations.

To conclude the chapter, we demonstrated how to take what you've learned about animation and apply it to a Flash gaming environment.

Keith Peters

Keith lives in the vicinity of Boston with his wife, Kazumi, and their new daughter, Kristine. He has been working with Flash since 1999, and he has coauthored many books for friends of ED, including *Flash MX Studio*, *Flash MX Most Wanted: Effects & Movies*, and the groundbreaking *Flash Math Creativity*.

In 2001 Keith started the experimental Flash site BIT-101 (www.bit-101.com), which strives for a new cutting-edge open source experiment each day. The site recently won an award at the Flashforward 2003 Flash Film Festival in the Experimental category. In addition to the experiments on the BIT-101 site are several highly regarded Flash tutorials, which have been translated into many languages and are now posted on web sites throughout the world.

Keith is currently working full-time doing freelance and contract Flash development and various writing projects.

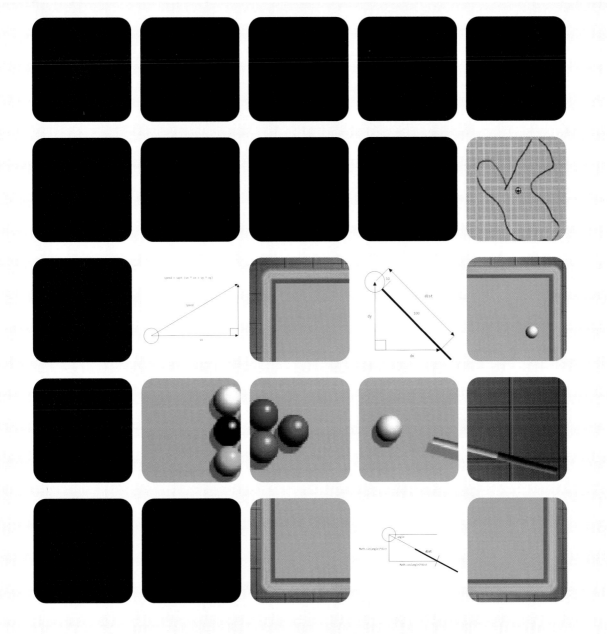

FRICTION AND COLLISION DETECTION

The purpose of this chapter is to introduce the concepts of friction and collision detection. By the end of this chapter, you should be able to get your head around the sorts of techniques needed to introduce these physical concepts to a game. Once you've grasped them, you'll find your games becoming solid and tangible—not just a bunch of dancing pixels on a screen!

Here's what to expect. Friction (or the amount you'll have to slow down an object as it rubs against a surface) is pretty simple. However, collision detection covers some pretty vast ground. There is one definite Most Wanted answer about collisions: When two round objects moving at different speeds and angles hit each other, how do you determine their resulting speeds and directions? The physics involved in this situation has been discussed so much that the subject has even gotten its own nickname: *billiard ball physics*.

The Color of Money

Well, because we'll be discussing billiard ball physics, we figured what better game to demonstrate it than billiards itself? So, that's the kind of game you'll make in this chapter. As a teaser of the kind of fundamental collision-detection techniques that you'll learn, take a look at the file pool_final.swf, which is available in the source code bundle associated with this chapter (you can download the files from www.friendsofed.com).

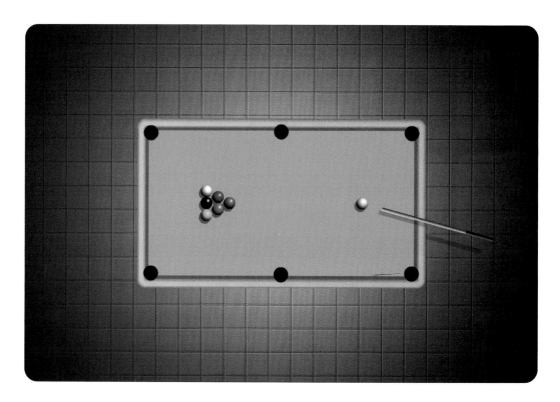

Before we begin, it's worth making a comment about programming styles. With Flash MX 2004, you have many possible methods of writing your code. You could go for a totally object-oriented approach or you could make each piece of the game into a Flash MX component; and you could use older Flash 5

onClipEvent code, the Flash MX event model, or even the new ActionScript 2.0 available with the latest version. You'll use the event methods provided in ActionScript 1.0, because of their power and flexibility, but at this point we won't delve too far into object-oriented programming (OOP) or components, as these can be entire subjects to learn in and of themselves. Once you understand *what* you're doing and *why*, you can easily transfer the principles into the coding method of your choice.

Pool Game Basics

Check out this chapter's source files, which are available for download from www.friendsofed.com. Open the file pool_01.fla and you'll see the basic setup. Here's a step-by-step breakdown of how to create this game.

1. Create a new movie. Click though Modify ➤ Document, make the stage 900x600 pixels, and set the frame rate to 60 fps.

> It's important to boost the frame rate for a game like this. This will allow the balls to travel a lesser distance on each frame, allowing for more accurate collision detection. If the frame rate is too low, and a ball is moving too fast, a ball could jump right "through" another ball without ever officially colliding with it!

2. Let's not dawdle around: create six new layers. The following screenshot should give you an indication as to where we're taking this.

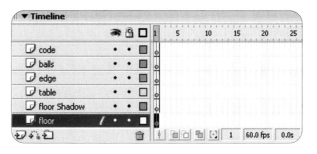

3. Create some nice graphics for that billiard-room feel. We created a tiled floor and pool table, as well as a beautifully shaded cue ball. The important thing here is to create the table and ball as separate movie clips, because you're going to rely on their dimensions for some of your math. Essentially, press *CTRL+F8* to create a new symbol and draw a green rectangle for your table. Call the movie instance table. Create another clip and call it whiteBall. Draw a ball on there and use the rulers to make it 20 pixels in diameter—it will become important later.

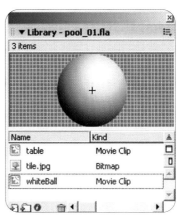

The rest of it is up to your own taste, but if you copy us you'll fill your six layers with a tiled floor, a shadow, and the edges of the table. Each of these is drawn directly onto its own layer.

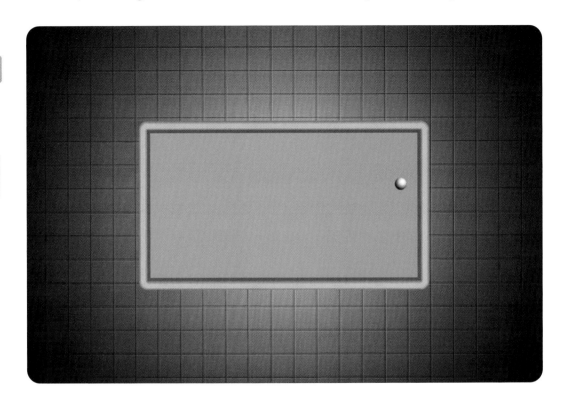

4. OK, now it's time to get busy coding. It's important to get a good understanding of what you're doing at this stage of the game, as you'll be adding a lot more throughout the chapter.

```
BALL_DIAMETER = 20;
BALL_RADIUS = BALL_DIAMETER/2;
TOP = table_mc._y-table_mc._height/2+BALL_RADIUS;
BOTTOM = table_mc._y+table_mc._height/2-BALL_RADIUS;
LEFT = table_mc._x-table_mc._width/2+BALL_RADIUS;
RIGHT = table_mc._x+table_mc._width/2-BALL_RADIUS;
BOUNCE = -1;
whiteBall_mc.vx = Math.random()*5+2;
whiteBall_mc.vy = Math.random()*5+2;
whiteBall_mc.onEnterFrame = ballMove;
function ballMove() {
  this._x += this.vx;
  this._y += this.vy;
```

```
        if (this._x>RIGHT) {
          this._x = RIGHT;
          this.vx *= BOUNCE;
        } else if (this._x<LEFT) {
          this._x = LEFT;
          this.vx *= BOUNCE;
        }
        if (this._y>BOTTOM) {
          this._y = BOTTOM;
          this.vy *= BOUNCE;
        } else if (this._y<TOP) {
          this._y = TOP;
          this.vy *= BOUNCE;
        }
    }
```

The top four lines define a few constants. These are values that will never change throughout the course of the program.

> You'll note we've used all CAPITALS as variable names for these constants. This is to signal that these are the final values and shouldn't be changed again.

LEFT, RIGHT, TOP, and BOTTOM are determined from the dimensions of the movie clip table_mc. By taking the position of the clip and its size, you can find the location of its left, right, top, and bottom edges by adding or subtracting half its width and height. You then offset these values by 10 (BALL_RADIUS), which is half the diameter of the ball. This gives you the limits of stage positions where the ball can go. BOUNCE is simply set to –1. This will be used to reverse the speed of the ball when it hits one of these edges.

5. You then give whiteBall_mc a random velocity in both the x and y axes. Math.random() returns a value between 0 and 1. Multiply that value by 5 and add 2, and you get a value between 2 and 7. You use vx and vy to hold these values. Next, the function ballMove is assigned as the onEnterFrame handler of whiteBall_mc, which causes that function to run 60 times per second, or at least it attempts to. The actual frame rate will vary depending on the physical capabilities of the system the movie is being run on. In that function, you simply add the ball's x and y velocity to its _x and _y positions.

6. You then venture into your first math-based collision detection. Ball-to-wall collision detection is pretty much the easiest you can do. If the ball moves past any one of the edges, you set it back so it sits exactly on the edge and reverse its velocity on that axis by multiplying it times the value of BOUNCE, -1.

You can test out this file and see the ball bouncing happily around all four walls. Can't you almost hear the soft baize rumble already? Again, we highly recommend that you make sure you understand all of what's going on so far before continuing.

Bounce and Friction

So, what do you improve next? You need to take two more steps to give the ball some realistic behavior.

1. First, you'll change the value of bounce. Why? Well, as it stands, after a bounce the ball simply reverses its direction but continues on with the same speed. However, some speed is always lost in a real collision; you can test this by bouncing a ball off of any surface—the floor, for example. Even the bounciest ball won't completely return to the point from which it's dropped. A billiard ball will bounce only a very small fraction of the distance it falls. To simulate this, simply set bounce to be a fraction of –1. You can play around with it, but we've found that -0.6 works pretty well. This means that when you get a hit, the ball moves away in the opposite direction with 60% of its original speed. Try that and see how it looks. It's a little better, but something is still wrong. . . .

2. On a real pool table, the baize surface of the table absorbs quite a bit of energy from the ball, slowing it not only when it bounces, but also every second the ball is in motion—all those tiny little fibers slow the ball down. What you're going to do is reduce the velocity by a fraction each frame. You can do this by multiplying it times a value such as 0.98 each time. In the file, you can set up another constant named DAMP, which will take care of how much friction the table is going to give off. Set it to 0.98. Then, in the existing ballMove function, multiply the vx and vy values by DAMP before adding them to the position values.

   Here you can see what you have so far, with the changes in bold:

```
BALL_DIAMETER = 20;
BALL_RADIUS = BALL_DIAMETER/2;
TOP = table_mc._y-table_mc._height/2+BALL_RADIUS;
BOTTOM = table_mc._y+table_mc._height/2-BALL_RADIUS;
LEFT = table_mc._x-table_mc._width/2+BALL_RADIUS;
RIGHT = table_mc._x+table_mc._width/2-BALL_RADIUS;
BOUNCE = -.6;
DAMP = .98;
whiteBall_mc.vx = Math.random()*5+2;
whiteBall_mc.vy = Math.random()*5+2;
whiteBall_mc.onEnterFrame = ballMove;
function ballMove() {
  this.vx *= DAMP;
  this.vy *= DAMP;
  this._x += this.vx;
  this._y += this.vy;
  if (this._x>RIGHT) {
    this._x = RIGHT;
    this.vx *= BOUNCE;
  } else if (this._x<LEFT) {
    this._x = LEFT;
    this.vx *= BOUNCE;
  }
  if (this._y>BOTTOM) {
    this._y = BOTTOM;
    this.vy *= BOUNCE;
```

```
    } else if (this._y<TOP) {
      this._y = TOP;
      this.vy *= BOUNCE;
    }
  }
```

Testing this, you should see a more realistic-looking rolling motion, but you can still improve it. If you watch it long enough, you'll see that the ball never quite achieves a full stop. It gets slower and slower, but it seems to keep rolling ever so slightly. You need a way to set a minimum speed, after which it will stop altogether.

3. Build in another constant, MINSPEED, and set it to 0.1.

Then you need to compare the actual speed against MINSPEED. If it is less, you can stop the ball. But first you need a way to determine the speed. You have the velocity on the x axis and on the y axis. You can use the Pythagorean theorem to determine the overall speed. This diagram shows you how:

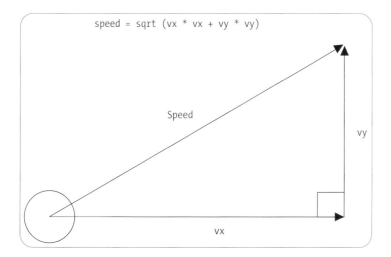

speed = sqrt (vx * vx + vy * vy)

Speed

vy

vx

4. If you square the vx, square the vy, add them together, and take the square root of that, you'll have the ball's speed. Sounds complex, but here's the actual code:

```
this.speed = Math.sqrt(this.vx*this.vx+this.vy*this.vy);
```

5. Now, you can compare this to MINSPEED. If it is less, you set vx and vy to 0, and then delete the ball's onEnterFrame handler. If you find the ball stops too suddenly, decrease the value of MINSPEED. Likewise, if it seems to take too long to stop, increase it.

> *Deleting the* onEnterFrame *handler is another efficiency point. If the ball isn't going to be moving, there's no use in running all this code on every frame. You can simply reactivate it later when you need it to move again.*

Here's the final code, which you can find in the file pool_02.fla:

```
BALL_DIAMETER = 20;
BALL_RADIUS = BALL_DIAMETER/2;
TOP = table_mc._y-table_mc._height/2+BALL_RADIUS;
BOTTOM = table_mc._y+table_mc._height/2-BALL_RADIUS;
LEFT = table_mc._x-table_mc._width/2+BALL_RADIUS;
RIGHT = table_mc._x+table_mc._width/2-BALL_RADIUS;
BOUNCE = -.6;
DAMP = .98;
MINSPEED = .1;
whiteBall_mc.vx = Math.random()*5+2;
whiteBall_mc.vy = Math.random()*5+2;
whiteBall_mc.onEnterFrame = ballMove;
function ballMove() {
  this.vx *= DAMP;
  this.vy *= DAMP;
  this._x += this.vx;
  this._y += this.vy;
  if (this._x>RIGHT) {
    this._x = RIGHT;
    this.vx *= BOUNCE;
  } else if (this._x<LEFT) {
    this._x = LEFT;
    this.vx *= BOUNCE;
  }
  if (this._y>BOTTOM) {
    this._y = BOTTOM;
    this.vy *= BOUNCE;
  } else if (this._y<TOP) {
    this._y = TOP;
    this.vy *= BOUNCE;
  }
  this.speed = Math.sqrt(this.vx*this.vx+this.vy*this.vy);
  if (this.speed<MINSPEED) {
    this.vx = 0;
    this.vy = 0;
    delete this.onEnterFrame;
  }
}
```

Using a Cue Stick

Well, that about covers friction. Before you get into collision between balls, you need to contrive a way to move the cue ball around where you want it, rather than just at a single random speed and direction. In real billiards you hit the ball with a stick, or cue. Following that example, let's make one.

1. Create a new layer underneath the code layer and call it stick.

2. Create a new movie clip (*Ctrl+F8*) and draw a good-looking stick. Make it 200 pixels in length. If you open the file pool_03.fla, you can see the stick we made, stick_mc. You should call yours the same.

Note that the registration point for the stick is exactly in the center. This will become important as you rotate the stick.

3. Add the following code to your existing accumulation on the code layer:

```
stick_mc.onEnterFrame = aim;
function aim() {
  var dx = whiteBall_mc._x-_xmouse;
  var dy = whiteBall_mc._y-_ymouse;
  angle = Math.atan2(dy, dx);
  this._rotation = angle*180/Math.PI;
  this._x = _xmouse;
  this._y = _ymouse;
}
```

This code is simply in addition to the code we've already covered up to now in the earlier versions (we've also now deleted the two lines that assign a random initial speed to the cue ball). You add this code right after the line assigning the onEnterFrame of whiteBall_mc (which you can delete now if you wish, along with the two lines assigning a random vx and vy to the cue ball—they were there to help test the movement, bounce, and friction, but they've become unnecessary as you use the stick to start the ball in motion).

Here's an explanation about what the code is doing. It assigns the function, aim, as the onEnterFrame handler for the stick. This function creates two variables, dx and dy. These variables represent the distance from the stick to the mouse, on the x and y axes. Note the use of the keyword var. This keeps the variables local to the function. Because you'll use variables with the same name in other functions, this avoids any possibility that they'll be confused with each other. It also has the added benefit of giving an increase in speed and efficiency.

You then use a bit of trigonometry to rotate the stick. With reference to the first diagram in the following section, the angle that the cue makes with the horizontal is that which you're looking to find. This is retrieved by use of the atan2 function, where *Tan (angle) = opposite / adjacent* and, more specifically, *Tan (angle) = dy/dx* (see the "Racing Cars" chapter for more discussion of trigonometric functions). This function takes a y value and an x value and returns an angle.

```
angle = Math.atan2(dy, dx);
```

Note that in this case you don't use var with the variable angle. Although it isn't obvious now, you'll need this angle value later, in another function. Rather than recalculate it, you'll just leave it as a timeline variable so it will be available to any function on the timeline.

Unfortunately, all of the Flash trigonometry values return their values in radians, rather than degrees. You need to convert this in order to use it with _rotation, which takes degrees. The conversion formula is as follows:

```
Degrees = Radians*180/PI
```

You can see that the next line uses the keyword this to affect the rotation of the clip directly. Finally, you just set the position of the stick to the current mouse coordinates. You can play around with this file to see how the stick will always point toward the cue ball, no matter where you move it.

Hitting the Cue Ball

Now comes your next foray into math-based collision detection. First off, you need to determine when you're aiming and when you're shooting. It makes sense that you would simply aim by moving the mouse around and then press the mouse button to go into "shooting mode." For that, you need to add some onMouseDown and onMouseUp handlers.

1. Return to your coding. Just above the function aim() line, add the following code:

```
onMouseDown = function () {
  stick_mc.onEnterFrame = shoot;
};
onMouseUp = function () {
  stick_mc.onEnterFrame = aim;
};
```

From this code you can see that, when the mouse is pressed down, stick_mc's onEnterFrame handler is switched over to a function named shoot. When you release the mouse, it goes back to the aim function. Simple enough. Now let's determine what happens inside shoot.

2. At the bottom of your code, add the following:

```
function shoot() {
  this._x = _xmouse;
  this._y = _ymouse;
  this.vx = this._x-this.oldx;
  this.vy = this._y-this.oldy;
  this.oldx = this._x;
  this.oldy = this._y;
  var dx = whiteBall_mc._x-this._x;
  var dy = whiteBall_mc._y-this._y;
  var dist = Math.sqrt(dx*dx+dy*dy);
  if (dist<110) {
    whiteBall_mc.vx = this.vx;
    whiteBall_mc.vy = this.vy;
    whiteBall_mc.onEnterFrame = ballMove;
    this.onEnterFrame = aim;
  }
}
```

So what's happening here? Well, for now, you'll continue to have the stick stay with the mouse—that's the first two lines. Then you need to find out how fast the stick is moving. This is so you can transfer the stick's velocity to the ball once it hits the ball. You do this by taking the stick's current position and subtracting it from where it was the last time this function was run, which was on the previous frame. You store its location in oldx and oldy each frame, so it can be compared on the next frame. You'll just store vx and vy for now, and come back to these velocity components later, as required.

Next, you need to determine when the tip of the stick is hitting the ball. Again, you'll use the Pythagorean theorem, this time to determine the distance from the cue stick to the ball. If the distance is less than a certain amount, then the cue stick has hit the ball. The following diagram should give you a good idea of how this works:

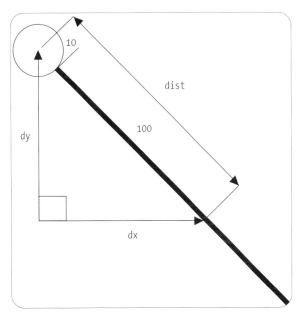

You store the x and y distances in dx and dy. Note that var keeps these values local to the function. Finally, you calculate the distance, dist.

The magic number in this particular case is 110. This is because the stick happens to be 200 pixels long. The registration point, as mentioned earlier, is in the exact center. This means that it's 100 pixels from center to tip. Add to this 10 pixels as half the diameter of the ball and you have the minimum distance between the two. If the distance is less than this, then you have a collision. Obviously, if you change the size of any of your objects, you'll need to adjust this number. Normally, you'll try to avoid coding in numeric values for sizes of things like this. If you use the _width and _height properties of the movie clips themselves, you wind up with a more flexible program. For the sake of simplicity and clarity, we've left these as numeric literals. (Note: You already have BALL_RADIUS assigned. To remove this magic number, you only have to assign a single new constant at the start to define the pool cue width.)

Finally, if dist is less than 110, you give the ball the current velocity of the stick. You then assign its onEnterFrame handler, so that it will start moving. Finally, you switch the stick's onEnterFrame back to aim, so you don't accidentally keep hitting the ball. You can test that out and see that you can actually start knocking that cue ball all over the table!

3. Here's an extra bit of refinement related to the feel of the shooting. There's too much side-to-side motion and it's possible to try to whack the ball with the stick sideways, which gives you some very odd results. Note, though, that while shooting, you don't alter the stick's rotation, which is an effect we wanted. But we wanted the stick to stay lined up with the ball as you move it back and forth, just as if you had it rested on your left hand and were sliding it back and forth with your right. This took another bit of tricky math. The following bold lines are the ones you should add to the shoot function you've just created. (Note that you can find this version in the support file pool_05.fla.)

```
function shoot() {
  var dx = whiteBall_mc._x-_xmouse;
  var dy = whiteBall_mc._y-_ymouse;
  var dist = Math.sqrt(dx*dx+dy*dy);
  this._x = whiteBall_mc._x-Math.cos(angle)*dist;
  this._y = whiteBall_mc._y-Math.sin(angle)*dist;
  this.vx = this._x-this.oldx;
  this.vy = this._y-this.oldy;
  this.oldx = this._x;
  this.oldy = this._y;
  dx = whiteBall_mc._x-this._x;
  dy = whiteBall_mc._y-this._y;
  dist = Math.sqrt(dx*dx+dy*dy);
  if (dist<110) {
    whiteBall_mc.vx = this.vx;
    whiteBall_mc.vy = this.vy;
    whiteBall_mc.onEnterFrame = ballMove;
    this.onEnterFrame = aim;
  }
}
```

Note that you should remove the following code from the previous shoot() function:

```
this._x = _xmouse;
this._y = _ymouse;
```

OK, so let's break down what you've just written. It's those first five lines that are important. The first three should seem pretty familiar. Once again, you're using the theorem of your good friend, Pythagoras, to find the distance of the mouse from the ball. You want to keep the stick at that same distance, but rather than being directly attached to the mouse, you want it to stay lined up at that angle you just chose while aiming.

Remember earlier, in the aim function, that you left the variable, angle, on the timeline, rather than using var to make it local? Here's where you take advantage of that. You now know the distance you want the stick from the ball, and you know the angle. You dive into some more trigonometry to find out its exact location. The next diagram illustrates what you're doing:

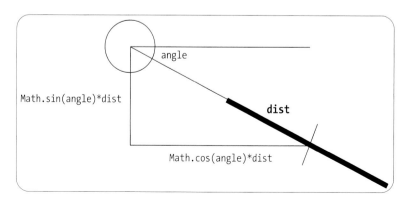

The formulas you use to find the x and y distance from the ball are as follows:

```
Xdistance = cos(angle)*dist
Ydistance = sin(angle)*dist
```

Don't forget that you also need to take into account the ball's location to get the actual stage location of the stick. It all comes together in these two lines:

```
this._x = whiteBall_mc._x-Math.cos(angle)*dist;
this._y = whiteBall_mc._y-Math.sin(angle)*dist;
```

4. There's one more change to make. It's in the onMouseDown section at the top of the code. Type in the following bold code to make the whole thing look like this:

```
onMouseDown = function () {
  var dx = whiteBall_mc._x-_xmouse;
  var dy = whiteBall_mc._y-_ymouse;
  var dist = Math.sqrt(dx*dx+dy*dy);
  if (dist>110) {
    stick_mc.onEnterFrame = shoot;
  }
};
```

Without this fix, if you put the stick over the ball and then click the button to shoot, it will immediately register a hit, and the ball will shoot off in some wild direction. This code checks the distance beforehand. If the distance is less than that magic 110, the stick is already hitting the ball. In that case, nothing happens. This forces the user to pull back a bit before shooting.

Colliding Balls

You've been doing great so far! And if all you wanted to do was shoot a cue ball around an empty table, you'd be golden. But now you'll add at least one more ball to make it interesting. This is going to require a deep breath. Open pool_06.swf for a sneaky preview of the next stage. To get there, here's what to do:

1. In your Library, duplicate the whiteBall movie clip and name it redBall. Double-click the new movie clip and recolor it to comply with its name. Drag an instance of it onto the balls layer and name it REDBALL_mc.

   There are a number of different strategies regarding where to put your collision-detection code. You could put it right in the ballMove function, but when you look into that, you'll see that the red ball would be checking to see if it hit white and the white ball would be checking to see if it hit red. That would be double the work! Once you start adding more balls, each one would have to check every other one, which could add up to a fantastic amount of excess code.

   We like to have the collision code as a separate function running as an onEnterFrame handler on the main timeline. It will check for a collision between the two balls, and if it finds that they've hit each other, it will update their positions and their velocities.

2. You need to set `onEnterFrame` to your new function, which will be called `checkCollison`. At the top of the code after you defined your constants, type in the following line:

   ```
   onEnterFrame = checkCollision;
   ```

3. Next, you need to define the `checkCollision` function. The actual checking for collision is pretty simple. It's almost the same thing you did when you checked if the cue stick hit the ball. You simply find the distance between the two balls, and if the distance is less than a certain amount, you have a hit. The "certain amount" in this case is 20, which is stored in `BALL_DIAMETER`. That's 10 for one half of the diameter of each ball, as you can see in this diagram:

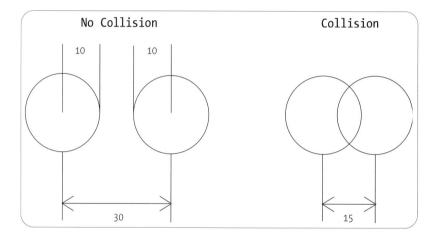

Here's the beginning of the function, showing the detection part. Place this at the bottom of your code:

```
function checkCollision() {
  var dx = redBall_mc._x-whiteBall_mc._x;
  var dy = redBall_mc._y-whiteBall_mc._y;
  var dist = Math.sqrt(dx*dx+dy*dy);
  if (dist<BALL_DIAMETER) {
// the code for the reaction will go here
  }
}
```

OK, so you know that you've achieved a collision. The question is, what do the balls do now? More specifically, in what direction and at what speed do they now move off? To figure this out, you need to learn a bit of physics. Don't panic, we'll go through the theory step by step.

4. To approach the next stage, you'll need to be familiar with a few terms:

   ■ **Speed** is the simple term used to tell how *fast* something is going.

   ■ **Velocity** includes the extra information about both the *speed* at which an object is moving and the *direction* in which an object is moving.

- **Mass** is basically how much something weighs, in simplistic terms. (Of course, strictly speaking, weight is a force, but it's certainly related to the mass. We can see an army of angry physicists marching toward us with torches, much like the final scene of *Frankenstein*!)

- **Momentum** is defined as mass times velocity, and the principle of conservation of momentum says that the total momentum of the two objects before the collision is equal to the total momentum after the collision.

It often helps to simplify things to one dimension to see how momentum works. For example, consider one ball moving left to right at 10 pixels per frame (a vx of 10), and another ball moving right to left at 5 pixels per frame (a vx of –5). Assuming that they hit head on, you can probably predict that each one will bounce off in the direction opposite the one in which it was originally headed. In other words, the first ball will now move right to left, and the other one will now move left to right. But how fast?

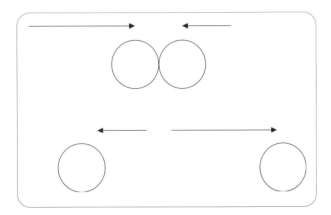

Now this could all get very complex, but you've got luck on your side: both balls are the same size, and they're made of the same material, so they have the same mass. And here's the kicker: When two balls of the same mass collide in one dimension, they simply swap their velocities. In other words, `ball1.vx` now gets the value of `ball2.vx`, and `ball2.vx` takes on the former value of `ball1.vx`:

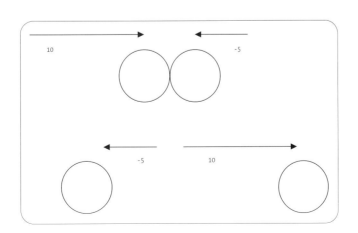

5. Take a quick look at a small Flash movie that demonstrates this concept: `collision_1d.fla`. This movie was constructed by creating a new movie with a frame rate of 20 fps and placing a red ball and a white ball on the stage with the instance names `ball1` and `ball2`. We placed the following code in the first frame:

```
ball1.vx = 10;
ball2.vx = -5;
onEnterFrame = function () {
  ball1._x += ball1.vx;
  ball2._x += ball2.vx;
  var dist = ball2._x-ball1._x;
  if (dist<20) {
    ball2._x = ball1._x+20;
    var vxTemp = ball1.vx;
    ball1.vx = ball2.vx;
    ball2.vx = vxTemp;
  }
};
```

In this file, you simply add the velocities to each ball, and then check their distance. This is, in fact, pretty straightforward because you're working in only one dimension. If the distance is less than 20, then the balls have hit. Remember in the code for bouncing off a wall, when the ball hit the wall, you repositioned the ball so that it was resting right on the edge of the wall? Well, you need to do the same thing with this collision. Otherwise, the balls will momentarily appear to overlap. This can also cause the balls to stick together in circumstances in which the resulting velocities are not enough to separate them.

There are complex methods to determine where each ball would actually be placed at the moment of the collision. We're going to skip them and simply move one of the balls to the edge of the other one. (Those angry physicists are getting closer!) This is another one of those cases in which you can stray from reality for the sake of simplicity, as long as the result looks OK. If you were trying to land a rocket on a distant planet, you couldn't get away with this. Just remember, this is only a game! As long as your inconsistencies aren't noticeable and distracting to the player, you can take a few liberties with reality.

Next, you just swap the vx's of each ball. Note that you need to assign one ball's velocity component to a temporary variable first, or it will be lost when you give it the value of the other one. Test this out with different values for the velocities. Something that might seem a little unreal at first is if you give one ball a vx of 0. When the other ball hits it, the moving ball will stop, and the stationary ball will start moving with the other's velocity. Though it may look a bit strange, be assured it's a realistic reaction. If you've played much pool in real life, you've undoubtedly seen similar occurrences on the table.

Now that you've figured this all out in one dimension, you can jump to the world of two dimensions. In this case, some advanced math is unavoidable, but we'll try to keep it as painless as possible.

Take a look at the following diagram:

In the diagram, two balls have just collided. You can see a dark arrow extending out from each of them, which shows each ball's velocity. The arrow is known as a *vector*. A vector shows direction and magnitude. Remember that velocity is a certain speed in a certain direction. In the diagram, the length of the arrow shows the speed of the ball, and obviously the arrow is pointing in the direction the ball is heading. We also put in some dotted arrows that show each ball's velocity on the x axis and y axis. You can see how these add up to the total velocity.

You can see also that we drew a double line between the two balls. This is the angle of collision, and it's very important. The only part of the balls' momentums that you care about is the amount that lies along this angle. If you can find that, you can figure the resulting velocities exactly as you did previously for a one-dimensional collision.

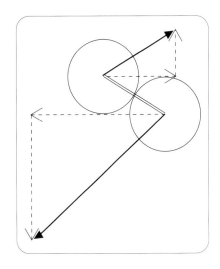

So how do you figure out how much of the momentum or velocity lies on that line? Well, look at the next diagram. It's actually the same image rotated a bit to make the angle of collision lie flat and adjusted the x and y velocities of each ball. These are now labeled vx1, vy1, vx2, and vy2.

Because the angle of collision now lies exactly on the x axis, all you're concerned about is the x velocity of each ball: vx1 and vx2.

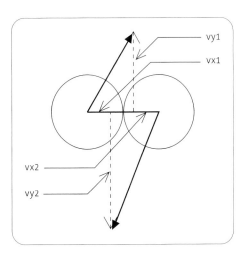

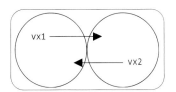

You can then swap the x velocities. The y velocities will stay the same.

Finally, rotate the whole thing back, which gives you the final velocities for each object (we've only shown the final vx and vy of one ball here).

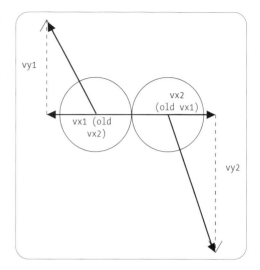

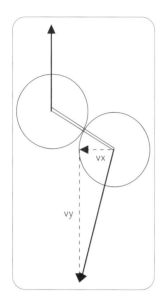

All right, so how do you go about rotating this thing? First off, you need to know how much to rotate it. You need to know what that angle is. If you think back to when you were rotating the cue stick, you got the distance between the stick and the ball on the x and y axes, and you used `Math.atan2(dy, dx)` to get the angle. You'll do the same thing here to get the distance between the two balls.

6. Head back to your ongoing pool game (or the `pool_06.fla` file). You already figured dx and dy to check the distance, so you just need to plug it into the `atan2` function. Go to the handily commented line at the bottom of the code, which tells you "the code for the reaction will go here". Amend it to look like the following:

```
if(dist<BALL_DIAMETER){
  var angle = Math.atan2(dy, dx);
```

7. To do the rotation, you'll use the sine and cosine of this angle several times. Rather than figuring them out over and over, you'll do the calculations only once and save them in a couple of variables:

```
if(dist<BALL_DIAMETER){
  var angle = Math.atan2(dy, dx);
  var cosa = Math.cos(angle);
  var sina = Math.sin(angle);
```

8. Now for the rotation part. With reference to the previous diagram, you have a vector going out to x, y at a certain angle; let's call that angle A. If you rotate that vector by that angle, counterclockwise, you'll get a new vector, x1, y1. Here's the formula you use to accomplish that:

    x1 = cos(A)*x + sin(A)*y
    y1 = cos(A)*y − sin(A)*x

    If you instead want to rotate the vector *clockwise* by angle A, you use a very similar formula:

    x1 = cos(A)*x - sin(A)*y
    y1 = cos(A)*y + sin(A)*x

    All you do is change the + and the −.

9. Let's pull this all together. Keeping in mind the earlier figure that illustrates the swapping of the x velocities, in the game code you want to rotate the vector represented by redBall_mc.vx, redBall_mc.vy, and the vector represented by whiteBall_mc.vx, whiteBall_mc.vy. This will give you roughly the image shown in last diagram (the one illustrating the final velocities), with vectors represented by vx1, vy1, vx2, and vy2. Here's the code for that part:

    ```
    if(dist<BALL_DIAMETER){
        var angle = Math.atan2(dy, dx);
        var cosa = Math.cos(angle);
        var sina = Math.sin(angle);
        var vx1 = cosa*redBall_mc.vx + sina*redBall_mc.vy;
        var vy1 = cosa*redBall_mc.vy - sina*redBall_mc.vx;
        var vx2 = cosa*whiteBall_mc.vx + sina*whiteBall_mc.vy;
        var vy2 = cosa*whiteBall_mc.vy - sina*whiteBall_mc.vx;
    ```

10. Now you just swap vx1 and vx2 and rotate the vector back clockwise. Note that in this next rotation you're rotating the temporary vxs and vys and the result is the actual vx and vy of each ball:

    ```
    var tempvx = vx1;
    var vx2 = vx1;
    var vx1 = tempvx;
    redBall_mc.vx = cosa*vx1 - sina*vy1;
    redBall_mc.vy = cosa*vy1 + sina*vx1;
    whiteBall_mc.vx = cosa*vx2 - sina*vy2;
    whiteBall_mc.vy = cosa*vy2 + sina*vx2;
    redBall_mc.onEnterFrame=ballMove;
    whiteBall_mc.onEnterFrame=ballMove;
    ```

    Don't forget the last step. You want to make sure that both balls are now running the ballMove function and acting on their newfound velocities.

11. In playing around with this and trying to make it a bit more manageable, we found one pretty cool shortcut. Because you're figuring vx1 and assigning it to vx2, and figuring vx2 and assigning it to vx1, you could simply just assign them to their opposite right as you figure them, and avoid all the swapping as follows:

```
    if(dist<BALL_DIAMETER){
      var angle = Math.atan2(dy, dx);
      var cosa = Math.cos(angle);
      var sina = Math.sin(angle);
      var vx2 = cosa*redBall_mc.vx + sina*redBall_mc.vy;
      var vy1 = cosa*redBall_mc.vy - sina*redBall_mc.vx;
      var vx1 = cosa*whiteBall_mc.vx + sina*whiteBall_mc.vy;
      var vy2 = cosa*whiteBall_mc.vy - sina*whiteBall_mc.vx;
      redBall_mc.vx = cosa*vx1 - sina*vy1;
      redBall_mc.vy = cosa*vy1 + sina*vx1;
      whiteBall_mc.vx = cosa*vx2 - sina*vy2;
      whiteBall_mc.vy = cosa*vy2 + sina*vx2;
      redBall_mc.onEnterFrame=ballMove;
      whiteBall_mc.onEnterFrame=ballMove;
    }
```

We know this looks like a lot, but trust us, after you do this a few times, it really does start to make sense. And try as we definitely have, we haven't yet found a simpler way of doing all this. At any rate, when you run the file and see just how realistic the play is, you'll see it's worth the typing, if not the aggravation of trying to figure out exactly what's going on.

12. There's just one more thing you want to add to this function. Recall in the small `collision_1d.fla` file that you repositioned one of the balls to be just touching the other. Although it doesn't seem to make a big difference here, once you add a bunch more objects into the mix, it will. So you'll just take care of it now. Because you're now working in two dimensions, it's a bit more complex than just adding the ball diameter on the x axis. You need to add the diameter along the angle of collision.

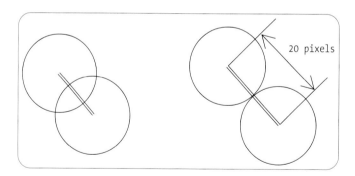

This is done by the following two lines:

```
    redBall_mc._x=whiteBall_mc._x+cosa*BALL_DIAMETER;
    redBall_mc._y=whiteBall_mc._y+sina*BALL_DIAMETER;
```

These can go in right after you figure the values for `cosa` and `sina`. Here's the whole function:

```
    function checkCollision() {
      var dx = redBall_mc._x-whiteBall_mc._x;
      var dy = redBall_mc._y-whiteBall_mc._y;
```

```
    var dist = Math.sqrt(dx*dx+dy*dy);
    if(dist<BALL_DIAMETER){
      var angle = Math.atan2(dy, dx);
      var cosa = Math.cos(angle);
      var sina = Math.sin(angle);
      redBall_mc._x=whiteBall_mc._x+cosa*BALL_DIAMETER;
      redBall_mc._y=whiteBall_mc._y+sina*BALL_DIAMETER;
      var vx2 = cosa*redBall_mc.vx + sina*redBall_mc.vy;
      var vy1 = cosa*redBall_mc.vy - sina*redBall_mc.vx;
      var vx1 = cosa*whiteBall_mc.vx + sina*whiteBall_mc.vy;
      var vy2 = cosa*whiteBall_mc.vy - sina*whiteBall_mc.vx;
      redBall_mc.vx = cosa*vx1 - sina*vy1;
      redBall_mc.vy = cosa*vy1 + sina*vx1;
      whiteBall_mc.vx = cosa*vx2 - sina*vy2;
      whiteBall_mc.vy = cosa*vy2 + sina*vx2;
      redBall_mc.onEnterFrame=ballMove;
      whiteBall_mc.onEnterFrame=ballMove;
    }
  }
```

The only remaining problem is one that only presents itself with the new version of Flash. In Flash MX and earlier, an undefined variable, when evaluated within a mathematical operation, defaulted to zero. In Flash MX 2004, it will evaluate as undefined, and so will most likely cause a result of NaN, or "Not a Number." You can demonstrate this with the following code in a new Flash document:

```
trace(34 + y);
```

In Flash MX, this would have returned "34" in the Output window, but now it will return "NaN". How does this affect your current code? Well, you have yet to assign vx and vy values for the red ball (the white ball gets assigned these values in the shoot function). For the collision to work, you need to declare these variables at the start.

13. Head to the top of the code and add the following bold lines:

```
DAMP = .98;
MINSPEED = .1;
redBall_mc.vx = 0;
redBall_mc.vy = 0;
onEnterFrame = checkCollision;
```

Now you have some default values for your red ball's velocity and your operations in checkCollision will work like a charm. Test it and see.

And there you have it: a 99.9% realistic billiard-ball collision! Once you've convinced yourself that this will fool all but the most finicky of physicists, you can move on and throw some more color on the table.

Multiple Collisions

When you open up the next incarnation of the game, pool_07.fla, you'll immediately see that we've added five more balls to the table. We know what you're thinking: Shouldn't there be ten balls, plus the cue? Of course there should be! But we saved that for your after-class assignment. You'll get rolling with what you see there.

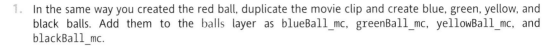

1. In the same way you created the red ball, duplicate the movie clip and create blue, green, yellow, and black balls. Add them to the balls layer as blueBall_mc, greenBall_mc, yellowBall_mc, and blackBall_mc.

   Now here's a problem. In the last version, the names of the balls were hard-coded. The checkCollision function would work with—and *only* with—two objects named redBall_mc and whiteBall_mc. There are two issues with that.

   One issue is that it isn't flexible. Already the function is obsolete because you have to completely recode it to work with your new additions. And when you go to do your homework, you'll have to recode it again to work with whatever you add.

   The other issue is that if you hard-code each ball's name, you wind up with a huge, redundant, inefficient function. All that code you wrote for collision and reaction was just for two balls. You'd have to have a section of the function with all that code just for comparing white to red. Then you'd need another section the same size for white to blue, another for white to purple, and so on. When you got through with all of the colors compared to white, there would be another section for red to blue, red to purple, and so on. And then another section for blue compared to all the others. . . .

   Of course, that would be ridiculous. Instead, you'll write the code just once and use some variables instead of the actual names of the balls. That's easy enough. Then you just need a way to loop through and get the ball's names and plug them into the variables.

2. If you look at the code in the file, you see the first line accomplishes this. You just put the names of all the balls into an array. Put the following line at the top of your code. Then you can loop through the array with a for loop and get each ball to test.

   ```
   balls = [whiteBall_mc, redBall_mc, blueBall_mc, yellowBall_mc,
   ➥purpleBall_mc, greenBall_mc, blackBall_mc];
   ```

   Now personally, the first time I ever did something like this, I thought I was pretty clever. I made a double, nested for loop. The outer loop stepped through all of the elements to get the first object to test. So, for instance, the first time through it would grab the white ball.

   Then the inner loop would again step through the array, testing the white ball against each object. It looked something like this:

   ```
   for(var i=0;i<balls.length;i++){
     for(var j=0;j<balls.length;j++){
       // test for collision between balls[i] and balls[j]
     }
   }
   ```

   Pretty cool—it will test each ball against every other ball! But the first bug appeared on the first loop, where it tried to test the white ball against the first element of the array, which was the white ball. Hmm . . . not good. So I added an if statement to make sure that the two objects being tested weren't the same object. A bit clunky, perhaps, but it handled the bug.

   Then I realized another problem. On the first outer loop, the white ball is tested against every other ball for collision. Excellent. Then, on the second outer loop, the red ball is tested against every other ball—including the white ball. But I already checked for red and white. On the next loop, the blue ball checks against white and red, both of which have already been checked. It turns out I was doing twice the number of tests necessary.

I'd like to say that I put together a simple and elegant solution that totally handles this, but I can't. However, I can say that I finally read about the simple and elegant solution that totally handles this and is used by anyone programming this stuff.

Basically, you just start the inner loop with an index one higher than the current outer loop. If the outer loop is on the fourth element, the inner loop only has to pick up the fifth onward. Also, because all will have been tested by the time the outer loop gets to the last element, you don't need to test that against anything. So you can end the outer loop at length-1. Here's how the revised version looks:

```
for(var i=0;i<balls.length-1;i++){
  for(var j=i+1;j<balls.length;j++){
    // test for collision between balls[i] and balls[j]
  }
}
```

Not bad! Four extra characters for twice the efficiency!

3. Now, plug that into the checkCollision function you wrote in the last exercise:

```
function checkCollision() {
  var len=balls.length;
  for (var i=0; i<len-1; i++) {
    ball1_mc = balls[i];
    for (var j=i+1; j<len; j++) {
      ball2_mc = balls[j];
      var dx = ball1_mc._x-ball2_mc._x;
      var dy = ball1_mc._y-ball2_mc._y;
      var dist = Math.sqrt(dx*dx+dy*dy);
      if (dist<BALL_DIAMETER) {
        var angle = Math.atan2(dy, dx);
        var cosa = Math.cos(angle);
        var sina = Math.sin(angle);
        ball1_mc._x = ball2_mc._x+cosa*BALL_DIAMETER;
        ball1_mc._y = ball2_mc._y+sina*BALL_DIAMETER;
        var vx2 = cosa*ball1_mc.vx+sina*ball1_mc.vy;
        var vy1 = cosa*ball1_mc.vy-sina*ball1_mc.vx;
        var vx1 = cosa*ball2_mc.vx+sina*ball2_mc.vy;
        var vy2 = cosa*ball2_mc.vy-sina*ball2_mc.vx;
        ball1_mc.vx = cosa*vx1-sina*vy1;
        ball1_mc.vy = cosa*vy1+sina*vx1;
        ball2_mc.vx = cosa*vx2-sina*vy2;
        ball2_mc.vy = cosa*vy2+sina*vx2;
        ball1_mc.onEnterFrame = ballMove;
        ball2_mc.onEnterFrame = ballMove;
      }
    }
  }
}
```

You can plainly see the two for loops, which are exactly as you just wrote them. After each loop, you assign the array element to a temporary variable. Although this might indeed be easier to write, the most obvious benefit of using the temporary variable is that it's a lot more efficient to deal with a simple variable than to access an array like that. It works out a little faster. For this same reason, you store the length of the array in the variable len instead of accessing it every iteration of each loop.

There are, of course, other changes in your code in the midst of these new loops. Whereas before you had redBall_mc and whiteBall_mc, you now have the generic ball1_mc and ball2_mc, which will change on each loop through. Make sure those are changed in your code.

4. As a final step, you need to make sure to assign default vx and vy values to all of the table's balls. You can do this in a single line for..in loop at the top of your code, running through your balls array:

```
balls = [whiteBall_mc, redBall_mc, blueBall_mc, yellowBall_mc,
➥purpleBall_mc, greenBall_mc, blackBall_mc];
for (i in balls) balls[i].vx = balls[i].vy = 0;
```

Sinking the Balls

You're now approaching the end of the line for your billiards game. There has been one really obvious omission so far: holes. Sure, you can knock the balls around, but they need somewhere to go eventually. Check out pool_08.fla if you want to see where you're headed.

Now we're going to teach you yet another time- and code-saving trick for collision detection. Obviously, you're going to need six holes on the table, two on the sides and one in each of the four corners. You can make a round black shape, somewhat larger than a ball, turn it into a movie clip, and put it in place. You wind up with something that looks like this:

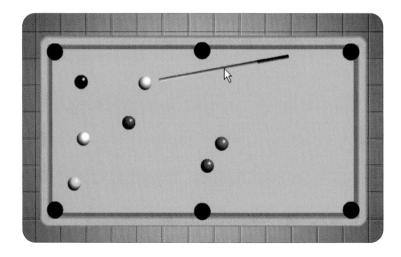

Now, each ball will need to test to see if it has hit any of the holes. Naturally, this would be best done in the ballMove function, and it would have to occur right after the final positioning of the ball. The built-in hitTest function serves just fine for this.

The two versions of this command are this:

        movieClip1.hitTest(movieClip2)

and this:

        movieClip.hitTest(x, y, shapeflag)

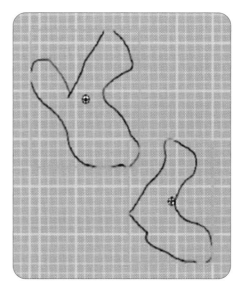

The first version merely tests if movieClip1 has collided with movieClip2. It does this by using bounding boxes. A *bounding box* is an imaginary rectangle that completely surrounds a movie clip. Although this is the quickest method, it's also the least accurate. As long as the two bounding boxes of the clips overlap at any point, hitTest will return true. Here's a simple example of a couple of irregularly shaped movie clips and their associated bounding boxes:

You can see that although the two shapes are not touching at all, the bounding boxes are. Thus, Flash would consider that a collision between the two had taken place. This is fine for rectangular-shaped clips and often passable for small, fast-moving objects. But in this case, it's not nearly good enough.

Let's look at the second version. You see this has an x and a y as arguments. It will return true if the stage coordinates represented by that x and y are hitting the movie clip. If you pass an argument of true to the shapeflag argument, Flash will look at the shape of the visible movie clip. If that x, y location represents an area that has some color on it, it returns true. If you give shapeflag an argument of false, it goes back to using the bounding box of the clip. But remember, now you're testing a specific point to see if it's within the box.

If you look into it closely, you see that the x, y version with shapeflag set to true is best for our purposes. The x and y will be the _x and _y location of the ball, which is its center. If you imagine the following two examples, the first shows a ball close to, and somewhat overlapping, a hole. But the center would still be solidly on the table, so it won't fall in. The second example shows the ball at the point at which it will actually drop into the hole and, in this case, will generate a collision.

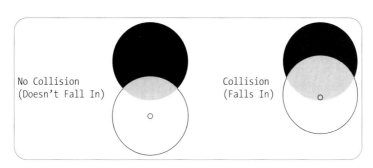

No Collision
(Doesn't Fall In)

Collision
(Falls In)

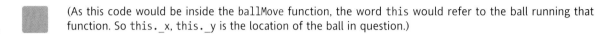
The relevant code would look like this:

```
if(hole_mc.hitTest(this._x, this._y, true)){
  // do something here
}
```

(As this code would be inside the ballMove function, the word this would refer to the ball running that function. So this._x, this._y is the location of the ball in question.)

Now that you know how to check one hole, you need to figure out how to do all six. Here's where we reveal the neat trick we mentioned a few paragraphs back.

The key to this is that you don't really care which hole the ball has fallen in—you just want to know if the ball has hit any hole. So, you put all of these holes into one otherwise empty movie clip called holes and then do a hit test on that entire movie clip. This works just fine as long as you're still using shapeflag. Otherwise, the bounding box covers the entire table and will always register a hit. This little trick lets you get away with one hit test, rather than six.

All right, now that you've gone through the theory, open the file pool_08.fla. The first thing you'll see is that the table now has some holes in it. If you're working on your own movie, here's how to go about making them:

1. Create a new layer underneath the balls layer and call it holes. Use a circular black paint brush and paint the holes directly onto the layer.

2. With the holes in place, click the layer to select everything and select Convert to Symbol (F8). Call the symbol holes, and give it an instance name of holes_mc in the Property inspector.

    The positioning of the holes is tough, so be prepared to nudge them around until they give good play. If the balls are too far onto the table, they'll fall in too often. If they're too far off the table, they'll always bounce off the side before they get a chance to register a hit. We found the corner pockets particularly tough.

3. So what about coding? Well, the only change here is in the existing ballMove function. Here it is with the hit test section included:

```
function ballMove() {
  this.vx *= DAMP;
  this.vy *= DAMP;
  this._x += this.vx;
  this._y += this.vy;
  if (this._x>RIGHT) {
    this._x = RIGHT;
    this.vx *= BOUNCE;
  } else if (this._x<LEFT) {
    this._x = LEFT;
    this.vx *= BOUNCE;
  }
```

```
    if (this._y>BOTTOM) {
      this._y = BOTTOM;
      this.vy *= BOUNCE;
    } else if (this._y<TOP) {
      this._y = TOP;
      this.vy *= BOUNCE;
    }
    if (holes_mc.hitTest(this._x, this._y, true)) {
      this._x = 10000;
      this._y = Math.random()*10000;
      delete this.onEnterFrame;
    }
    this.speed = Math.sqrt(this.vx*this.vx+this.vy*this.vy);
    if (this.speed<MINSPEED) {
      this.vx = 0;
      this.vy = 0;
      delete this.onEnterFrame;
    }
  }
```

Here's what the code does. When a hit test comes back positive, you need to remove the ball. Had you originally attached the balls using attachMovie, you could simply use removeMovieClip here. But because you created the balls in the authoring environment, you have to resort to the old-fashioned method of removing movie clips—essentially shooting them off into the void. In other words, you just give them an _x or _y position that's way off the stage so they'll never be seen. In this case, you also want to make sure that subsequent balls don't land in the same position, thus triggering later collisions, so you add in a random factor that should pretty much keep the balls away from each other 99.9% of the time. Finally, you delete the onEnterFrame handler, which stops them from moving. (As a side note, in fact it *is* possible to remove a movie clip created and placed on stage in the authoring environment by first swapping the clip to a positive depth. In this case, however, this would require you to then reattach the balls upon the stage if a new game was to begin, which is additional code that we don't cover in this chapter.)

We admit there are a few improvements that could be made to this whole system. One thing that could be done is to remove the ball's name from the array using Array.splice. This would keep the collision-detection code from trying to check the ball now that it's out of play. Our only justification is that the code has been optimized enough to work smoothly with all the balls on the table, as it must at the beginning of the game. Although you could make it more efficient as the game goes on by removing balls from the array, we decided not to fix something that worked. (Oh, and also, it's an extra-credit homework assignment if you want to take it on!) Furthermore, we wanted to spend the last few pages of this chapter making a few enhancements that will improve the visual and audio experience.

As an additional note, you may want to determine which ball was just sunk so you can code in penalties for scratching, or sinking, the eight ball. You do this by testing if the current ball is equal to the ball of choice:

```
if (holes_mc.hitTest(this._x, this._y, true)) {
  if(this == whiteBall_mc){
    // code here for what happens if you "scratch"
  } else {
    // otherwise, it was a colored ball:
    this._x = 10000;
    this._y = Math.random()*10000;
    delete this.onEnterFrame;
  }
}
```

Realistic Shadows

Now let's add a few visual enhancements. First off, you'll give the balls a shadow. It would be relatively easy to edit each ball and add a little shadow shape under the color of the ball. It would look fine all by itself. But then you would soon see that each ball is either above or below each other ball. And that means all of the graphics for that ball. Therefore, if the white ball was on top of the red ball, the white ball's shadow would also be on top of the red ball. That would look very strange, to say the least.

In fact, a simple way around this is to keep all the shadows on their own layer and move them around as the corresponding balls are moved. Although this adds a bit to the computation required, it ends up not taking up too many CPU cycles to have much of an impact.

To break down the finished product, open pool_09.fla.

1. Create a new layer just above the table layer and call it ball shadows.

2. Create a new movie clip composed of a dark green circle, with a size of 20x20 pixels. Instead of making its registration point dead center, move it up and to the right just a little to offset the shadow from the ball.

3. On your ball shadows layer, drag seven copies of the shadows movie clip. Give them instance names of sh01 through sh07.

4. The code amendments are once again quite simple. Add these few lines to the top:

```
balls = [whiteBall_mc, redBall_mc, blueBall_mc, yellowBall_mc,
➥purpleBall_mc, greenBall_mc, blackBall_mc];
for (i in balls) balls[i].vx = balls[i].vy = 0;
shadows = [sh01, sh02, sh03, sh04, sh05, sh06, sh07];
for (i=0; i<7; i++) {
  balls[i].shadow = shadows[i];
  shadows[i]._x = balls[i]._x;
  shadows[i]._y = balls[i]._y;
}
```

Here, you put the names of the shadows in an array, just like you did with the balls. Then you loop through and assign each ball its very own shadow. You do this by giving the ball a property called shadow. This holds a reference to a particular shadow movie clip.

5. Move further down into the ballMove function again, and you'll see how easy it is to manipulate these shadows. You simply wait until the ball has reached its final _x, _y position, and then you move the shadow to the same place. Because all the shadows are on a layer below all the balls, they will look just right. The code to add is in bold:

```
function ballMove() {
  this.vx *= DAMP;
  this.vy *= DAMP;
  this._x += this.vx;
  this._y += this.vy;
  if (this._x>RIGHT) {
    this._x = RIGHT;
    this.vx *= BOUNCE;
  } else if (this._x<LEFT) {
    this._x = LEFT;
    this.vx *= BOUNCE;
  }
  if (this._y>BOTTOM) {
    this._y = BOTTOM;
    this.vy *= BOUNCE;
  } else if (this._y<TOP) {
    this._y = TOP;
    this.vy *= BOUNCE;
  }
  if (holes_mc.hitTest(this._x, this._y, true)) {
    this._x = 10000;
    this._y = Math.random()*10000;
    delete this.onEnterFrame;
  }
  this.shadow._x = this._x;
  this.shadow._y = this._y;
  this.speed = Math.sqrt(this.vx*this.vx+this.vy*this.vy);
  if (this.speed<MINSPEED) {
    this.vx = 0;
    this.vy = 0;
    delete this.onEnterFrame;
  }
}
```

Well, that was too easy, and it really adds some depth to the whole game.

Why not take it a step or two further? Let's give the stick a shadow. Actually, you'll give it two shadows: one shadow for the table and another for the floor. If you offset them a bit differently, it will give an incredible sense of depth and really make the table itself seem to pop right up off the floor.

Check out the next iteration: pool_10.fla.

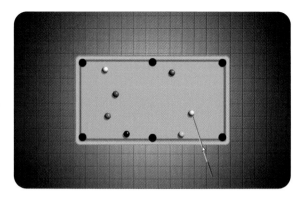

6. In your Library, duplicate the stick movie clip and call it stick shadow. Select the whole thing and fill it using the Paint Bucket tool set to black with a 30% alpha setting (you can set this in the Color Mixer palette).

7. Create two new layers. The first, named floor stick shadow, should be right above the floor shadow layer. The second, table shadow, lies right above the balls layer. Each layer has an instance of the new stick shadow movie clip, named floorShadow_mc and tableShadow_mc.

8. All you need to do is position them each time the stick moves. This takes a mere six lines of code. You'll change the _x and _y position of each shadow, and then the rotation. This code will go in two places: the aim and shoot functions. Here they are:

```
function aim() {
  var dx = whiteBall_mc._x-_xmouse;
  var dy = whiteBall_mc._y-_ymouse;
  angle = Math.atan2(dy, dx);
  this._rotation = angle*180/Math.PI;
  this._x = _xmouse;
  this._y = _ymouse;
  tableShadow_mc._x = this._x-5;
  tableShadow_mc._y = this._y+5;
  tableShadow_mc._rotation = this._rotation;
  floorShadow_mc._x = this._x-20;
  floorShadow_mc._y = this._y+20;
  floorShadow_mc._rotation = this._rotation;
}
function shoot() {
  var dx = whiteBall_mc._x-_xmouse;
  var dy = whiteBall_mc._y-_ymouse;
  var dist = Math.sqrt(dx*dx+dy*dy);
  this._x = whiteBall_mc._x-Math.cos(angle)*dist;
  this._y = whiteBall_mc._y-Math.sin(angle)*dist;
  this.vx = this._x-this.oldx;
  this.vy = this._y-this.oldy;
  this.oldx = this._x;
  this.oldy = this._y;
  dx = whiteBall_mc._x-this._x;
  dy = whiteBall_mc._y-this._y;
```

```
    dist = Math.sqrt(dx*dx+dy*dy);
    if (dist<110) {
      whiteBall_mc.vx = this.vx;
      whiteBall_mc.vy = this.vy;
      whiteBall_mc.onEnterFrame = ballMove;
      this.onEnterFrame = aim;
    }
    tableShadow_mc._x = this._x-5;
    tableShadow_mc._y = this._y+5;
    tableShadow_mc._rotation = this._rotation;
    floorShadow_mc._x = this._x-20;
    floorShadow_mc._y = this._y+20;
    floorShadow_mc._rotation = this._rotation;
  }
```

As you see, the table shadow is offset 5 pixels from the stick, and the floor shadow is offset 20 pixels. This makes for a great optical illusion of depth. Because the floor shadow layer is under the table, you only see that shadow on the floor. Unfortunately, the table shadow will appear not only on the table, but also on the floor. Because the stick shouldn't cast a double shadow like that, it ruins the effect a bit. You need a way of limiting the table shadow to the table itself.

9. What you need is a simple mask. There are two ways you can use a mask here. You can either create a mask layer and draw a mask or use a scripted mask. Although a scripted mask is pretty cool, it's easy enough to use a simple mask layer here. Just make a new layer above the table shadow layer. Draw a filled rectangle with any color in it. Adjust the size to completely cover all parts of the table but not extend onto the floor. Then right-click (CMD+click on a Mac) that layer in the timeline and set it to be a mask layer.

Now test the file and you'll see that you've got all the basics of a very nice little Flash pool game. We hope it's inspired you to take things further. We leave it up to you to extend the game to include rules and player details. And wouldn't some nice sound effects enhance the player experience and help put some emphasis on your wonderful collision detection?

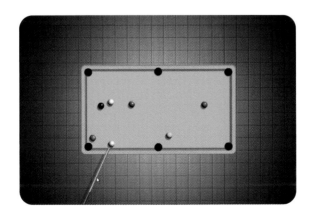

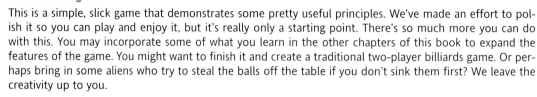

Summary

This is a simple, slick game that demonstrates some pretty useful principles. We've made an effort to polish it so you can play and enjoy it, but it's really only a starting point. There's so much more you can do with this. You may incorporate some of what you learn in the other chapters of this book to expand the features of the game. You might want to finish it and create a traditional two-player billiards game. Or perhaps bring in some aliens who try to steal the balls off the table if you don't sink them first? We leave the creativity up to you.

In any case, in this chapter we covered a variety of types of collision detection: object to wall, object to object using calculated distance, and object to object using hitTest with bounding boxes and shapes. We also covered how to test multiple objects against each other and one object against many objects, and how to react to a collision between two moving objects when they have the same mass. If you're interested, you can easily find the formulas for conservation of momentum and work out how to fit them into checkCollision. This will enable you to handle objects of different masses, and it opens the door to many new possibilities for physically realistic games.

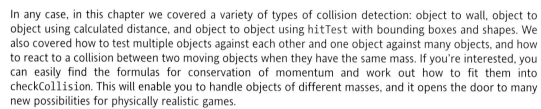

Keith Peters

Keith's bio can be seen on page 68.

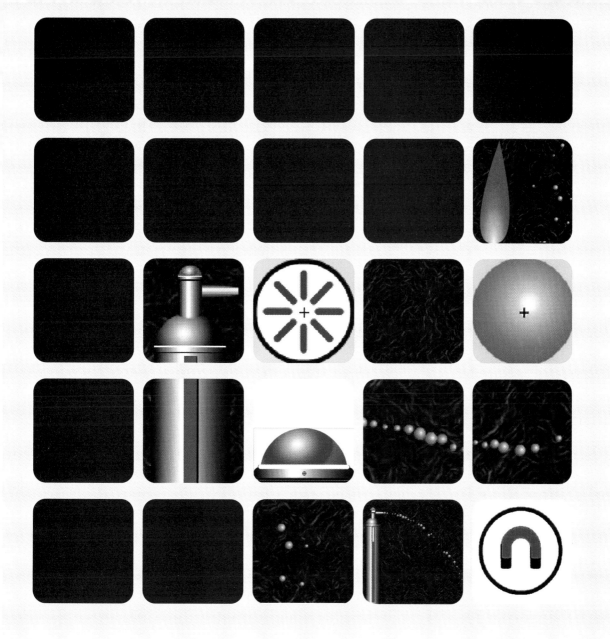

GRAVITY AND PHYSICS

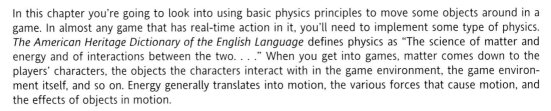

In this chapter you're going to look into using basic physics principles to move some objects around in a game. In almost any game that has real-time action in it, you'll need to implement some type of physics. *The American Heritage Dictionary of the English Language* defines physics as "The science of matter and energy and of interactions between the two. . . ." When you get into games, matter comes down to the players' characters, the objects the characters interact with in the game environment, the game environment itself, and so on. Energy generally translates into motion, the various forces that cause motion, and the effects of objects in motion.

Game developers have been amateur physicists since day one. For examples of this, you can go back to the old classics such as Pong. You have a ball: matter. The ball is moving: energy. If the ball hits a paddle: more matter also moving with energy, and there is a physical reaction that changes the energy of the ball, sending it moving off in another direction. Some books on game-programming physics make college physics books look tame. Basically, as you model your game environment according to real-world physics formulas, it looks more and more like something that would happen in the real world.

One important distinction to make between game physics and serious, real-world physics is that in games, you can cheat! If you read the last chapter, you saw a few examples of this; you'll see a few more in this chapter. There is a principle in fiction writing known as the "suspension of disbelief." It's what makes fiction work, and it also applies to games. When you read a novel, you know it's not true, but if it's interesting enough and the situations and events are portrayed in a realistic manner, you become willing to ignore the fact that you're reading a made-up story, and you believe it for a while. If the storyline is confusing or it's poorly written, you're continually reminded that you have a book in your hands, not a little universe.

This principle also applies to games. You know that you're not really shooting aliens, but if the game plays well, it draws you in and lets you pretend for a while. No doubt you've also played a poorly designed game that continually reminded you that you were sitting in front of a computer trying to play a game. Realistic physics goes a long way toward suspending disbelief, but it's not the only factor, and it doesn't need to be perfect as long as the rest of the game elements (the storyline, the graphics, and so on) do their job in pulling the player in.

That said, in this chapter we concentrate on physics alone. The original idea for this game came from an old game called **Bill's Tomato Game**. In this game, a tomato would appear in a particular starting spot on your screen. You had various trampolines, fans, springs, and other paraphernalia available to position around the screen. You then launched the tomato, and hopefully all your gadgets would guide it past various hazards—fire, acid, tomato-eating monsters, and so forth—to the exit point.

The game you'll construct in this chapter is quite a bit simpler than Bill's Tomato Game, but it follows the same idea of guiding something from a start point to a goal by positioning various devices.

Fire-Fighting Game

Every good game has a story. Here's this game's story:

You are the science officer on an intergalactic spaceship. Some faulty under-floor wiring has a tendency to cause small fires, which you need to extinguish before they get out of control. You have a tank of water to spray on the fires, but it's much too large to lug around and aim. Luckily, you've just discovered a revolutionary new material that acts as a water magnet. Certain forms of this material will attract water, and others will repel it. By positioning these magnets around the lab, you can direct a flow of water to a fire.

Spraying Water

In this section we take you step by step through the creation of the movie, and then we unpick the code at length. If you want to skip all this or just work with the file we used, open water_01.fla from the downloadable files for this chapter, which you can obtain from the friends of ED website at www.friendsofed.com. You'll see a water tank against a background.

To create the file, follow these steps:

1. Create a new Flash document with the dimensions 800x400 and a frame rate of 20 fps. Create three layers: background, tank, and code.

2. You need to create a tank with a gauge, a nozzle, and a button. Create a new movie clip symbol (*CTRL+F8*) and call it tank. Draw your tank, which should look something like this:

3. Create another new movie clip and name it gauge. This is basically a vertical metallic bar, but make sure the center-point crosshairs are at the bottom of the bar.

   Create yet another movie clip and call it waterLevel. This is an identical bar, only this time in watery blue. Drag a copy of this bar onto the metallic gauge and call it waterLevel_mc. Then close the gauge movie clip.

4. Drag a copy of this movie clip onto the newly created tank and name the instance gauge_mc. Close the movie clip tank.

5. Create another new movie clip and call it nozzle. Do your best rendering of a nozzle, with the center point at the leaky end, and return to the main timeline.

6. Create another new symbol—this time a button. Call it start.

7. When you have all your movie clips, drag an instance of each onto the main timeline. Call them waterTank_mc, nozzle_mc, and start_btn.

8. Create a new movie clip symbol and call it drop. It should represent one drop of water. You can see ours here:

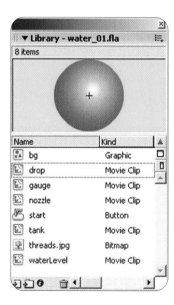

9. You'll need a whole lot more than a single drop of water. Use attachMovie to create drops as you need them. To do that, you need to export the movie clip from the Library. You can do this as you create the clip, by checking the Export for ActionScript box in the Convert to Symbol or Create New Symbol dialog boxes. If you've already done that, you can right-click (CMD+click for Mac users) the symbol in the Library, and choose Linkage. Give the clip a linkage name of drop. Now it's available to the attachMovie command.

10. In the first frame of the code layer, add the following:

```
RIGHT = Stage.width;
LEFT = 0;
TOP = 0;
BOTTOM = Stage.height;
GRAV = .5;
depth = 0;
dropSize = 0;
waterLevel = 100;
// start spraying
start_btn.onPress = function() {
  squirtInt = setInterval(squirt, 50);
};
// stop spraying
start_btn.onRelease = start_btn.onReleaseOutside=function () {
  clearInterval(squirtInt);
};
function squirt() {
  // make a drop of water
  var drop_mc = attachMovie("drop", "d"+depth, depth++);
  // vary its size
  drop_mc._xscale = drop_mc._yscale=125+Math.sin(dropSize += .9)*50;
  // position it at end of nozzle
  drop_mc._x = nozzle_mc._x+5;
  drop_mc._y = nozzle_mc._y;
  // give it some speed
  drop_mc.vx = 10;
  drop_mc.vy = Math.random()-.5;
  // assign enterFrame handler
  drop_mc.onEnterFrame = move;
  // reduce water level
  waterLevel -= .1;
  // adjust gauge
  waterTank_mc.gauge_mc.waterLevel_mc._yscale = waterLevel;
  // check if water is gone
  if (waterLevel<=0) {
    // disable button
    delete start_btn.onPress;
    // stop spraying
    clearInterval(squirtInt);
  }
}
function move() {
  // add gravity
  this.vy += GRAV;
  // add velocity to position
  this._x += this.vx;
  this._y += this.vy;
  // if off stage, remove
```

```
        if (this._x>RIGHT || this._x<LEFT) this.removeMovieClip();
        // if hit floor, splash a bit, then change onEnterFrame handler
        if (this._y>BOTTOM) {
          this._x += Math.random()*20;
          this._y = BOTTOM;
          this.onEnterFrame = evap;
        }
      }
    }
    function evap() {
      // shrink a bit
      this._xscale -= 2;
      // squash it down, as it is now like a puddle
      this._yscale = this._xscale/2;
      // if all gone, remove
      if (this._xscale<1) {
        this.removeMovieClip();
      }
    }
```

We've tried to comment this code pretty well, but we'll go through the basics here. First, you define some constants for the edges of the playing area based on the stage size, and you define one constant for gravity. You then set the water level at 100 and initialize the variables depth and dropSize.

Next come a couple of functions to activate the button on top of the tank. The first one is assigned as the onPress handler. The next one is assigned as both the onRelease and onReleaseOutside handlers. These functions are now called each time you click the button and release it. We highly recommend using onReleaseOutside anytime you use onRelease, when you're using release to cancel an action started by an onPress. This prevents a situation in which the user clicks the button and then accidentally shifts his mouse hand a bit, causing the cursor to be off of the button when it's released. If you don't handle onReleaseOutside, you never start or stop the action intended for onRelease, causing the user to frantically click away in an attempt to handle the unexpected consequences. Another little trick is that if you go in and edit the button and check the hit state, you'll see a shape much larger than the visible shape of the button. This makes the button much easier to "hit." It's a good idea to do this whenever you have smallish buttons, if you don't want the user's hand to cramp up constantly trying to find that tiny specific spot where the button actually works.

The button functions make use of one of Flash's most exciting features: setInterval. This causes a function to execute over and over every so many milliseconds:

```
    start_btn.onPress = function() {
      squirtInt = setInterval(squirt, 50);
    };
```

The preceding few code lines tell Flash to execute the squirt function every 50 milliseconds, or 20 times per second. When you run setInterval, it also returns a value called the **interval ID**. You use this when you want to stop the function, and it occurs on the onRelease/onReleaseOutside handlers right here:

```
    start_btn.onRelease = start_btn.onReleaseOutside=function () {
      clearInterval(squirtInt);
    };
```

You use the command clearInterval to tell Flash to stop executing the function connected to that particular interval ID. So what happens here is that you click the button and the squirt function repeats, every 50 milliseconds. When you release the button, the function stops repeating. Pretty simple, actually.

So, what does the squirt function do? It creates one drop of water and starts it moving. As mentioned, the movie clip drop is exported from the Library. The first thing squirt does is attach an instance of it on the stage:

```
var drop_mc = attachMovie("drop", "d"+depth, depth++);
```

It then varies the drop's size slightly, using a sine function. Math.sin() will return a number from –1 to +1, depending on the number fed to it as an argument. If you continually increase that argument, the result will go up and down smoothly, in a sine wave. Here, you use the variable dropSize and increase it by .9 each time the function is run:

```
Math.sin(dropSize += .9)
```

You then multiply that times 50, which gives you a number from –50 to +50. Adding that to 125 and assigning the result to _xscale and _yscale gives you a nice range of varying drop sizes, from 75% to 175% of their original size.

```
drop_mc._xscale = drop_mc._yscale = 125 + Math.sin(dropSize += .9)*50;
```

Then you position this newly formed droplet on the edge of the nozzle and assign it a velocity on both x and y:

```
drop_mc._x = nozzle_mc._x+5;
drop_mc._y = nozzle_mc._y;
drop_mc.vx = 10;
drop_mc.vy = Math.random()-.5;
```

Note the last line. Math.random() returns a random number from 0 to just under 1. If you subtract .5 from that, you get a number from roughly –0.5 to +0.5, which gives you a slight variation or spray in the stream of water.

The last thing you do with the drop is assign it a function to run each frame, move, which obviously enough takes care of moving it:

```
drop_mc.onEnterFrame = move;
```

The rest of the function keeps track of the water level. Each time a drop is shot, the water level goes down a bit. At the top of the file, you can see that the variable waterLevel is set to 100. You now can use that variable to scale a nested clip called waterLevel_mc, which as you recall you put inside gauge_mc, which in turn is inside waterTank_mc. This is just the blue strip you see on the side of the tank. As the water level goes down, the strip shrinks, giving a visual indication of how much water is left. When the water level hits zero, you disable the button by deleting its onPress handler, and you kill the interval by using clearInterval to stop any water from squirting.

Next up you make the water move by defining the move function. This is pretty simple, and it's where physics first comes in. You have an **x component** and a **y component** to the water's velocity. Note that the term **velocity** refers specifically to a speed in a particular direction. In simple terms, you can just add the x and y velocities of the drop to find the distance that it will move each frame. That is the basic formula for any motion.

Now you're going to add some simple gravity. This takes into account **acceleration**. Any force that acts to change an object's velocity can be thought of as an acceleration. Velocity changes position, so you add velocity to position (adding vx to _x, for example), and acceleration changes velocity, so you add acceleration to velocity. You can see this in the line

```
this.vy += GRAV;
```

You defined GRAV as .5 at the top of the file. For sake of argument, say vy started off as 0. You add .5 to it, making it .5 after the first frame. Now the drop is falling at .5 pixels per frame (ppf). The next frame you add .5 again, and the drop is falling at a rate of 1 ppf. The next frame is 1.5, and then 2. So, simply put, the longer the drop falls, the faster it falls. This is how gravity, or any force, works. If you dropped a baseball from your right hand, you would have no problem catching it with your left hand. However, if your friend dropped a baseball off the Empire State Building, you'd probably do your best to avoid it! As the ball fell through the air, gravity would act upon it to increase its speed until the ball reached a **terminal velocity**— the maximum velocity reached by an object falling through the air, as determined by its drag.

Another way to look at it is to throw an object up into the air. In Flash terms, you could say the object is traveling at a negative y velocity. But gravity is *adding* to its velocity, bringing it closer and closer to zero. Eventually the object slows down, stops, and starts falling. Then the object speeds up on its way down.

OK, simple enough. The water drop leaves the nozzle and travels at its designated speed, with gravity accelerating it downward. You do a couple of checks to make sure it hasn't gone off the left or right side of the stage. If so, you remove it.

```
if (this._x>RIGHT || this._x<LEFT) this.removeMovieClip();
```

Finally, you see when it hits bottom. At that point you vary its _x position a bit, as if it has splashed. You set its _y position to be right at the bottom (in case it went a ways beyond it) and change its onEnterFrame handler to a new function, evap.

```
if (this._y>BOTTOM) {
  this._x += Math.random()*20;
  this._y = BOTTOM;
  this.onEnterFrame = evap;
}
```

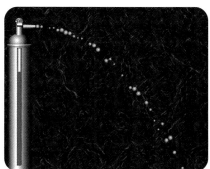

The evap function is pretty simple too—it merely shrinks the _xscale and _yscale of the drop until it is gone, then removing it.

Here's the overall result of what you have so far:

You click the button and a stream of water comes out of the nozzle, shooting left to right and falling to the floor, where it splashes a bit and then evaporates. You release the button and it stops. The gauge on the side of the tank keeps track of how much water is left, and when it's gone, that's that.

You learned a bit of elementary Flash physics there. Now you'll move on to learn some more.

Magnetic Attraction

Check out the water_02.fla file to see the next step.

1. Create a new movie clip and call it magnet. Draw an icon you think is going to prove most attractive to water. (Come to think of it, it should probably be a sponge!)

2. Drag an instance of the icon onto the tank layer and call it mag_mc.

3. Next up, you should have another go at that code. Toward the top of the code, just before the start spraying code, enter the following:

```
// set up magnet
mag_mc.power = 10000;
mag_mc.onPress = doDrag;
mag_mc.onRelease = noDrag;
mag_mc.onEnterFrame = rotate;
mag_mc.onReleaseOutside = noDrag;
function doDrag() {
  this.startDrag();
}
function noDrag() {
  stopDrag();
}
function rotate(){
  this._rotation += 5;
}
```

None of this code actually turns the icon into a magnet, but let's look at what it does do. First you assign the magnet a property called power and set it to 10000. Why 10000? Because, after several hours of playing with it, we found that this seemed to be a pretty workable value. We'll get to exactly what this is in a minute.

The next nine lines are the ones you need to use to make a movie clip—any movie clip—draggable. All you do is set handler functions for the onPress and onRelease/onReleaseOutside handlers. The functions, doDrag and noDrag, simply tell the clip to start and stop dragging.

OK, now you have a magnet with power that you can drag around. The last function for the onEnterFrame handler simply makes it spin around, which serves no real purpose, except that we thought it looked cooler than just sitting there! Actually, it does kind of draw attention to itself this way, which may help tell the user that it isn't just part of the background and invite her to interact with it.

4. Essentially, you now have a spinning, draggable movie clip. Although the clip does have a power value, at this point it's just a simple number that doesn't do anything useful. To see the magnet in action, jump down to the move function, which has been modified a bit:

```
function move() {
  // handle magnetism
  var dx = mag_mc._x-this._x;
  var dy = mag_mc._y-this._y;
  var distSQ = dx*dx+dy*dy;
  var force = mag_mc.power/distSQ;
  var dist = Math.sqrt(distSQ);
  this.vx += force*dx/dist;
  this.vy += force*dy/dist;
  // add gravity
  this.vy += GRAV;
  // add velocity to position
  this._x += this.vx;
  this._y += this.vy;
  // if off stage, remove
  if (this._x>RIGHT || this._x<LEFT) this.removeMovieClip();
  // if hit floor, splash a bit, then change onEnterFrame handler
  if (this._y>BOTTOM) {
    this._x += Math.random()*20;
    this._y = BOTTOM;
    this.onEnterFrame = evap;
  }
}
```

The changes to the function are in bold. To convey what the modifications are doing, we need to discuss a bit more physics. First of all, we have to admit that what we've modeled isn't necessarily the physics for a magnet. Actually, we don't know what formulae you would use to model a magnet. What we used is a very simple formula, and that is a scaled-down formula for gravity. Now, we aren't telling you that gravity is the same as magnetism. But it has similarities—enough to use for our purposes.

Earlier, you used gravity with the line this.vy += GRAV; and we explained that gravity is as simple as adding a value to the y velocity. But obviously the preceding formula in bold is a bit more complex than that. So let's backtrack a bit.

You can look at gravity in two ways. One way is how we look at it here on Earth. We drop an apple and it falls down, picking up speed as it drops. In that framework, gravity is a totally workable model.

But if you back off a couple of million miles, you see a different picture. You see a large mass (a planet) pulling things toward it. The concept of "down" kind of loses its meaning. Close up, you can be one dimensional about gravity and represent it as a force acting on one axis: the y axis. But as you move away, it becomes necessary to view things in two dimensions: x and y. (In reality, of course, it's three dimensions, but for the sake of our rather flat game, two will do.) The following diagram may help:

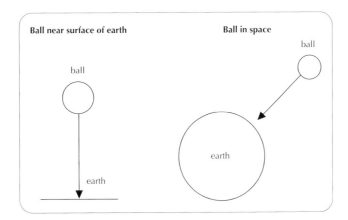

In the first example, a ball falling to earth, the line of force exerted on the ball can be, for all practical purposes, considered as completely vertical. Thus you only have to consider the y axis. In the second example, the planetary attraction can be on virtually any angle, depending on your particular viewpoint. So you have to translate that force into one force on the x axis and one force on the y axis, to align with your velocities on these lines. You'll learn how to do that in a moment.

Also, in the first example, you can usually consider gravity to be a constant value. In fact, gravity changes depending on your altitude. Technically, you weigh a bit less on Mount Everest than you do at sea level. But you need a pretty good scale to measure this difference, so in most situations, you can ignore it.

When you look at the next picture, though, and start figuring in some real distances, you start to see a much more profound effect of distance on the force of gravity. The actual formula for the force of gravity is this:

$$force = \frac{G \times mass_1 \times mass_2}{dist^2}$$

G is the "universal gravitational constant," which is basically a number you use to represent the force of gravity. It applies to all gravity, thus it is universal, and it never changes, thus it is constant. Don't worry about it for now. Next you have the mass of each object in question. In the preceding diagram, that would be the mass of the ball and the mass of the earth. You multiply these times each other, then times the gravitational constant, and then you divide by the square of the distance. This gives the overall force exerted between the two objects.

Sound complicated? Well, the good news is that you can throw away about half of the equation for this particular game. Here, you'll have the drop gravitating toward a magnet. The magnet's mass will never change. You can decide here and now that all the water drops will have the same mass as well. Because you aren't dealing in real-world measurements of miles and pounds, you don't need to worry about the standard value for G; you just need to use some constant number.

Now, here comes the fun part. Because the top three items will be the same for every drop every time, you don't need to calculate them for every drop, every frame. You can just make up a number that works there and use that. In fact, we already made up that number: it's mag_mc.power. This number, which was arbitrarily set at 10000, represents the gravitational constant times the mass of the magnet times the mass of a typical water drop. And once again, this is simply a number we came up with through trial and error. If you were doing a realistic solar system model or something like that, you would need to convert all your pixel distances to miles, use actual masses of planets and the sun, and look up and use the actual value of *G*.

Thus you get the following first lines to determine force:

```
var dx = mag_mc._x-this._x;
var dy = mag_mc._y-this._y;
distSQ = dx*dx+dy*dy;
var force = mag_mc.power/distSQ;
```

As you can see, the first three lines calculate the square of the distance. The fourth divides the power value by this value.

All right, now that you've figured the force between the two, what do you do with it? Well, you need to translate this into a force on the x and y axes. You can do this with some simple trigonometry, but there's an even easier way. First, you get the distance between the two. Because you have the distance already, you just take the square root of that:

```
var dist = Math.sqrt(distSQ);
```

If you multiply force by dx/dist, the result is the force on the x axis. force times dy/dist is the force on the y axis. As these forces are accelerations, you simply add them to the vx and vy of the drop.

```
this.vx += force*dx/dist;
this.vy += force*dy/dist;
```

For the physics purists out there, we must admit that we took yet another liberty with the rules of the universe. The force we calculated was the entire force between the two objects. In the case of a ball in space, not only would the ball be pulled toward the earth, but also the earth would be pulled toward the ball. In a more realistic simulation, you would need to divide the force by the mass of each object to get how much of the force would go toward accelerating that object. Because the ball's mass is very small, it winds up with most of the force. When you divide the same force by the mass of the earth (very large), you see why the force from the earth to the ball is pretty negligible.

In this case, you've already fudged things so much that you can pretty much ignore this factor. Because you aren't allowing the magnet to move at all anyway, you just give all the force to the ball.

This is a pretty good point at which to stop and play with the file (water_02.swf). You can move the magnet around and spray a bit of water. See how the closer each drop is to the magnet, the more it is attracted. In some cases, it barely bends the path of the water drops; get it a little closer and you can see a serious influence. Get just the right distance and you can even set up a permanent orbit! Too close and the drops will shoot off at a very high speed. This is known as the **slingshot effect**, and it's used to send space probes such as *Voyager* into the far reaches of the solar system.

Also, play around with the power variable to see if you can get a more natural feel using a different number, or if you agree with our choice.

Repulsion

Now for the next element to our story. Not only did this cutting-edge science officer develop a magnet that attracts water, but also he somehow reversed the formula and created a substance that repels water too!

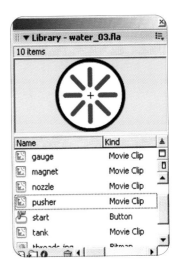

Open the Library in water_03.fla to see our version of this pusher movie clip, and then follow these instructions:

1. If you're working on the game from scratch, create a new movie clip and call it pusher. Drag an instance of it onto the stage and call it push_mc.

2. Head for the code layer and add the following, right next to your magnet code:

```
// set up pusher
push_mc.power = -5000;
push_mc.onPress = doDrag;
push_mc.onRelease = noDrag;
push_mc.onEnterFrame = rotate;
push_mc.onReleaseOutside = noDrag;
```

This is almost exactly the same as the setup code you used for mag_mc. The only difference is that you assign a power value of –5000 rather than 10000. The result is that rather than being attracted to the new magnet, the water is repelled. The closer the water is to the magnet, the stronger the repulsion.

3. Now you need to write the code into the move function to account for this new object. One way to do this is to copy and paste the code that deals with mag_mc and change the names to push_mc. This gives you the following within move:

```
// handle magnetism
var dx = mag_mc._x-this._x;
var dy = mag_mc._y-this._y;
var distSQ = dx*dx+dy*dy;
var force = mag_mc.power/distSQ;
var dist = Math.sqrt(distSQ);
this.vx += force*dx/dist;
this.vy += force*dy/dist;
// handle repulsion
dx = push_mc._x-this._x;
dy = push_mc._y-this._y;
distSQ = dx*dx+dy*dy;
force = push_mc.power/distSQ;
dist = Math.sqrt(distSQ);
this.vx += force*dx/dist;
this.vy += force*dy/dist;
```

Note that you don't need to duplicate the var keyword, as the local variable has already been created. You're just reassigning its value.

4. Now, this works just fine—there's nothing logically wrong with it at all. However, when you start to duplicate that many lines of code, you have to start thinking of moving it into its own function. If you aren't convinced, consider that you may want to make further levels of game in which additional magnets are placed around the screen. That's seven more lines of code for each magnet. Before long, the function gets way too long. Thus the new file has a new function, handleMag:

```
function handleMag(magnet, drop) {
    // handle magnetism
    var dx = magnet._x-drop._x;
    var dy = magnet._y-drop._y;
    var distSQ = dx*dx+dy*dy;
    var force = magnet.power/distSQ;
    var dist = Math.sqrt(distSQ);
    drop.vx += force*dx/dist;
    drop.vy += force*dy/dist;
}
```

This function takes two arguments: a reference to a particular magnet and a reference to a particular drop. The rest of the function does exactly the same thing as when the lines were in the move function; it simply uses the two clips given to it.

The beautiful thing about this code is that one function handles both the push and the pull magnets. The difference is just in the sign of the power factor.

5. Move back to the move function and see how this is called:

```
function move() {
    handleMag(mag_mc, this);
    handleMag(push_mc, this);
    var dx = mag_mc._x-this._x;
    var dy = mag_mc._y-this._y;
    distSQ = dx*dx+dy*dy;
    var force = mag_mc.power/distSQ;
    var dist = Math.sqrt(distSQ);
    this.vx += force*dx/dist;
    this.vy += force*dy/dist;
    // add gravity
    this.vy += GRAV;
    // add velocity to position
    this._x += this.vx;
    this._y += this.vy;
    // if off stage, remove
    if (this._x>RIGHT || this._x<LEFT) this.removeMovieClip();
    // if hit floor, splash a bit, then change onEnterFrame handler
    if (this._y>BOTTOM) {
        this._x += Math.random()*20;
        this._y = BOTTOM;
        this.onEnterFrame = evap;
    }
}
```

You call it once for each magnet. Remember that the handleMag function takes a reference to a drop movie clip. Because this function is being called by the onEnterFrame handler of a drop, the keyword this contains a reference to the drop. Thus you pass this to the function.

In case you're wondering why we chose −5000 as a power rather than −10000, once again we found that it looked good! When a pushing magnet had the same power as an attracting one, it just seemed too strong. The drops wouldn't go anywhere near it. Cutting it in half allowed the drops to get pretty close. It then seems like they realize where they are and say, "Whoa! I'm outta here!" Again, play around with the values here and see what looks good to you. Save your file now—you're about to take a brief detour.

Creating a Realistic Flame

Now that you have water, it's time to make some fire. You're going to make a scripted flame with the drawing API that was inspired by a candle flame done by Mario Klingemann at www.quasimondo.com. The concept for the simple flame is a couple of curved lines with a gradient fill inside. That's easy enough to draw one time. But then you have to consider how to move it around in a flamelike fashion. There's obviously a random factor there: a flame rises, falls, turns fat and thin, and leans this way and that, sometimes slowly, sometimes with a quick flicker. To learn about this randomness, we'll take a short side-trip into a subject called **Brownian motion**.

Before we explain exactly what this is, consider the problem: How do you make something move around randomly? My first experiments in this were some years ago, long before Flash, in BASIC on a Commodore 128. I basically took the object's current position and added a random value to it. That should be good enough, right?

Random Effects

If you open the file random.fla, you'll see the Flash equivalent of this.

1. To start your own experiment, open up a new FLA file. Create a new movie clip symbol and call it dot. Within the symbol, dab a little speck with your paint brush. Place an instance called dot_mc on the timeline.

2. Place the following code on frame 1:

    ```
    dot_mc.onEnterFrame = function() {
      this._x += Math.random()*2-1;
      this._y += Math.random()*2-1;
    };
    ```

    If you test this, you'll see a little dot kind of quivering around the center of the stage. All you're doing is adding a random value from −1 to +1 to its _x and _y positions on each frame. It's definitely moving kind of randomly, but not very much. Certainly not enough motion for a flame.

3. Remedy this by changing the random values, moving them into a higher range:

    ```
    dot_mc.onEnterFrame = function() {
      this._x += Math.random()*8-4;
      this._y += Math.random()*8-4;
    };
    ```

Well, that gets it moving more, but wow, it's way too jittery. Looks more like a bug on a hot frying pan than a flame. The problem is, the more motion you give it, the more jittery it gets. You want your flame to move around, but not look like it's in a hurricane. How do you smooth it out?

> Brownian motion is simply random motion as it's actually seen in the real world. It's most often exemplified by the idea of a speck of dust or a drop of ink in a container of water. Even if the water is completely still, the dust (or ink) moves around in a random manner. There's no current moving in the water, but something is causing the dust to move around.
>
> The solution comes when you get down to a molecular level. From that viewpoint, the water is far from still. Even if the water itself is perfectly calm, the molecules it's made up of are frantically bouncing around in every possible direction. They're bouncing off the walls of the container, bouncing off each other and, of course, bouncing off the dust speck.
>
> As each molecule strikes the speck, it accelerates it slightly in that direction. A single H_2O molecule is a lot smaller than a speck of dust, of course, so it's not a lot of acceleration, but multiply that times millions or billions of collisions per second, and it has a small visible effect.
>
> Remember that these molecules are bouncing in all possible directions. One molecule may come in from the left, adding slightly to the speck's velocity in that direction. Next, another one may hit the speck from the right, all but canceling out any velocity it just gained. Over time, these pretty much average out and the speck doesn't move a whole lot. But, for a short period of time it may receive more hits on one side, and may start visibly moving in a particular direction. Eventually, it gets enough hits from the other side to slow it down, or maybe stop it and get it going in the other direction for a short bit. Imagine that in three dimensions, and you pretty much have what you see with a speck of dust in a glass of water.
>
> To duplicate this in Flash, pay attention to two important words we introduced earlier in the chapter. The molecule **accelerates** the speck; it adds to the **velocity** of the speck.

In the random example, you gave the dot a random velocity to move on each frame. For more realistic Brownian motion, you'll give it a random acceleration, adding to its velocity on each frame. Because you'll only change the dot's velocity slightly each time, you'll get a much smoother motion.

4. Replace the code in frame 1 with the following (you can find this code in the support file brownian_01.fla):

```
dot_mc.vx = dot_mc.vy = 0;
dot_mc.onEnterFrame = function() {
  this.vx += Math.random()*.2-.1;
  this.vy += Math.random()*.2-.1;
  this._x += this.vx;
  this._y += this.vy;
};
```

As mentioned, you're now adding a random amount to the velocity of the dot, and then you're adding the velocity to the position. Note that the random amount is much, much smaller in this case, because you're looking for an accumulating effect.

If you test this code, you'll see a much smoother but still completely random motion. It looks more like the dot is wandering, so you're getting closer. The next problem is that the dot eventually seems to choose a direction and start heading off that way, never to return. This happens because for a while it's getting more accelerations in a particular direction, and it speeds up more and more in that direction—too fast for a few hits in the opposite direction to effectively slow it down. Theoretically, it should eventually hit a period where it gets more hits in the other direction and return to the general area. But you probably don't want to wait for that.

5. The first fix you can apply is a kind of damping factor. As a clip starts going faster in a certain direction, you reduce its speed in that direction. The faster it goes, the more you reduce it. You do this simply by multiplying the velocity by a damping factor such as .95. Replace your code with the following (or view it in `brownian_02.fla`):

```
damp = .95;
lineStyle(1, 0, 100);
moveTo(dot_mc._x, dot_mc._y);
dot_mc.vx = dot_mc.vy = 0;
dot_mc.onEnterFrame = function() {
  this.vx += Math.random()*.6-.3;
  this.vy += Math.random()*.6-.3;
  this.vx *= damp;
  this.vy *= damp;
  this._x += this.vx;
  this._y += this.vy;
  lineTo(this._x, this._y);
};
```

Here you define the variable damp. This is simply multiplied by the velocities on each frame, and it kind of artificially evens out the Brownian effect. Also notice that you have a higher random amount now. Because the velocity is constantly being dampened, you need to add a bit more acceleration to get some good motion going. As you test this, you'll see that the dot still wanders around, but it never gets going too fast in any one direction. It pretty much stays in its own backyard, so to speak. We added in some lines as well, so you can see where the dot is going and where it has been.

Don't forget why you're looking at this now. You'll eventually use this damping code for the control points of a curve drawing a flame shape. That said, there are a couple more qualifications you need to add to this motion. A flame's shape may wander for a while in a particular direction, but it goes only so far. Think of a candle flame. It's not going to reach the ceiling or the wall. Also, after you've done all this work to smooth out the motion, you occasionally want the flame to flicker a bit. You can combine these two actions by setting some limits. If the point goes beyond those limits, it should jump back.

6. Replace your code with the following (see `brownian_03.fla`):

```
damp = .95;
dot_mc.xMax = 290;
dot_mc.xMin = 250;
```

```
dot_mc.yMax = 220;
dot_mc.yMin = 180;
dot_mc.vx = dot_mc.vy = 0;
dot_mc.onEnterFrame = function() {
  this.vx += Math.random()*.6 - .3;
  this.vy += Math.random()*.6 - .3;
  this.vx *= damp;
  this.vy *= damp;
  this._x += this.vx;
  this._y += this.vy;
  if (this._x > this.xMax || this._x < this.xMin) {
    this.vx *= -2;
  }
  if (this._y > this.yMax || this._y < this.yMin) {
    this.vy *= -2;
  }
};
```

This assigns four properties, which are maximum and minimum x and y positions. At the end of the onEnterFrame function, you check to see if you've gone beyond any of those limits. If so, you reverse the velocity on that particular axis, multiplying it by –2. This sends it back into range with a bit of a jerk. You'll note we've removed the line-drawing code, but you can see how the dot stays in the center area, mostly moving quite smoothly, but with an occasional jump.

Applying the Results to Your Flame

OK then, it's time to apply the results from the previous section to a flame. For these next two files, you create everything through code on the first frame of the timeline. Open the file flame_01.fla and you'll see the following lines of code:

```
damp = .95;
top = {x:0, y:-80, w:25, vx:0, vy:0, vw:0, xMax:10, xMin:-10, yMax:-60, yMin:-100,
➥wMax:40, wMin:20};
createEmptyMovieClip("flame", 0);
flame._x = 270;
flame._y = 200;
flame.onEnterFrame = function() {
  // draw curves
  this.clear();
  this.lineStyle(1, 0, 100);
  this.moveTo(0, 0);
  this.curveTo(-top.w, 0, top.x, top.y);
  this.curveTo(top.w, 0, 0, 0);
  // draw control lines for demonstration
  this.moveTo(0, 0);
  this.lineStyle(1, 0, 20);
  this.lineTo(-top.w, 0);
  this.lineTo(top.x, top.y);
  this.lineTo(top.w, 0);
  this.lineTo(0, 0);
```

```
// randomize
top.vx += Math.random()*.6-.3;
top.vy += Math.random()*.6-.3;
top.vw += Math.random()*.6-.3;
// damp
top.vx *= damp;
top.vy *= damp;
top.vw *= damp;
// add velocity
top.x += top.vx;
top.y += top.vy;
top.w += top.vw;
// check limits
if (top.x>top.xMax || top.x<top.xMin) {
  top.vx *= -1.2;
}
if (top.y>top.yMax || top.y<top.yMin) {
  top.vy *= -1.2;
}
if (top.w>top.wMax || top.w<top.wMin) {
  top.vw *= -1.2;
}
};
```

This code looks complex, but if you understood the last Brownian file, this one shouldn't be too tough to grasp. First you create a generic object called top. This object has x and y properties that correspond to the top of the flame. It also has a w property that is the width of the flame.

The top object then goes on to define maximum and minimum values for these three properties. Looking it over, you can see that the tip of the flame can go from –10 to +10 on x as well as –60 to –100 on y. The w property can be between 20 and 40. Not as complex as it might first seem!

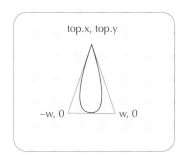

Then you create a movie clip called flame and center it on the stage. In flame you draw two curves, one from 0, 0 to top.x, top.y and another back to 0, 0. The control points for these curves are –w, 0 and w, 0. In case you're having trouble visualizing this, the next few lines draw some straight lines to these control points so you can see where they are.

The rest of the code is quite similar to the last Brownian file. You're randomizing the top x, y point as well as the width, w. You simply add some random acceleration to its velocity, dampen it, add the velocity to the position, and then check if it has gone past its limits. If so, you bounce it back. Notice that here, you bounce it back only –1.2 rather than –2 for a little more subtlety.

All you've really done is taken your original randomly wandering point and made that the top of the flame. Then you have another randomly wandering variable, w, that you use for width. If you test this file, you see a pretty decent attempt at a realistically moving flame shape. Now you need to color it in.

Adding Color

Open the next file, `flame_02.fla`. The file loses the lines and throws in a gradient fill instead.

```
damp = .95;
top = {x:0, y:-80, w:25, vx:0, vy:0, vw:0, xMax:10, xMin:-10, yMax:-60, yMin:-100,
➥wMax:40, wMin:20};
createEmptyMovieClip("flame", 0);
flame._x = 270;
flame._y = 200;
colors = [0xffff00, 0xff0000];
alphas = [100, 80];
ratios = [0, 155];
flame.onEnterFrame = function() {
  // draw curves
  this.clear();
  matrix = {matrixType:"box", x:-top.w, y:top.y, w:top.w*2, h:-top.y*2, r:0};
  this.beginGradientFill("radial", colors, alphas, ratios, matrix);
  this.moveTo(0, 0);
  this.curveTo(-top.w, 0, top.x, top.y);
  this.curveTo(top.w, 0, 0, 0);
  this.endFill();
  // randomize
  top.vx += Math.random()*.6-.3;
  top.vy += Math.random()*.6-.3;
  top.vw += Math.random()*.6-.3;
  // damp
  top.vx *= damp;
  top.vy *= damp;
  top.vw *= damp;
  // add velocity
  top.x += top.vx;
  top.y += top.vy;
  top.w += top.vw;
  // check limits
  if (top.x>top.xMax || top.x<top.xMin) {
    top.vx *= -1.2;
  }
  if (top.y>top.yMax || top.y<top.yMin) {
    top.vy *= -1.2;
  }
  if (top.w>top.wMax || top.w<top.wMin) {
    top.vw *= -1.2;
  }
};
```

Take a look at the lines in bold. First you define an array of two colors, yellow and red. Next is an array of alpha values for those two colors. This means that the yellow will be 100 percent opaque, and the red will have a bit of translucency. Next is ratios, which is often confusing. You can think of the ratio values as defining the point at which a particular color will appear in full. A value of 0 is the beginning of the gradient, and 255 is the end of the gradient. By specifying 0 and 155, you're indicating that the gradient will start out full yellow. A little more than halfway through (155 out of 255), it will fade to a full red and continue red from there on out.

You don't define the gradient matrix until you get into the loop, as this will change with the size and shape of the flame. The matrix is often the most misunderstood of all the gradient fill parameters. First, it's an object, not an array like the others. There are two formats for a matrix. One is to assign properties labeled a through i and use matrix multiplication to manipulate them—not for the faint of heart. You take the easy way out here by defining matrixType as "box". After that, you merely need to define the beginning point of the gradient (x, y) and its height and width (h, w). You also set a rotation factor, r, although this doesn't have much effect on a radial gradient.

The most confusing part of a radial gradient is realizing that the center of the gradient isn't the x, y point as you might expect:

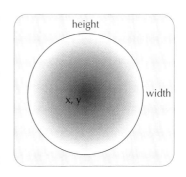

If that were the case, you could assign x, y as 0, 0. Width would be top.w and height would simply be top.y, as these two properties show the width and height of the flame. Unfortunately, the gradient looks a bit more like this:

If you want the yellow center of the gradient to appear at the bottom center of the flame, you need to do a bit of figuring. If you look at the flame diagram you used before, you see that the left control point is at –top.w. That's just about right for the left edge of the flame, so you can use that as x. You can also use top.y as y here. Using the original values of the flame, that puts x, y as –25, –80. The width and height aren't just the bottom right point, but the actual measurements of width and height. So width needs to be double the value of top.w, or 50. Height needs to be double the size of the flame, or 160. Because top.y is –80, you need to multiply it by –2. You can see all that in this line:

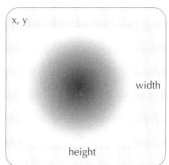

```
matrix = {matrixType:"box", x:-top.w, y:top.y,
    w:top.w*2, h:-top.y*2, r:0};
```

Finally, you plug everything into the beginGradientFill function, draw the curves, and end the fill. You might also notice that you don't set a line style here, which makes the lines invisible, leaving only the shape of the flame.

Well, you've pretty much completed your flame. We altered this slightly, removing the following two lines:

```
flame._x = 270;
flame._y = 200;
```

We then saved this as flame.fla, exporting the movie as flame.swf. Note that because we removed the two lines that position the flame, if you run the file now (which you'll need to do to create the SWF file), you may not see the flame at first. It will be way up in the top-left corner, at 0, 0. Note that you'll need that SWF file in the same directory as the main game file in the next step.

Back to the Game

This is the moment of truth, when you add the flame to the game already created. We first considered copying all the code for the flame into the main game, but we decided that was already getting too cluttered.

The flame.swf file that we just created was a nice, compact unit by itself, so we decided to keep it that way and load it in as is. This also gives us a chance to go into the basics of loadMovie, which is invaluable for building modular games.

If you open the file water_04.fla, the only difference in code you'll see is at the top in the following lines. If you're creating the game as you read along, type these lines into the top of your code pile, right after the constants:

```
createEmptyMovieClip("flame_mc", 1000000);
flame_mc.createEmptyMovieClip("flameHolder_mc", 0);
flame_mc._x = Math.random()*600+200;
flame_mc._y = 400;
flame_mc._xscale = flame_mc._yscale=30;
flame_mc.onEnterFrame = function() {
  this._xscale = this._yscale += .3;
};
flame_mc.flameHolder_mc.loadMovie("flame.swf");
```

The first line creates an empty movie clip. You have two ways to use loadMovie: you can load the external SWF file into a movie clip or you can load it into a new level. When we have a small movie that we want to position at a particular point on the stage, we like to load it into a movie clip. We generally reserve loading into a new layer for a large clip that will stay in place, such as an interface component. It doesn't have to be that way—you can reposition layers just as you can a movie clip, but the uses we just described seem the most intuitive.

Anyway, create a movie clip named flame_mc and give it a depth of 1000000. Why such a high depth? Remember that you're also attaching the drop movie clips here. If you attach a drop on the same level as the flame, it will replace the flame entirely. You most like won't ever use more than a million drops in one game, so you should be safe. Another option would be to keep flame_mc at depth 0 and start the drops at 1. Either way is fine as long as you ensure the drops never overlap.

Now, you could load the fire right into this newly created clip. But please don't. We almost always make an additional clip inside our target clip and load the external content into that. The reason for that is that when an SWF or JPEG file is loaded into a movie clip, it wipes out all the properties or content that was in that clip to begin with. Because flame_mc will be assigned some onEnterFrame code to run, this would be wiped out when flame.swf comes in. By creating another empty movie clip inside flame_mc, flameHolder_mc, and loading the SWF file into that, nothing on flame_mc itself gets affected at all.

After you create these nested clips, position the nest at a random _x and at the bottom of the screen. Scale the clip down to 30% and give it some onEnterFrame code that will slowly make it grow. Next, load in the external flame.swf. Make sure you use the full path to the internal holder clip, or everything in the external clip, including the holder, will be destroyed.

So far, so good—you have a flame onscreen! You can shoot water at it, but now you need to make the water and flame interact.

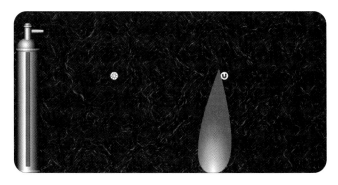

Putting Out the Fire

This process winds up being pretty simple. You use hitTest within the move function of each drop. When the drop moves to its new position, it checks if it's hitting the flame. If so, the drop reduces the flame a little. Yes, that means you need multiple hits to eventually put the fire out—one drop won't do. The bigger you let the fire become, the more water it will take.

The file water_05.fla gives you this additional code for the move function:

```
function move() {
  handleMag(mag_mc, this);
  handleMag(push_mc, this);
  var dx = mag_mc._x-this._x;
  var dy = mag_mc._y-this._y;
  distSQ = dx*dx+dy*dy;
  var force = mag_mc.power/distSQ;
  var dist = Math.sqrt(distSQ);
  this.vx += force*dx/dist;
  this.vy += force*dy/dist;
  // add gravity
  this.vy += GRAV;
  // add velocity to position
  this._x += this.vx;
  this._y += this.vy;
  // if off stage, remove
  if (this._x>RIGHT || this._x<LEFT) this.removeMovieClip();
  // if hit floor, splash a bit, then change onEnterFrame handler
  if (this._y>BOTTOM) {
    this._x += Math.random()*20;
    this._y = BOTTOM;
    this.onEnterFrame = evap;
  }
  if (flame_mc.hitTest(this._x, this._y, false)) {
    flame_mc._xscale -= 5;
    flame_mc._yscale = flame_mc._xscale;
    if (flame_mc._xscale<30) {
      flame_mc.reset();
    }
  }
}
```

The hitTest code is there in bold at the bottom. First, note that we chose to use false as the shape flag in hitTest (it is false by default, actually). This will register a hit when the drop just gets inside the bounding box of the flame. This isn't as accurate, but it makes hitting the target a little easier—not to mention faster! Feel free to change this to true for more of a challenge. This will require that the drop actually collides with the shape of the flame itself.

If you get a hit, you reduce the scale of the flame by 5%. If the scale goes below 30%, then you call a function of flame_mc called reset.

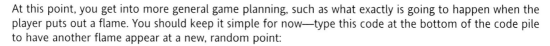
At this point, you get into more general game planning, such as what exactly is going to happen when the player puts out a flame. You should keep it simple for now—type this code at the bottom of the code pile to have another flame appear at a new, random point:

```
flame_mc.reset = function() {
  this._x = Math.random()*600+200;
  this._xscale = this._yscale=30;
};
```

This is the `flame_mc.reset` function, as seen at the end of the file. It rescales the flame to 30% and sets it at a random _x point. You don't need to change _y at all because it will always be on the floor.

There you have it—a pretty solid framework for a full game. To round things off, you'll create a few text boxes to hold a score and status message. You add 1 point to the score every time a drop hits the flame and 100 points if the player successfully douses the flame. Every time the score hits another 1,000 points, you give the player a bonus of 20 more units of water. When the water runs out, in addition to ending the game, you display a status message Game Over!

Here's the entire code to the final game, `water_final.fla`, with the previously mentioned additions:

```
score = 0;
nextBonus = 1000;
createEmptyMovieClip("flame_mc", 1000000);
flame_mc.createEmptyMovieClip("flameHolder_mc", 0);
flame_mc._x = Math.random()*600+200;
flame_mc._y = 400;
flame_mc._xscale = flame_mc._yscale=30;
flame_mc.onEnterFrame = function() {
  this._xscale = this._yscale += .3;
};
flame_mc.flameHolder_mc.loadMovie("flame.swf");
RIGHT = Stage.width;
LEFT = 0;
TOP = 0;
BOTTOM = Stage.height;
GRAV = .5;
depth = 0;
dropSize = 0;
waterLevel = 100;
// set up magnet
mag_mc.power = 10000;
mag_mc.onPress = doDrag;
mag_mc.onRelease = noDrag;
mag_mc.onEnterFrame = rotate;
mag_mc.onReleaseOutside = noDrag;
function doDrag() {
  this.startDrag();
}
function noDrag() {
  stopDrag();
}
```

```
function rotate() {
  this._rotation += 5;
}
// set up pusher
push_mc.power = -5000;
push_mc.onPress = doDrag;
push_mc.onRelease = noDrag;
push_mc.onEnterFrame = rotate;
push_mc.onReleaseOutside = noDrag;
function doDrag() {
  this.startDrag();
}
function noDrag() {
  stopDrag();
}
function rotate() {
  this._rotation += 5;
}
// start spraying
start_btn.onPress = function() {
  squirtInt = setInterval(squirt, 50);
};
// stop spraying
start_btn.onRelease = start_btn.onReleaseOutside=function () {
  clearInterval(squirtInt);
};
function squirt() {
  // make a drop of water
  drop_mc = attachMovie("drop", "d"+depth, depth++);
  // vary its size
  drop_mc._xscale = drop_mc._yscale=125+Math.sin(dropSize += .9)*50;
  // position it at end of nozzle
  drop_mc._x = nozzle_mc._x+5;
  drop_mc._y = nozzle_mc._y;
  // give it some speed
  drop_mc.vx = 10;
  drop_mc.vy = Math.random()-.5;
  // assign enterFrame handler
  drop_mc.onEnterFrame = move;
  // reduce water level
  waterLevel -= .1;
  // adjust gauge
  waterTank_mc.gauge_mc.waterLevel_mc._yscale = waterLevel;
  // check if water is gone
  if (waterLevel<=0) {
    // disable button
    delete start_btn.onPress;
```

```
      // stop spraying
      clearInterval(squirtInt);
      status_txt.text = "Game Over!";
    }
  }
  function move() {
    handleMag(mag_mc, this);
    handleMag(push_mc, this);
    var dx = mag_mc._x-this._x;
    var dy = mag_mc._y-this._y;
    distSQ = dx*dx+dy*dy;
    var force = mag_mc.power/distSQ;
    var dist = Math.sqrt(distSQ);
    this.vx += force*dx/dist;
    this.vy += force*dy/dist;
    // add gravity
    this.vy += GRAV;
    // add velocity to position
    this._x += this.vx;
    this._y += this.vy;
    // if off stage, remove
    if (this._x>RIGHT || this._x<LEFT) this.removeMovieClip();
    // if hit floor, splash a bit, then change onEnterFrame handler
    if (this._y>BOTTOM) {
      this._x += Math.random()*20;
      this._y = BOTTOM;
      this.onEnterFrame = evap;
    }
    if (flame_mc.hitTest(this._x, this._y, false)) {
      flame_mc._xscale -= 5;
      flame_mc._yscale = flame_mc._xscale;
      score++;
      if (flame_mc._xscale<30) {
        flame_mc.reset();
        score += 100;
      }
      if (score>nextBonus) {
        nextBonus += 1000;
        waterLevel += 20;
        if (waterLevel>100) {
          waterLevel = 100;
        }
        waterTank_mc.gauge_mc.waterLevel_mc._yscale = waterLevel;
      }
      score_txt.text = score;
    }
  }
  function evap() {
    // shrink a bit
    this._xscale -= 2;
```

```
    // squash it down, as it is now like a puddle
    this._yscale = this._xscale/2;
    // if all gone, remove
    if (this._xscale<1) {
      this.removeMovieClip();
    }
  }
function handleMag(magnet, drop) {
    // handle magnetism
    var dx = magnet._x-drop._x;
    var dy = magnet._y-drop._y;
    var distSQ = dx*dx+dy*dy;
    var force = magnet.power/distSQ;
    var dist = Math.sqrt(distSQ);
    drop.vx += force*dx/dist;
    drop.vy += force*dy/dist;
  }
flame_mc.reset = function() {
  this._x = Math.random()*600+200;
  this._xscale = this._yscale=30;
};
```

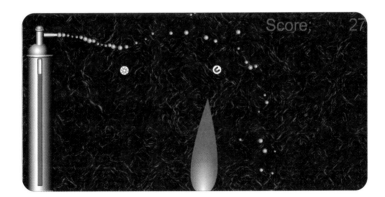

Summary

Where you take this game is up to you. You could build different levels with new backgrounds, multiple fires happening at once, more magnets, magnets of different powers, fixed magnets that can't be moved, and so on. Most likely, you'll want to start easy to give the player a good feel for how to direct the water, and you'll want to give him a goal—say, to put out five fires. When the player has accomplished that, he moves on to level 2, which has some added challenges.

We hope that you've gotten some interesting ways to model natural physics to use in your games out of this chapter. We covered gravity, magnetism, velocity, acceleration, random motion, and plenty of other little tidbits. We look forward to seeing some interesting new games hitting the Web soon!

Steve Young

Steve's been in the fast-moving world of multimedia for a number of years now. Originally starting out as a product designer, having studied at Glasgow School of Art, he somehow found himself in the new media industry, which, like most of his peers, he just seems to have "fallen into." Currently working at MMI (www.mmiweb.com) in Glasgow, Steve's still "living the dream" (aye, right) and can't believe he gets paid for larking around in the office. Prior to MMI, Steve was part of the team at Flammable Jam, which spearheaded Scotland's new media revolution, but that all seems such a long time ago now. Keep up to date with Steve's work at www.gimpster.net, assuming he can be bothered to update his site. He is, after all, a very busy boy.

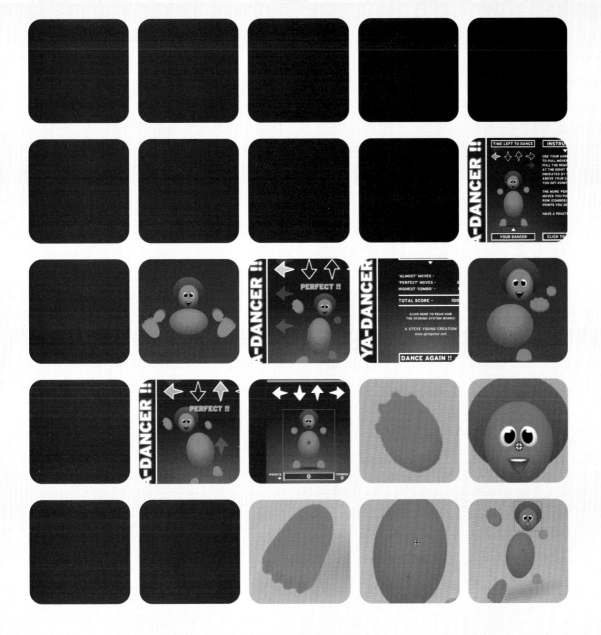

CONTROL

Control is arguably the most important aspect in any game. The graphics can be stunning, the characters can be really cool or cute, the concept can be really original, but if it's really difficult to play, navigate, and ultimately control the game, you're on to a real loser from the outset, guaranteed. The best online games don't necessarily have to look stunning, but they definitely have to be easy to understand and simple to use to stand any chance of being successful.

Keep It Simple

Always bear in mind, you shouldn't necessarily be trying to create the next Grand Theft Auto, Unreal Tournament, or Metal Gear Solid. If people want to play fantastic games like these, they're going to buy a games console or install a 3GB game on their PC and spend a good half an hour or so programming their brains with the multitude of different functions they'll need to get the most out of the game they've just spent $50 on. They aren't going to say, "I want to get into gaming big-time—I'll go and get the Flash plug-in!" That would just be crazy talk.

In our humble opinion, Flash should only be used to develop relatively simple online games that brighten someone's day and makes him smile. "Simple" doesn't necessarily mean garbage. One of the simplest online games/playthings in recent memory is Hoss Gifford's Spank the Monkey (www.mmiweb.com/spank/). All you do is click a hand and drag it over Spank as fast and hard as you can. The faster you move your mouse from right to left, the harder and faster you hit the monkey. Now that's simple! Who would have thought this game would be one of the most successful ever? It was launched on the same weekend as the *Star Wars, Episode II: Attack of the Clones* trailer and, due to the viral nature of something that has an element of humor, Spank beat *Star Wars* (Spank the Monkey got somewhere in the neighborhood of 750,000 hits on its first weekend). Strange but true. For more Flash fun from Hoss Gifford, be sure to check out his site at www.h69.net.

Some might say that Spank the Monkey is more of a play-thing than a game, and they'd probably be right. I created a game for Glasgow Rugby called Show's Yer Tackle (www.showsyertackle.com) that uses exactly the same functionality as Spank the Monkey. With some more elaborate graphics, slightly more in-depth game play, lots of amusing audio (voiced by one of Scotland's premier rugby commentators, I might add), and a high-score table, Show's Yer Tackle is what many would describe as a full-on game. This too has been incredibly successful. Some of the more astute readers among you will notice, after playing it, that Show's Yer Tackle isn't just a game. It has an ulterior motive, oh yes—it's a marketing tool! Gasp! Shock, horror—another sellout! Well, what do you expect in this day and age? Not everyone has the luxury of bags of free time to create games just for the fun of it. If you want to make online games for a living, someone's going to have to pay for it, and more often than not that someone is going to want something in return—advertising and click-throughs to their site (i.e., traffic/consumers).

For an online game to be successful, it should adhere to certain criteria. As well as being easy to understand and use, it should be addictive and/or humorous. If a game makes people laugh, chances are they'll pass it on to their friends, and those friends will pass it on to their friends, and so on. If a game is successfully passed on, its popularity tends to snowball, and before you know it you have a major success story on your hands. We refer to this as being "viral." The more viral a game is, the more people see the underlying message the game is promoting. The more people get the message, the happier your clients are, and the more likely they are to commission more games, keeping you in a job. The trick is, don't be too obvious about it. If you hit people with a big corporate message right from the start, they're just as likely to close the window—probably even more so—than if they were faced with lots of instructions. Which brings us to our next point.

Online games should be relatively intuitive. Unfortunately, due to the nature of the Internet, people seem to have no patience whatsoever. If people just don't "get it" in the first few seconds, they'll more than likely close the window and move on to the next thing. If you've just spent the last few days or weeks developing a game, you'll want your audience to at least get beyond the instructions page. Not that they're going to bother reading the instructions, but if they see reams of text explaining how to play your game, they'll simply say, "Whoa! This looks complicated. I don't have time to read all this text—I just want a quick fix of fun. Oh, forget it!" If they're a little more optimistic, they'll just click the Play Now button and see if they can work it out. But because your game needs lots of instructions to explain the intricacies of what on earth the players are supposed to do, they won't have the faintest idea how to play. (Click! What was that? Oh, they just closed your game and now they're checking their e-mail.)

Your game should be so easy to understand and play that potential players don't need instructions. You should still always supply the players with instructions, though, as long as those instructions are as simple as possible. Instructions don't have to be long-winded; they can be as simple as "Click this and drag it here as fast as possible" or "Shoot the critters, avoid the bullets."

What to Use and When

The old keyboard versus mouse debate is next on the agenda. Well, I suppose it boils down to what's appropriate, but my own personal preference is to design games that use the mouse. The reason for this is that people use the mouse to navigate the Web, and once they've opened your game they should just be able to click and play without their eyes leaving the screen to see where to put their fingers on the keyboard. I always find that using the mouse promotes "organic" game play—that is, the mouse is an extension of a user's arm and this helps the user feel more involved in the game. If the mouse controls a character, then

whenever the user moves the mouse in a certain way, the character apes the movement of the mouse. It's completely different if the user has to use the keyboard to move the character, which feels more removed.

On the other hand, the mouse isn't so good for controlling a driving game or the classic arcade game Asteroids. For games like these, the keyboard is much more appropriate. For example, in Asteroids you use the left and right arrow keys to rotate your ship, the up and down arrow keys to activate your thrust, and the spacebar to fire lasers at the asteroids. Notice already that you need two hands for this game. There's nothing wrong with using two hands to control a game, so long as your left hand (if you're right-handed) doesn't have to do too much other than press the spacebar. Anything more would probably confuse the heck out of most people.

Also, when you use the keyboard to control a game, it makes sense to use the obvious keys. By "obvious" we mean those keys that have become the industry standard for simple keyboard game control—for example, the arrow keys to move and the spacebar to fire. Chances are your users will have used these keys dozens of times before to achieve similar functionality within other games. If it ain't broke, why fix it? It's really annoying when some game developers use four keys somewhere in the middle of the keyboard (e.g., *A*, *S*, *P*, and *L*, plus the spacebar). If your fingers slip off the keys during a crucial part of the game, you'll probably have to look at the keyboard to make sure your fingers are back on the correct keys, by which time it'll be game over, no doubt.

Dance to the Music

With the game we've created to accompany this chapter, we've tried to use the keyboard in a slightly less conventional way. Rather than moving a character around an environment, you'll press certain keys or pairs of keys to make the character do a dance move. We've all seen these dance-mat games that are so popular these days. Well, we've tried to re-create the experience in Flash, only this time your feet are substituted for fingers, and instead of a dance mat you use the arrow keys. Just like the original arcade game, you're prompted to press certain keys at certain times in time to music.

Before you get our hands dirty, open dance.swf, turn up your speakers, and give this addictive little game a try. This is what you'll learn how to build in this chapter. Hopefully, you'll be suitably inspired!

You need three key elements to make this game:

- The **character**
- The **music**
- The **timing** (via the arrow generator, which shows which keys to press and when)

We usually start by making each element separately, and only once we're happy with each one do we start to make them interact. In the following sections you'll look at each of these essential game elements in detail.

Character Movement

For this particular game you should start with the character functionality, first of all creating the basic elements—that is, the head, hands, feet, and body. You can find these assets in the Library in a folder called character_parts. All the main elements that make up the character are suffixed by the word holder. We've kept things very simple—it's amazing what you can do with a few circles! Anyway, the simpler the elements are, the more processor-friendly the game's going to be. In case you're wondering, our character is a funky frog. You'll probably be able to create something much better, especially if you've already read the chapter on character animation in this book. It's amazing how much depth a simple eye blink makes. It really makes the little fella come alive, don't you think?

After putting together all of the character's elements, you'll then need to decide how to make the character move seamlessly from one move to the next. This isn't as straightforward as you might think, so we'll talk you through it.

1. Open this game's FLA file, dancer.fla, from your source code folder and go to the GAME scene (just click the Edit Scene button at the top right of the timeline to browse to a different scene). Don't be intimidated by this rather busy timeline. For now, just move to the keyframe labeled GAME_ON on the DANCER layer:

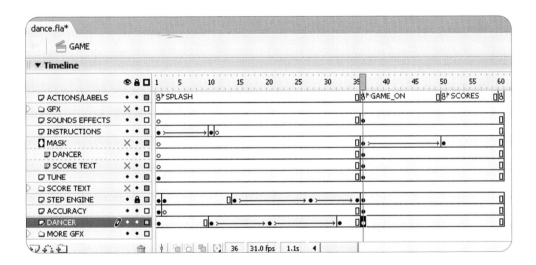

2. With this keyframe still selected, double-click the green character on the stage to open the movie clip.

3. Once inside the clip, you'll be able to look at all the different character components, as each is on a self-descriptive layer (e.g., head, body, etc.). You'll need to make them visible and unlock them first. Inside each of these movie clips is nothing more than a graphic—there are no actions, nothing fancy at all.

   Note that if you want to customize and change the appearance of the dancer, all you need to do is open one of the character's separate elements—for example, body—and change the shape, size, color, or whatever. This makes customizing and extending the game very simple indeed.

4. Now, lock and hide all the layers apart from the one entitled moves. Double-click the moves movie clip to open it (this should now be the only thing you can select on the stage). Inside you'll see exactly the same character components as you saw in the parent movie clip, all on their own layers just as before. Now look at all the frames and notice the names of the frame labels. Click each frame label and you'll see the same character components but in different positions:

5. When you press one or two arrow keys, a function called dancin on the root of this FLA file calls the gotoAndPlay() action to play the corresponding frame label in this moves movie clip. Take a look at the dancin function, which is attached to the first keyframe of the ACTIONS/LABELS layer of the GAME scene (you can use the navigation bar to browse back to the root timeline). Take a few moments to go over this code and you'll see that it's really quite undemanding:

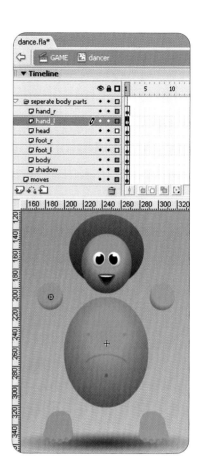

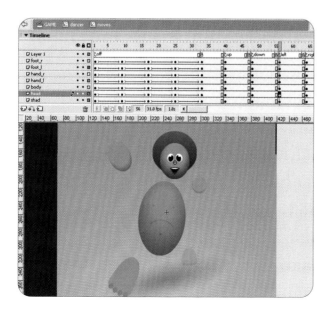

```
dancin = function () {
  if (Key.isDown(Key.RIGHT)) {
    mainDancer.moves.gotoAndPlay('right');
    _root.pressed = "right";
  }
  if (Key.isDown(Key.LEFT)) {
    mainDancer.moves.gotoAndPlay('left');
    _root.pressed = "left";
  }
  if (Key.isDown(Key.UP)) {
    mainDancer.moves.gotoAndPlay('up');
    _root.pressed = "up";
  }
  if (Key.isDown(Key.DOWN)) {
    mainDancer.moves.gotoAndPlay('down');
    _root.pressed = "down";
  }
  if ((Key.isDown(Key.UP)) && (Key.isDown(Key.RIGHT))) {
    mainDancer.moves.gotoAndPlay('upRight');
    _root.pressed = "upRight";
  }
  if ((Key.isDown(Key.UP)) && (Key.isDown(Key.LEFT))) {
    mainDancer.moves.gotoAndPlay('upLeft');
    _root.pressed = "upLeft";
  }
  if ((Key.isDown(Key.DOWN)) && (Key.isDown(Key.RIGHT))) {
    mainDancer.moves.gotoAndPlay('downRight');
    _root.pressed = "downRight";
  }
  if ((Key.isDown(Key.DOWN)) && (Key.isDown(Key.LEFT))) {
    mainDancer.moves.gotoAndPlay('downLeft');
    _root.pressed = "downLeft";
  }
  if ((Key.isDown(Key.LEFT)) && (Key.isDown(Key.RIGHT))) {
    mainDancer.moves.gotoAndPlay('leftRight');
    _root.pressed = "leftRight";
  }
  if ((Key.isDown(Key.UP)) && (Key.isDown(Key.DOWN))) {
    mainDancer.moves.gotoAndPlay('upDown');
    _root.pressed = "upDown";
  }
};
```

As you can see from the rest of the code on this keyframe, this function is called on an onEnterFrame function—it's simply a case of deciphering which arrow keys are pressed, via the various properties of this Key class (UP and RIGHT, for example), and then playing the appropriate move, which in this case would be going to the upRight frame of the moves movie clip. We've also set a variable on the root of the movie, pressed, to equal a string that describes, quite literally, which keys are being pressed. So in this case, if the UP and RIGHT keys are pressed, the variable _root.pressed equals upRight. The relevance of this variable flag will become clear later on, so don't worry about it just yet.

When no keys are pressed, this movie clip simply goes to the frame labeled off and loops around a little side shuffle until another arrow key is pressed.

6. When dancer.fla is published, the moves movie clip isn't visible at first; the alpha value is set to 0, and it's merely to act as a guide for the elements in the parent clip. A function called matchTheMove (nested inside the danceItUp function, again located on the ACTIONS/LABELS layer of the root timeline) makes the character components in the parent clip of moves glide to the position of the corresponding component in moves. This is what the important function looks like:

```
this.matchTheMove = function(part) {
  var proxyPart = this.moves[part._name];
  part._x += (proxyPart._x-part._x)/this.glide;
  part._y += (proxyPart._y-part._y)/this.glide;
  part._xscale += (proxyPart._xscale-part._xscale)/this.glide;
  part._yscale += (proxyPart._yscale-part._yscale)/this.glide;
  part._rotation += (proxyPart._rotation-part._rotation)/this.glide;
  part._alpha += (proxyPart._alpha-part._alpha)/this.glide;
};
```

We'll walk you through the first few lines of this function in detail (the remaining lines are pretty much the same: all they do is affect a different property of the dancer's body parts). The function is sent a reference to the dancer's body part movie clip and this is held in the variable part. Because the moves movie clip has the different body parts named the same, you can use the part movie clip's name to find the corresponding clip in moves and place it into the variable proxyPart. You then need to move and transform each part to match proxyPart. So, if you pass the head body part, the line of code for transforming the _x property will look something like this (the glide variable is just an approximation):

```
head._x += (moves.head._x - head._x)/4;
```

This equation is essentially a simple glide equation; all it does is ease the x position of the head to the x position of the head in the moves movie clip. So, when you duplicate this line and substitute x for the other properties (i.e., y, xScale, yScale, rotation, and alpha), the body part will ape its equivalent, which is in moves. Once you apply this theory to all the body parts, you're ready to roll. Sound confusing? We hope not. Now your dancer glides through his funky moves like John Travolta!

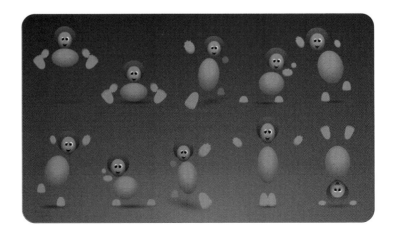

7. And that's it for setting up the character movement. If, however, you want to change the dancer's move when certain keys are pressed, that's also easy. Open the moves clip, go to the appropriate frame label, and rearrange the character components to look however you want. You can change the position, size, rotation, and alpha of each and every part of the character. If you're feeling ambitious and you understand the code sufficiently, why not add more components to the character and the game, such as lighting effects or maybe even different outfits for our intrepid dancer? You can really go to town with the design aspects of this game! You must also remember to add your new components, a nice kilt and a set of bagpipes, for example, to the bodyParts array in the mainDancerInit function on the root, like this:

```
this.bodyParts = [this.hand_l, this.hand_r, this.foot_l,
    this.foot_r, this.body, this.head,
    this.shad, this.kilt, this.bagpipes];
```

All parts that the dancer is set to move are stored in an array to make it easier to add such elements. Then in the onEnterFrame handler, you can run through all these elements and send each to the matchTheMove function you looked at previously:

```
mainDancer.onEnterFrame = function() {
    for (var i in this.bodyParts) {
        this.matchTheMove(this.bodyParts[i]);
    }
    _root.dancin();
};
```

So go ahead and customize the game however you want. But remember, if you add too many graphical components, the game will start to run slowly, depending on what kind of processor you have.

Music

The next important aspect of the game is the music. Without music, the dancing character doesn't have much purpose at all. The music can be anything you want, but it really helps if it has a good beat. Also, if you're going to publish your work online, make sure the music is royalty-free—you don't want to end up with a hefty fine now, do you?

1. Go to the scene called GAME, focus on the layer TUNE, and go to the frame labeled GAME_ON. The music is attached within the TUNE movie clip at the top of the game (we've labeled it TUNE to make things easier). Double-click it to look inside:

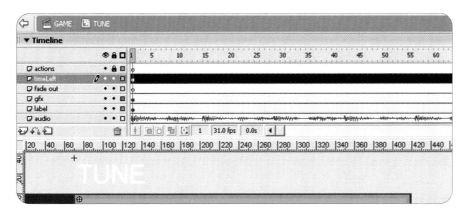

2. We've placed the music starting on frame 1 of the audio layer and set the Sync option in the Property inspector to Stream and Loop to 2 (see Chapter 6 for more advice on using sounds in your Flash games). We then added as many frames as we needed to the timeline so that the tune could play in its entirety.

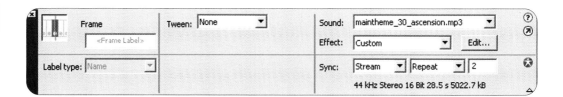

3. Under the Effect option we've simply faded the audio out at the end rather than having it stop dead (click the Edit button for information on this custom effect):

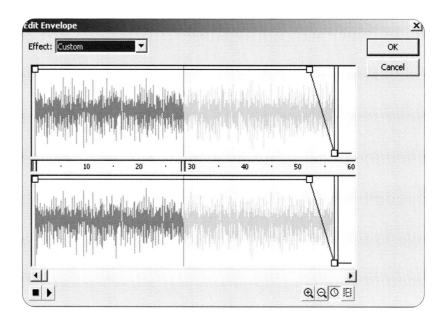

4. You might also notice some other elements within this movie clip. That's because this clip not only plays the music, but it also acts as a timer letting the user know how long she has to go before her time is up. This is done quite simply by measuring what frame the music has reached and setting the _xscale of the movie clip called timeLeft by using the following equation, which runs onEnterFrame on the parent movie clip (navigate one level back to the GAME scene, select the TUNE movie clip, and look in the Actions panel):

```
onClipEvent (load) {
  lab._visible = 0;
  goNow = true;
}
onClipEvent (enterFrame) {
  if (goNow) {
    timeLeft._xscale = 100/((this._totalframes-20)/this._currentframe);
  }
}
```

Note that this game uses the classic style of Flash coding from pre-MX days, when code was placed on individual clips throughout the movie and contained within onClipEvents. *With the introduction of Flash MX and the ability to dynamically assign handlers for events, many developers began centralizing their code on a single frame on the main timeline. The biggest benefit of this method is that all the code is located in one place, and developers can easily find, edit, and debug their code, without having to hunt through many clips and timelines searching for where they placed their code (this can become extremely frustrating as time passes between stages in development—you forget where everything is!).*

However, using onClipEvents *and placing code directly on movie clips can still have its benefits. For instance, if you have a clip with a unique functionality that you can use in multiple movies/projects, it's easy to copy and paste from one movie to another and be certain that all relevant code is copied too. In the case of this game, you're using* onClipEvents *here because the* timeLeft *movie clip really stands on its own and it therefore makes sense to keep its code separate from the meat of the game. And, of course, it goes without saying (which we guess is why we're writing it) that if you're working alone you should code in the style you're most comfortable with and works best for you.*

So, when this movie clip is loaded, you hide the movie clip lab, as this is only needed when you're editing, and set the variable goNow to true. The equation that sets the _xscale of the timeLeft movie is very simple. The reason you subtract 20 from the total frames (1,780 frames) is because that's when the audio ends and the last 20 frames are transitional fade-out frames. Also, on frame 1760 you set the goNow variable to false so that the timeLeft movie doesn't continue to grow even though the music has stopped.

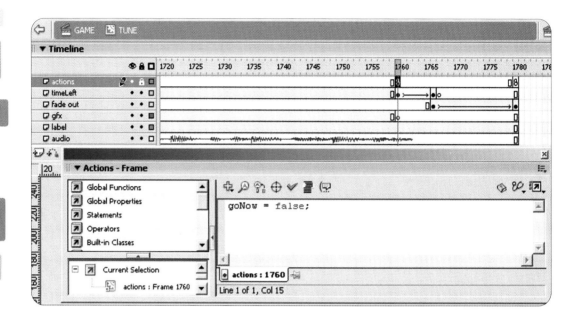

This effectively kills two birds with one stone and helps keep things simple. If you want to change the music, all you have to do is replace the sound on the audio layer, set it to Stream, and loop it as many times as you want. It's best to use loops, or a combination of loops, just for the sake of keeping the file size of the overall game as small as possible. Nobody wants to spend half his lunch break waiting for a game to load! Once you're happy with the music, add or delete as many frames as are necessary to keep the timeline just slightly longer than the end of your music. You might want to fade the music out at the end, too, using the sound edit envelope. Once you've done this, the timer functionality will work perfectly!

Anyone want a cup of tea? Maybe it's time to take a short break here—I don't know about you, but my eyes are starting to gloss over. You'll need to be nice and alert in a short while when things get slightly more complicated. . . .

Timing

OK, break's over! The final significant element that makes up this game is the arrow generator. Without this, the player wouldn't know what dance move to do and when to do it. This is a little more complicated than what you've seen so far, so before we explain a bit more about this part of the game we feel we should cover a concept imperative to the success of this game.

The beat of the music never changes, so the movement of the arrows must remain accurate and consistent. Therefore, the upward movement of the arrows must be governed by time as opposed to frames. With us so far? If the "beats per second" of the music is 1, then the arrows must move at the same consistent speed as the music (i.e., 1 arrow per second). Because users have different processors in their computers, the frame rate could vary considerably, so it would be impossible to rely on the _y position of each arrow being governed by an onEnterFrame function.

Another, possibly better, way to explain the concept behind animation over time as opposed to frames is to use the old Flash cliché of fading between images. Everybody's done this at one time or another. Imagine you're running your movie at 30 fps and you have two fairly large bitmaps in their own movie clips and on their own layer. You make your timeline 30 frames long and add a keyframe, on the top layer, on frame 30. You then make the alpha value of the image on this keyframe 0 and create a motion tween between frames 1 and 30. Now when you run this movie, it should take just 1 second to fade the top image out to reveal the image on the bottom layer. But, if your machine has a rather poor level of performance, it may well take as long as 5 seconds—maybe even longer! So this would be when you should animate with code over time. By using the timer within Flash and decreasing the alpha value of the top image depending on how much time has elapsed, it will take just 1 second to fade between your images. If your machine is fast, then you'll see a nice, smooth alpha fade; if your machine isn't fast, then it certainly won't be as slick a transition but it will do what it's supposed to do in the time you want. That's exactly what must happen with this game—the arrows must move exactly in time with the music.

To change the speed of the movement of the arrows, you must change the bps (beats per second) variable on the root, inside the reset function. Increasing this value will make the arrows move faster and, as you'd expect, decreasing the value will slow the arrows down. We're afraid the process of finding the correct value of the bps variable for a particular piece of music is one of trial and error. Once you've chosen and inserted your music, publish the movie and see how the arrows move in time with your music. Increase or decrease the number until the arrows move in perfect time with the music. It could take some time as you have to wait until the end of the music—if it's even 0.001 off, the arrows could be out of sync by the time the music ends. This process is painstaking, but necessary. On the other hand, the game we've supplied to accompany this chapter goes slightly out of sync toward the end. "Why didn't they make sure it was perfect?" I hear you cry. "These people are hypocrites!" Yes, we are—and lazy as well. Do as we say, not as we do!

Well, we'd better dive right into the tricky stuff and get up to our necks in code.

1. Unlock the STEP ENGINE layer of the main timeline in the GAME scene and return to the frame labeled GAME_ON. Select the four white arrows at the top of the game—this is the stepDisplay movie clip, with an instance name of stepTemplate. Double-click it to delve inside:

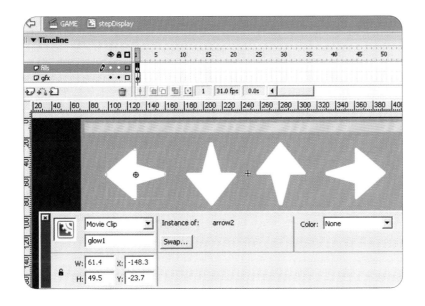

2. Now you'll see two layers: fills and gfx. The gfx layer is simply static graphics, just the outlines of the arrows, and the fills layer contains four arrow movie clips with the instance names glow1 to glow4. There's nothing mysterious or tricky about these elements. Their purpose is simply to flash and fade out when prompted to do so by code elsewhere in the movie, which we cover later. Probably the most important thing to note is that all the arrows are centered along the x axis (i.e., they all have a y position of 0).

For the code that controls the flash and fade, you need to head back to the main timeline and ACTIONS/LABELS. Scroll down through the code until you reach the letsDance function and the stepTemplateInit function, which is applied to the stepTemplate (all references to this inside the stepTemplateInit function will, in fact, refer to stepTemplate). Inside this function, you'll find the following:

```
checkAlpha = function() {
  if (this.goNow) {
    if (this._alpha > 0) {
      this._alpha -= 5;
    } else {
      this._alpha = 0;
      this.goNow = false;
    }
  }
}
for (var i = 1; i < 5; i++) {
  this["glow" + i]._alpha = 0;
  this["glow" + i].onEnterFrame = checkAlpha;
}
```

As you can see in the for loop at the bottom of the code, you set the initial alpha to 0 for each glow clip so it's not visible. You also give each clip a function to run every frame, checkAlpha. Whenever you want a particular arrow to flash, you target it, set its alpha to 100, and set the goNow variable to be true. All that happens next is that in each frame that follows, the clip fades down until it reaches 0 when the goNow variable is set to false.

3. To see how this function is applied to the stepTemplate movie clip, look at this line:

```
stepTemplateInit.apply(stepTemplate);
```

Pretty easy, isn't it? It does exactly what its name implies by applying the function to the object or movie clip specified. Now any reference to this inside the function will in fact refer to stepTemplate. You apply the mainDancerInit function in the same way to the mainDancer clip.

4. Let's take a look at the rest of stepTemplateInit. This initialization function sets the important code for stepTemplate, the movie clip you've just been looking at.

```
stepTemplateInit = function() {
  this.bps = _root.bps;
  this.bpb = 3;
  this.count = 1;
  this.startTime = getTimer();
  this.pauseTime = 1000/bps;
```

```
        this.currentRoutine = _root.routine_1;
        this.step.goNow = false;
        this.stepCount = 0;
        _root.score = 0;
        this.goNow = true;
```

5. Next up comes its onEnterFrame function, which is basically a timer:

```
    stepTemplate.onEnterFrame = function() {
        if (this.goNow) {
          this.timeNow = getTimer();
          this.elapsed = this.timeNow - this.startTime;
          if (this.elapsed >= this.pauseTime) {
            var newName = 'step' + this.count;
            var clip = this.attachMovie("step", newName, this.count++);
            clip._y = (100*this.bpb);
            clip.goNow = true;
            clip._alpha = 5;
            if (this.stepCount >= this.currentRoutine.length) {
              this.stepCount = 0;
            }
            this.whatStep = this.currentRoutine[this.stepCount];
            clip.step.gotoAndStop(this.whatStep);
            clip.posi = this.whatStep;
            this.stepCount++;
            this.startTime = getTimer();
          }
        }
    };
```

At first glance the onEnterFrame function looks a bit complex, so we'll break it down and explain it in bite-size chunks. Let's start with the main timer functionality:

```
    stepTemplate.onEnterFrame = function() {
      if (this.goNow) {
        this.timeNow = getTimer();
        this.elapsed = this.timeNow - this.startTime;
        if (this.elapsed >= this.pauseTime) {
          //
          // THIS IS WHERE YOU PUT THE CODE YOU WANT TO ACTION
          // EVERY TIME pauseTime HAS ELAPSED
          //
          this.startTime = getTimer();
        }
      }
    };
```

This function runs if goNow is true—basically if the game is in progress. When the game comes to an end, goNow is set to false. Now on every frame, timeNow increments and the time elapsed is constantly being calculated. Whenever the time elapsed is greater than or equal to pauseTime, it calls the action you want to happen and then resets the startTime variable to timeNow, and the whole process starts over again. We use this timer functionality all the time, more often than not for a game countdown. You'd be well advised to make a mental note here—better still, put a sticky note next to this code.

Now we'll start to cover what happens every time pauseTime elapses. The first chunk of code within the timer is as follows:

```
var newName = 'step' + this.count;
var clip = this.attachMovie("step", newName, this.count++);
clip._y = (100*this.bpb);
clip.goNow = true;
clip._alpha = 5;
```

The first line creates a newName for the movie you're about to attach, step plus the count variable, which you initialize as 1 in the onLoad function. The next line takes the movie clip you've identified as step in the linkage properties of the promptHolder element in the Library, attaches it to (places it inside) the stepTemplate movie, names it newName, and sets the depth of this newly attached movie to equal count. The ++ after count increments it by one, ready for the next one, as you can't have two movie clips with the same name or at the same depth (note that attachMovie returns a reference to the newly attached clip, which you can store directly in the variable clip). The next three lines set some basic properties and variables for this new clip: the y position, its alpha, and the goNow variable.

The next chunk of ActionScript looks like this:

```
if (this.stepCount >= this.currentRoutine.length) {
  this.stepCount = 0;
}
this.whatStep = this.currentRoutine[this.stepCount];
clip.step.gotoAndStop(this.whatStep);
clip.posi = this.whatStep;
this.stepCount++;
```

The last bit of code is quite simple, really. Its function is to set the "step" movie clip that's just been attached to display the arrow combination that should be pressed when the _y of this "step" equals 0. The stepCount variable was initialized as 0 when the onLoad function was called, and currentRoutine.length is the number of individual dance steps in the routine_1 array (more on this in the next section). So, if stepCount is less than the routine length, which at the start it will be, you set the variable whatStep to equal a value from the routine_1 array in sequential order.

The next line tells the "step" movie clip to go to the appropriate frame label and display the desired arrow combination for that step. You also set a variable called posi to equal whatStep in the next line. The last line increments stepCount by one. However, if stepCount is greater than or equal to currentRoutine.length, you simply reset the stepCount variable back to 0 and the whole routine runs again from the beginning. So now you're generating a different clip for every beat, and you're one "dance" step closer to a finished game.

At this point, you might be wondering about the "step" movie clip we referenced in the previous few paragraphs. Open the Library and scroll until you find the movie clip symbol called promptHolder, which you'll notice—if you're on the ball—is exported as step (look under the Linkage tab in the Library). Double-click promptHolder to open it up. Once it's open there's not really much to see, is there? Select the movie clip (the text that says steps in here) and look in the Actions window. Here you'll find another attached script—but don't despair! You're right, it does look imposing (maybe for the novices among you, anyway), but as with all the chapter's code so far we'll explain all.

First off, ignore all that code for the moment, and double-click the movie clip. Inside you'll see three lay-ers: the ever-familiar actions layer; a layer named label, which contains the text steps in here and bears no importance (it's hidden during game play anyway); and finally a layer named arrows. The frame labels on the actions layer should look familiar, and if you click the various points on the timeline you'll see arrows displaying exactly what you would expect them to:

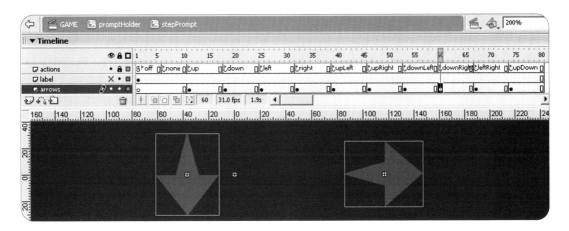

This is the straightforward bit, just a minor distraction from all the code. So now go back up a level to promptHolder, select the movie clip, which has the code on it, and go to the Actions panel. Now, the code here does quite a lot, as you've no doubt realized. We'll just start at the top and work our way down, and by the time we get to the bottom everything will hopefully be clear (as clear as mud!).

This first ream of code looks lengthy, but it doesn't do that much:

```
onClipEvent (load) {
  incScore = true;
  perfect = false;
  lab._visible = 0;
  startTime = getTimer();
  yPos = _parent._y;
  turnOn = function() {
    for (var i in arguments) {
      arguments[i]._alpha = 100;
      arguments[i].goNow = true;
    }
  }
  hitMe = function () {
    switch (_parent.posi) {
      case 'left':
        turnOn(_parent._parent.glow1);
        break;
      case 'right':
        turnOn(_parent._parent.glow4);
        break;
```

```
    case 'down':
      turnOn(_parent._parent.glow2);
      break;
    case 'up':
      turnOn(_parent._parent.glow3);
      break;
    case 'upDown':
      turnOn(_parent._parent.glow2, _parent._parent.glow3);
      break;
    case 'upLeft':
      turnOn(_parent._parent.glow1, _parent._parent.glow3);
      break;
    case 'upRight':
      turnOn(_parent._parent.glow4, _parent._parent.glow3);
      break;
    case 'downRight':
      turnOn(_parent._parent.glow2, _parent._parent.glow4);
      break;
    case 'downLeft':
      turnOn(_parent._parent.glow2, _parent._parent.glow1);
      break;
    case 'leftRight':
      turnOn(_parent._parent.glow1, _parent._parent.glow4);
      break;
  }
};
}
```

The first five lines within load onClipEvent simply initialize some variables used further down in the code. The remaining code in this segment consists of just two functions, turnOn and hitMe. The turnOn function is quite simple in that it sets a movie clip or clips' _alpha to 100 and the goNow variable to true. What's neat is that you actually run through the arguments sent to the function to find the clips. You see, every function has a built-in array named arguments that holds whatever is sent to the function. Because you address the movie clips that will be found in the arguments array, you're able to send as many or as few movie clips as you need to the function—whether one or one hundred, the function will deal with them the same!

When the hitMe function is called, it makes the arrows at the top of the game flash and fade out. It does this by checking the value of the posi variable in a handy and readable switch statement and sending the appropriate glow movie clips to the turnOn function described previously. If you can't remember our description of the stepTemplate movie clip, it's worth your while to go back a couple of pages and quickly refresh your memory. With that in mind, here's an explanation of the preceding hitMe function:

```
// sample code chunk...
case 'upLeft':
  turnOn(_parent._parent.glow1, _parent._parent.glow3);
  break;
```

This part of the function is taken, roughly, from the middle. As you can see, in the case that the variable posi equals upLeft, you send the glow1 and glow2 movie clips to the turnOn function. This will make the two arrows in stepTemplate appear, by setting the alpha value of each to 100, and then the onEnterFrame handler for each arrow makes them fade out. That's all this hitMe function does; it makes the appropriate arrows appear before they fade out.

We go through the next section of code, which is undoubtedly the most complex in the entire game, piece by piece because it's rather lengthy. The first snippet is as follows (ignoring the first two lines from the code, as they only establish that this code runs on an enterFrame and this only happens when the game is in full swing):

```
elapsed = getTimer()-startTime;
_parent._y = yPos-((elapsed/10)*_parent._parent.bps);
if (_parent._alpha<100) {
  _parent._alpha += 5;
}
if (_parent._y<=-90) {
  _parent.goNow = false;
  _parent.removeMovieClip();
}
if (_parent._y<5) {
  _parent._alpha -= 7;
}
```

The first line calculates the variable elapsed, which is the length of time elapsed since the movie clip was attached. This variable is used by the next line, which moves the y position of the movie clip upward. Remember when we covered animation over time as opposed to frames? Well, this is it in action! The next piece of this code is an if statement that increases the alpha value if it's less than 100, gradually increasing the opacity to display the movie clip such that it doesn't just suddenly "appear." The next if statement stops and deletes the movie clip when it gets beyond a certain y position, as it then ceases to become relevant to the game. The last if statement fades the movie clip out after it has reached the end of its usefulness and before it's removed.

Next up, another if statement calls the hitMe function when the key combination displayed has to be pressed—that is, when the movie clip's y position falls 12 pixels (_root.leeWayPerfect) either side of the origin, which is 0:

```
if ((_parent._y<(_root.leeWayPerfect)) && (_parent._y>(-_root.leeWayPerfect))) {
  hitMe();
}
```

The next section of code increments the scores, among other things, and falls into an if statement that allows it to happen only if the variable incScore is true:

```
if (incScore) {
  if (((_parent._y<(_root.leeWayOK)) && (_parent._y>_root.leeWayPerfect)) ||
➡ ((_parent._y>(-(_root.leeWayOK))) && (_parent._y<(-_root.leeWayPerfect)))) {
    _root.moveToPull = _parent.posi;
    if (_root.pressed == _root.moveToPull) {
      _root.scoreHolder.score++;
      _root.score++;
      _root.accuracy.gotoAndPlay('ok');
      _root.combo = 0;
```

```
        perfect = false;
        incScore = false;
    }
}
```

That's certainly one *big* if statement! Let's look at it again:

```
if ((((_parent._y<(_root.leeWayOK)) && (_parent._y>_root.leeWayPerfect)) ||
➡((_parent._y>(-X(_root.leeWayOK))) && (_parent._y<(-_root.leeWayPerfect)))) {
```

In simple terms, the content of this statement happens only when the movie clip's y position falls between 25 pixels (_root.leeWayOK) either side of the point 0 but outside a measurement of 12 pixels (_root.leeWayPerfect) on either side of the point 0—in other words, close (OK) but not perfect. Got that? When this is the case, a variable on the root called moveToPull is set to the variable posi. This is going to be up, down, left, etc., and it's the move the user has to match with his key combination. So, the next statement, if the keys pressed equal the variable moveToPull, the score is incremented by one, the accuracy movie clip on the root goes to and plays from the label ok, the variable combo on the root is set to 0, perfect is set to false, and so too is the variable incScore. If incScore wasn't set to false, the score would rapidly keep incrementing, which isn't what you want to happen.

The functionality of this section of the code is similar to the last section, in that it increments the score and so on, but this code happens only when the movie clip falls into the perfect area (i.e., within 12 pixels on either side of the point 0).

```
    else if ((_parent._y<(_root.leeWayPerfect)) && (_parent._y>(-_root.leeWayPerfect))) {
      if (_root.pressed == _root.moveToPull) {
        howClose = Math.round(_parent._y);
        if (howClose<0) {
          howClose = howClose*-1;
        }
        tempScore = (_root.leeWayPerfect-howClose)+3;
        if (_root.combo == 0) {
          _root.scoreHolder.score += tempScore;
          _root.score += tempScore;
        } else if (_root.combo>0) {
          _root.scoreHolder.score += tempScore*_root.combo;
          _root.score += tempScore*_root.combo;
        }
        _root.accuracy.gotoAndPlay('great');
        _root.combo++;
        if (_root.comboHi<_root.combo) {
          _root.comboHi = _root.combo;
        }
        soundToPlay = Math.floor(Math.random()*_root.sounds.noOfSounds)+1;
        _root.sounds.gotoAndPlay('snd'+soundToPlay);
        perfect = true;
        incScore = false;
      }
    }
```

So, if the keys pressed equal the variable moveToPull on the root timeline, the following will happen. A variable is set that captures the movie clip's y position at the time the keys were pressed, so it's going to be somewhere between 12 and −12. If howClose is less than 0, it's multiplied by −1 so that it's a positive number; otherwise you'll end up with a minus score. Next, a variable tempScore is established that subtracts howClose from the leeWayPerfect variable and then adds 3, so for a perfect hit the user's score can vary from 3 to 15 depending on how accurate she is. Now, if the variable combo on the root equals 0 the score is incremented by the tempScore; otherwise, if combo is greater than zero the score is incremented by "tempScore multiplied by combo." This starts to create quite diverse scoring, because combo is incremented by one every time a user gets it perfect. If the user misses one "perfect," the combo variable is reset to 0. The movie clip _root.accuracy is then told to go and play from the frame labeled great so that the user knows she's hit a "perfect" move. The next if statement just sets a variable on the root called combiHi to be the highest number of "perfect" moves pulled consecutively. The last few lines of this code reward the user with a randomly selected funny sound effect, set the variable perfect to be true, and set incScore to be false, again, so the user gets her score only once.

This last if statement sets the combo variable to 0 if the three cases are true (this was just a minor bug fix):

```
if ((_parent._y<=(-_root.leeWayPerfect)) && (!perfect) && (_parent.posi != 'none')) {
    _root.combo = 0;
}
```

Whew! Take a deep breath and relax. Believe it or not, all the complicated stuff is now out of the way. You can go and have another cup of tea if you understand it all—you deserve it!

In a previous paragraph we mentioned the accuracy movie clip, so we thought we'd better show you where it's located, just to satisfy your curiosity. Go to the root of the game, unlock the ACCURACY layer, and go to the frame labeled GAME_ON. The accuracy movie clip sits just in between the four white arrows and the dancer's head in the middle of the game. Double-click it and you can look inside to see what it's all about.

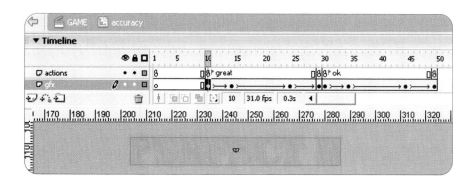

Dance Routine

All right, you've got your character, your music, and the arrows are moving in perfect time. Now what you want to do is design a dance routine. Time to don your choreographer's hat and design some slick moves! If you look at the code on the ACTIONS/LABELS layer on the root timeline, you should see an array called routine_1. This array contains a series of arrow key combinations that correspond to the moves:

```
routine_1 = new Array('left', 'left', 'left', 'none',
➡'right', 'right', 'right', 'none', 'up', 'down', 'none', 'none', 'up', 'left',
➡'right', 'down', 'none', 'upDown', 'none', 'none', 'upLeft', 'none', 'upRight',
➡'none', 'upLeft', 'none', 'upRight', 'none', 'downLeft', 'downRight', 'downLeft',
➡'downRight', 'none', 'leftRight', 'none', 'none');
```

Here you have a mixture of 11 different possibilities. To make your own routines, you just need to create a new array in this fashion:

yourRoutineName_# = new Array(your moves go in here);

Or you can use this shorthand:

yourRoutineName_# = [your moves go in here];

Here you would start adding the different arrow key combinations, one after the other. Once you've finished, you must remember to change the value of another variable, currentRoutine, to equal the name of your new array name. This is also defined on the root, just below the array of moves. This lets you create lots of different routines and alternate them easily.

Now, publish your movie and see how the moves work together. If you're happy, great; if not, just change the moves to something else, no problem. One word of warning, though: make sure your character doesn't end up dancing like your dad—that would be very embarrassing indeed!

What's the Score?

You have the main elements of the game and they do what you want them to do. This is all well and good, but the user will play your game once or twice and say, "Oh, that was nice, what's next?" Where's the incentive to play it again and again? You need to have a quality scoring system that lets users see how well they've performed and enables them to establish a benchmark for themselves and others to try harder. Let's briefly consider how this game's scoring system works.

When the user presses an arrow key or combination of arrow keys, the dancing character does a dance move—we've established that. Recall that earlier in this chapter we mentioned that at the same time the function dancin tells moves which frame to go to, it also sets a variable on the root called pressed to the corresponding value; for example, if the user presses the left and up arrow keys, _root.pressed will equal upLeft. Well, when the rising arrows that prompt the user to press the corresponding arrow keys reach the point at which keys should be pressed, it sets another variable on the root called moveToPull to equal that value. So if the up and left arrow keys are to be pressed, _root.moveToPull will equal upLeft also, but only within a certain slot either side of the absolute 0. Got that? We hope so—it sounds much more confusing than it actually is, honest! Therefore, if _root.pressed and _root.moveToPull are the same value at the same time, the user is going to be due some points, but just how many points depends on how close the user is to pressing the keys at the exact time they were supposed to be pressed (i.e., exactly on the beat).

On the root we've set the `leeWayOK` variable to equal 25 and the `leeWayPerfect` variable to equal 12. As these variable names suggest (we recommend naming variables in the most descriptive manner possible, within reason, because you may forget what they're for if you give them obscure names), if the user presses the keys when the y coordinate of the arrow(s) to be pressed is less than `leeWayOK` but greater than `leeWayPerfect`, or if the value is less than minus `leeWayPerfect` but greater than minus `leeWayOK`, then the score falls into the "almost" category and minimal points are awarded. However, if the keys are pressed when the y coordinate is less than `leeWayPerfect` and greater than minus `leeWayPerfect`, then the score is categorized as "perfect" and the user is awarded more points depending on how close he was to the exact time of the beat (i.e., the 0 position).

Another facet to the scoring system is the "combos." If the user gets a "perfect," the combo variable is incremented by one. Each time the user gets a "perfect," the value of that "perfect" is multiplied by the combo variable, rewarding the user considerably for her consistency. If the user misses a move or gets an "almost," the combo variable is reset to 0. This just adds more depth to an otherwise predictable scoring system.

So, if the user gets a great score, he's going to want to immortalize that score along with his name in a high-score table or "hall of fame." Having a high-score table means the difference between a user playing your game several times or 50 times. It gives the user a chance to measure his score against others. Most people's competitive streak takes over at this point, and before you know it your user has developed a bit of a dancing addiction: "Hi, my name's Steve, and I'm a dance-aholic!" Anyway, we hope we've prompted you enough to pay particular attention to "Online Gaming with PHP and MySQL," in which you'll learn how to collect data and set up an online scoring system.

Spit and Polish

Now you know how everything works, and hopefully you'll find the game highly playable. However, unless it looks slick and professional, and it functions with a high level of robustness, nobody will hold your game with any great regard. People are shallow, we know. . . .

So the final thing to do is make sure everything is exactly right. If you're using pixel fonts, make sure they're exactly on a rounded pixel. When you're making buttons, be sure to make them all look and function the same way, and make it blindingly obvious what to press and when. Do you really need that splash screen? Probably not, but everyone still insists on putting one in there because that's what "proper" games have. Forget that—get the user to the game with as few clicks as possible. Of course, there will be times when clients overrule your better judgment. Be pedantic about every little detail; paying particular attention to that last 5% is what's going to make your games stand out from the crowd.

Another noteworthy point is to ensure that you include a quality preloader that tells the user exactly how long she has to go before she can play. Few things prompt users to instantly close a window more than the word Loading flashing hypnotically before their eyes. People need to know how long they have to wait, because their time's precious.

So, before we say our good-byes, we'll explain briefly how the preloader works:

1. Go to the scene called LOADER, unlock the layer called loader, and select the loader movie clip (also notice that there's a `stop( )` action on frame 1):

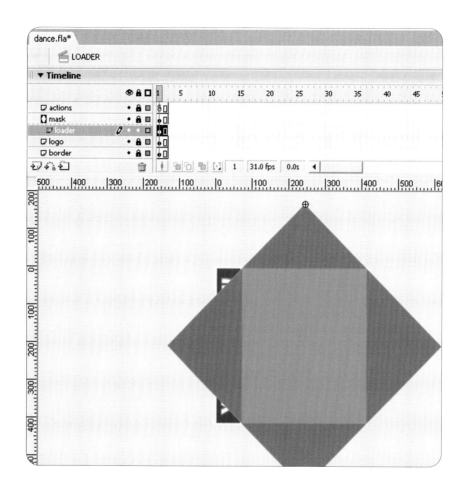

2. You'll find the following code attached to the loader movie clip:

```
onClipEvent (load) {
  this._visible = 0;
  loadBar._xScale = 0;
  loading = function () {
    var total = _root.getBytesTotal();
    var soFar = _root.getBytesLoaded();
    perc = soFar/total*100;
    if ((!perc>0) && (!perc<=100)) {
      perc = 1;
    }
```

```
      var dl = perc-loadBar._xScale;
      loadBar._xScale += dl/10;
      if (perc>=100) {
        _parent.play();
      }
    };
    loading();
  }
  onClipEvent (enterFrame) {
    this._visible = 1;
    loading();
  }
```

All this code really does is work out exactly how much of the total file size has loaded as a percentage. It then sets the _xscale of the loadBar (inside loader), and when the percentage loaded is greater than or equal to 100%, it plays the root of the movie. Very easy, and something you'll use time and time again.

> *Note that Flash MX 2004 provides a new object designed specifically for loading content and returning meaningful information about the load process. The* MovieClipLoader *object is a fantastic addition to the ActionScript arsenal. Unfortunately, you can't use it for the main timeline of a movie it's created in. In other words, although the* MovieClipLoader *object may be very useful for loading content into movie clips or other levels, for movies loaded into the main timeline you must resort to the traditional methods demonstrated previously in this chapter.*

Finally, you may notice when you play the game that when you get a "perfect" not only do you increment your score, but also you're rewarded with a Michael Jackson–esque squeal of some description. One of five additional sound effects that add that something extra, a little bit of humor which should bring a wry smile to even the most miserable chap sitting at the back of the office. On the root timeline, back in the GAME scene, you'll find the sounds movie clip (with associated code attached):

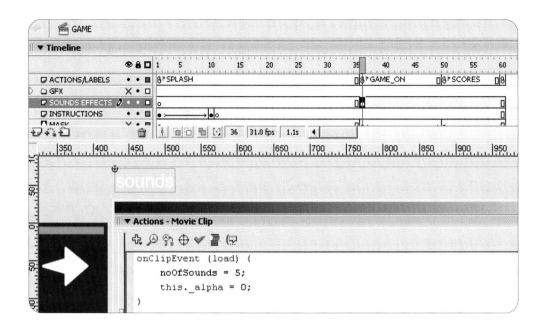

Double-click sounds and you'll see that can easily add your own sound effects by editing it from within. You'll also need to change the noOfSounds variable to equal the number of sounds you've included. Simple and very effective!

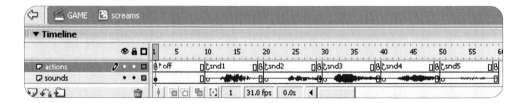

Summary

All the features we discussed in this game combine to make it stand out from all the garbage that's out there in the vastness of cyberspace, where the emphasis is on quantity rather than quality. So please, don't be another "bedroom" developer churning out mediocre Flash work—there's enough of that already cluttering up the Web and giving Flash a bad name. Set your goals high, and don't upload anything until you know it's worth uploading. You'll know when your game is going to be a runaway success when you can't stop playing with it yourself!

Just one more thing: try to avoid simply taking the games supplied with this book, reskinning them, and selling them to the highest bidder—show a bit of originality and creativity. Take what we've provided you with, make sure that you truly understand the work, and then make something better. After all, just how long do you think it's going to be before the Web is overrun with dancing games? Good luck!

Brian Monnone

Brian is the senior multimedia producer/developer for Tocquigny Advertising in Austin, Texas. Tocquigny Advertising received the Austin Business Journal's Top 25 Web Developers #1 position for 2002/2003 in web design and development in Austin. Brian has been computing for over 18 years and has found himself doing what he loves to do. He works on projects with AMD, Dell, HP, USAA, UPS, Seagate, and a host of other companies, creating cool Flash demos, websites, videos, and other types of multimedia. Brian has won awards for his work and many accolades.

Living in the heart of Texas, Brian finds inspiration for his work and enjoys spending time with his wife, Julie, and two daughters, Madison and Lauren. Although Brian currently creates multimedia content, he hopes to someday become a filmmaker.

Brian would like to thank a few people for putting up with him during the last few years. First and foremost, he'd like to thank his wife, Julie, for dealing with the long hours in front of the computer away from her. He could not have done any of this without her. He'd also like to thank his parents, Gabrielle, David, Cheryl, Robert, and Joe; his children for reminding him about the real reason he's here; and Josh Dura and Daniel Dura for advising him during the development of this project. According to Brian, "The fact is this: I work with lots of people on a daily basis, listening to ideas and reviewing storyboards, but it really does boil down to one simple concept for me. I'm just a guy who wants to make some cool s*!t."

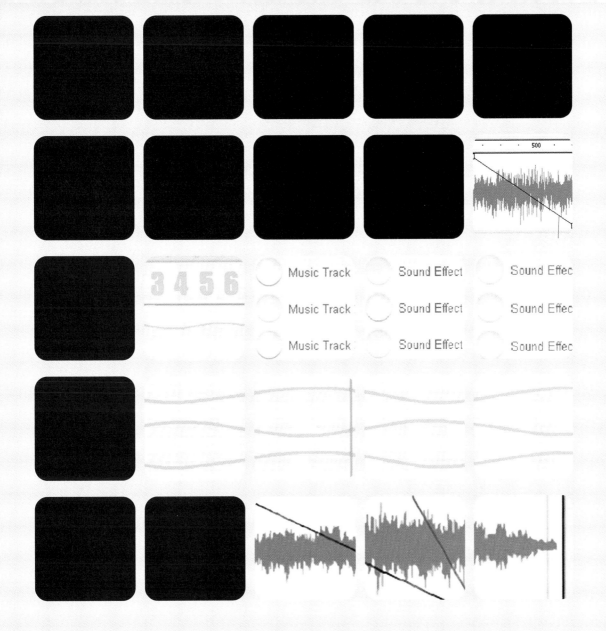

SOUND FOR GAMES

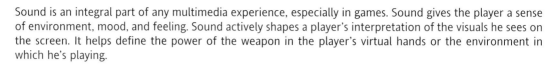
Sound is an integral part of any multimedia experience, especially in games. Sound gives the player a sense of environment, mood, and feeling. Sound actively shapes a player's interpretation of the visuals he sees on the screen. It helps define the power of the weapon in the player's virtual hands or the environment in which he's playing.

Sound can be used in advanced ways—for example, sound can alert the player to enemies lurking around a corner, beyond the range of vision, warning the player of an impending threat. Sound can enhance game play by startling the player with a sudden loud bang or even reassuring the player that she has won by playing cheerful music. Imagine playing your favorite game with the sound turned down. All of a sudden that creepy game you're playing is less creepy. Sure, the visuals are great and scary, but you probably won't feel scared due to the lack of sound effects.

Subtle ambient sounds such as crickets, insects, wind, rain, and even traffic provide a physical sensation. On the flip side, sound also creates the context for silence. *Not* using sound in certain parts of a game can add drama, suspense, or importance.

So it's only natural that games made in Flash have sound. In this chapter you'll learn how to add and control sounds with Flash MX 2004 to be used in your games. You'll explore a "sound box" that will dynamically attach music tracks and sound effects to buttons, and will give you an idea of how sound objects work. We'll discuss what kind of sounds you can import and the way Flash MX 2004 uses them. Because sound can also dramatically increase the size of your Flash game, it's important to discuss how to optimize your sound to get the smallest possible file size from Flash MX 2004. We'll take you through two different examples of how to dynamically use sound with Flash MX 2004. The first is a straightforward approach with three simple buttons. The second is the aforementioned more elaborate "sound box" that will play different music tracks and sound effects when the user clicks buttons.

There are many ways to use sound in Flash MX 2004. You can import each sound into the main movie (SWF), or you can create a separate SWF to hold the sounds—a "sound container," for instance. Creating a separate SWF to hold the sounds requires that you create references from the main SWF to play them. This is a good method, but it can cause issues with playback because of preloading or if you want to have the sound specifically track with the visuals such as a "streaming" sound. If your sounds are small enough in file size, creating SWF holders may be the route to go. On the other hand, a great default method is to simply import the sounds in the main movie and create sound objects to play them back. More on that in a bit—first you need to import the sounds into Flash.

Importing Sounds

Importing sounds into Flash is rather straightforward, but you do need to take certain issues into consideration. You want to import these sounds straight into the Library, not the stage like you would a graphic. Select File ➤ Import to Library and choose the sound or sounds you want to import. The imported sounds will now live in the Library, not the timeline. Make sure the drop-down menu is set to "All formats"—this way, you have the opportunity to use all the sound formats Flash MX 2004 can import.

So what are the different sound formats, you ask? There are three main types: MP3, WAV, and AIF. If you don't know already, MP3 is the standard compression type for music stored in a computer. An MP3 file is compressed, meaning that the sound quality is actually not as good as a CD's file but is much smaller in size. Even though the compression in an MP3 file is high, it's still very clear and nice sounding. Some people can't even tell the difference between an MP3 file and a CD file with regard to sound.

Note that sound is a wavelength that displays the vibration of air molecules. Technically speaking, the sound source that produces sounds vibrates the air molecules, creating vibration wavelengths that in turn are recognized by our ears, such as a violin or guitar, or even the speakers on your PC. In air, sound propagates via small, rapid changes in the air pressure above and below atmospheric pressure. These pressure variations travel in the form of a pressure wave with an inherent amount of energy. When the rapid variations in pressure occur between about 20 and 20,000 times per second (i.e., at a frequency between 20 Hz and 20 kHz), sound is potentially audible by humans even though the pressure variation can be, and typically is, very small with respect to the mean pressure (e.g., atmospheric pressure). Louder sounds are caused by greater variation in pressure. The sound we hear is usually described in analog wavelength vibration and the amplitude of vibration is periodically divided into a frequency. This audible frequency band range differs among animals, and a bat, for instance, can hear ultrasonic waves that exceed a human's audible band range.

We won't delve too much into the topic of sound compression, but the basic concept you should understand is that sound is compressed by removing small amounts of sound that are barely audible to the human ear.

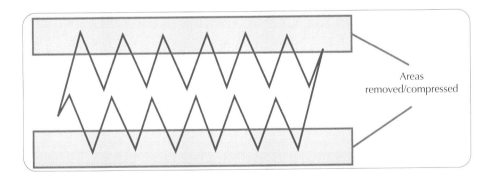

Areas removed/compressed

So maybe with compression we can actually help those bats by eliminating sounds that irritate them?! Anyway, this compression produces a much smaller file than a raw WAV or AIF file. WAV is a standard PC format; AIF is a standard Mac format. WAV and AIF files are basically uncompressed sound files. For example, if you play a song on a keyboard into your computer and save it as a WAV file, it will be large—very large. A 1-minute WAV file can be as large as 20MB, whereas the same file compressed as an MP3 would be only 1MB. The stunning news is that the file would sound virtually the same in both the MP3 and WAV formats!

So it seems obvious to use MP3 files, right? Wrong. Although Flash can import MP3 files, it has a difficult time dealing with MP3s that are compressed in certain ways. Yes, that's right, all MP3 files are not created equal. When you encode an MP3 file with an MP3 encoding program, the main thing to consider is bit rate.

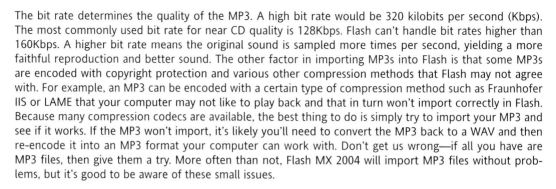

The bit rate determines the quality of the MP3. A high bit rate would be 320 kilobits per second (Kbps). The most commonly used bit rate for near CD quality is 128Kbps. Flash can't handle bit rates higher than 160Kbps. A higher bit rate means the original sound is sampled more times per second, yielding a more faithful reproduction and better sound. The other factor in importing MP3s into Flash is that some MP3s are encoded with copyright protection and various other compression methods that Flash may not agree with. For example, an MP3 can be encoded with a certain type of compression method such as Fraunhofer IIS or LAME that your computer may not like to play back and that in turn won't import correctly in Flash. Because many compression codecs are available, the best thing to do is simply try to import your MP3 and see if it works. If the MP3 won't import, it's likely you'll need to convert the MP3 back to a WAV and then re-encode it into an MP3 format your computer can work with. Don't get us wrong—if all you have are MP3 files, then give them a try. More often than not, Flash MX 2004 will import MP3 files without problems, but it's good to be aware of these small issues.

To ensure that your sound will import correctly, it's best to use WAV or AIF files. Even though they're essentially uncompressed and yield very high file sizes, Flash can compress them to manageable MP3s on export of your final SWF. There is a catch, however. Unless you have QuickTime 5 or 6 installed, when you run Windows you can't import AIF, and on the Mac you can't import WAV. A simple solution for Windows users is to just download and install the free QuickTime software from www.apple.com and you'll be able to import files in AIF format.

The other thing to consider when using an MP3 rather than a raw WAV file is that some sound-editing programs such as Sound Forge by Sonic Foundry by default will add a tiny amount of silence at the beginning and at the end of the sound during MP3 creation. This being the case, and to avoid the situation altogether, we recommend using WAV files. Although the FLA will yield a higher file size, the SWF won't, and the final results are more predictable.

For the purpose of these exercises and to keep file sizes low, we use MP3 files for the music tracks, but we use WAV files for the sound effects.

Flash Sound Types and Effects

If you chose to add your sounds to the timeline, which you may want to do, there are several ways in which Flash MX 2004 will handle syncing those sounds. Adding sound to the timeline is rather painless:

1. If the frame on the timeline doesn't have a keyframe, create one now (press *F6* or select Insert ➤ Timeline ➤ Keyframe) and then import the sound into Flash (*CTRL+R/CMD+R* or File ➤ Import ➤ Import to Library).

2. After successfully importing, the sound won't show up in the timeline just yet, as you imported it directly into your Library. You need to select the keyframe you just added and then choose the sound name from the Sound menu in the Property inspector.

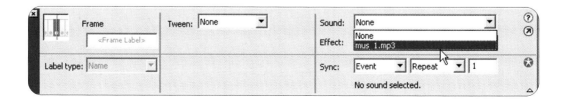

3. To see more of the music file in the timeline, you need to add some frames in the timeline. As you can see in the following image, we inserted the frames to 75 to see more of this sound.

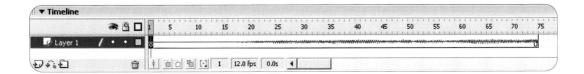

By default, Flash will Sync the sound as an Event. You really don't need to be able to see the entire music file in the timeline for it to play back completely—more on that in a moment. You'll ultimately control your sounds dynamically with ActionScript, leaving them in the Library. Sound objects called upon from within the Library are set to Event sounds, meaning they'll play regardless of the animation because they aren't placed directly on the timeline. This being the case, you don't really need to worry too much about sync types, but they're good to know about. As you'll see, the sync types described here are timeline based. Seeing these sync types and how they work is essential to understanding how sound works on the timeline.

Sync Settings

- Event is the default setting and, generally, the best performance choice, especially for sound effects and other "incidental" sounds. When you choose Event, sounds will start to play when the keyframe is reached and keep playing until they're done. Event sounds might not sync up with visual elements the same way on different computers. Sounds won't play slower or faster, but a slower computer may take longer to display visual elements.

- Start is almost the same as Event, except that multiple instances of the same sound are prevented. With Event, a sound can be layered on top of itself. Think of Start as playing a sound if it's not already playing.

- Stop is for when you want a specified sound to stop playing. For example, if you import a sound called "background music," and by whatever means have it playing, when a keyframe is encountered with the same sound (background music) set to Stop, just that sound will stop. Any other sounds already playing will continue. This seems awkward because you use the Properties panel to specify the sound (just like when you want the sound to play), but you're specifying it as the particular sound you want to stop. Think of Stop as "stop this sound if it's playing."

- Stream causes the sound to remain perfectly synchronized with the timeline. Because, again, you can't have sounds playing slowly if the user's machine can't draw frames quickly enough, Flash will skip frames to keep up. Stream sounds start playing when the first frame is reached and continue to play as long as there's space in the timeline. In other words, if your sound is 3 seconds long and you're playing at 12 fps, the timeline has to be at least 36 frames; otherwise, part of the sound will never be reached. Just remember that when you're using Stream, you have to ensure there are enough frames in the timeline to accommodate the length of the sound. Finally, Stream sounds are previewed as you "scrub," whereas Event sounds aren't, thus making the process of synchronizing audio to images possible.

163

Editing Sounds

Let's take a brief look at the editing capabilities for sound that you can use within Flash.

1. Continuing on from the previous exercise, click the keyframe or anywhere on the layer in the timeline that the sound occupies. Next, click the Edit button in the Property inspector.

2. The Edit Envelope dialog box opens, and the drop-down box at the top has preset envelopes. The envelope handles the volume of the sound; for example, if you drop the first envelope handle down in the left channel, then the sound will only play out of the right channel's speakers. You can fade the sound in and out with these handles. Let's take a closer look at the Edit Envelope dialog box and its various elements:

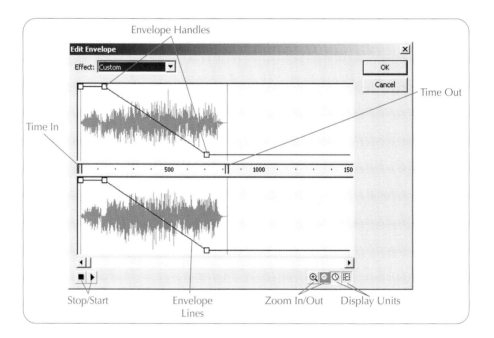

- Left Channel/Right Channel displays different waveforms if your original sound was in stereo. Even if you only use mono sounds, you'll get the left and right channels so that you can still create panning effects.

- Envelope lines indicate the volume level at any particular time in the sound. When the line is at the top, the sound plays at full 100% volume.

- Envelope handles are like keyframes within the sound. If you want the envelope lines (indicating volume) to change direction, you'll need to insert a handle, which acts almost like a keyframe for sound. All you need to do is click anywhere on a line and a handle will be inserted. You can only have a total of eight keyframe points on each line.

- Time In lets you establish the starting point of a sound, trimming the extra sound (or silence) at the beginning of the sound file. You're not telling the sound to start any later, but the sound you hear will begin wherever the Time In marker is placed.

- Time Out lets you trim extra sound off the end of a sound file.

- Stop/Start lets you preview all the settings you've made. This is important because although the waveform can let you "see" a sound, you ultimately want to hear the new effect.

- Zoom in/Zoom out lets you zoom out so the entire sound fits in the current window or zoom in close to control precisely how you place the Time In/Time Out markers or envelope handles.

- Display units (Time or Frames) simply changes the units displayed (in the center portion) from time units (seconds) to frame units.

Controlling Sound with ActionScript

You can accomplish most of the previous settings with nothing more than ActionScript. This is the ideal situation for creating games in Flash MX 2004 because you can control the sound dynamically rather than relying on the timeline to play your sounds. With sounds controlled though ActionScript, you can get a better handle on when they're played and not played, and how they're played, as opposed to simply adding the sound to a frame in the timeline.

When you create sound objects, you never drag the sound from the Library onto the stage or even place it in a frame. Instead, you define the sound through ActionScript in a frame or from a movie clip and give an identifying name to the sound while it's in the Library.

Using the Sound Object

For Flash MX 2004 it's typically a good idea to define all of your sound objects and button actions in the root of your movie. This makes accessing them easier for Flash and you. Another important consideration is naming conventions. Things can get confusing rather quickly because you're going to want to use names that have some sort of resemblance to each other. For example, the music track music1.wav will probably have a sound object name of myMusic1 and a linkage identifier as music1. Other things might include myMusicPosition or myMusicVolume. We'll take a look at starting and stopping this dynamically called track.

In this exercise you're going to go through a simple example of using sound objects. You can re-create this exercise from the starting point of empty_button_object.fla—we've provided all the assets you'll need in the Library. You can also refer to the finished piece, button_object.fla, for reference.

Open empty_button_object.fla and create three layers called Actions, Text Boxes, and Buttons. In the first layer, Actions, place this code in frame 1:

```
myMusic1 = new Sound();
myMusic1.attachSound("music1");
myMusic1.onSoundComplete = function() {
  status.text="NOT PLAYING";
  playing = false;
};
//Start button
startButton.onRelease = function(){
  if (!playing) {
    myMusic1.start(0, 1);
    myMusic1Volume = 100;
    volStatus.text="Volume Level "+myMusic1Volume;
    myMusic1.setVolume(myMusic1Volume);
```

```
        status.text="PLAYING";
        playing = true;
    }
};
startButton.onRollOver = function(){
    startButton.gotoAndStop(2);
};
startButton.onRollOut = function(){
    startButton.gotoAndStop(1);
};
//Stop Button
stopButton.onRelease = function(){
    myMusic1.stop("music1");
    volStatus.text="Volume Level "+myMusic1Volume;
    status.text="NOT PLAYING";
    playing = false;
};
stopButton.onRollOver = function(){
    stopButton.gotoAndStop(2);
};
stopButton.onRollOut = function(){
    stopButton.gotoAndStop(1);
};
//Volume Button
volButton.onRelease = function(){
    myMusic1Volume=25;
    myMusic1.setVolume(myMusic1Volume);
    volStatus.text="Volume Level "+myMusic1Volume;
};
volButton.onRollOver = function(){
    volButton.gotoAndStop(2);
};
volButton.onRollOut = function(){
    volButton.gotoAndStop(1);
};
```

We break this code down and explain it in the following subsections.

Defining a Sound Object

1. Create your sound object in a frame in the root of the main timeline:

   ```
   myMusic1 = new Sound();
   ```

2. Set a new sound object called myMusic1. You'll use this object for only one actual sound, making it a unique identifier for that sound for ActionScript:

   ```
   myMusic1.attachSound("music1");
   ```

   Here you're attaching the sound in the Library that you'll identify as music1 to the new sound object myMusic1.

3. Next, link the sound mus_1.mp3 located in the Library with your new sound object, myMusic1. Right-click (Windows) or CMD+click (Mac) the sound file in the Library and choose Linkage:

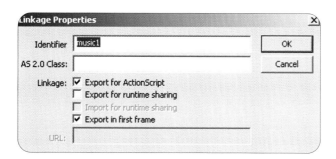

4. Select Export for ActionScript and give the file a name. We called our sound clip music1. This tells us the new sound object called myMusic1 is referencing a music track in the Library linked as music1.

onSoundComplete

5. What if you want something to happen based on when a sound is complete? You can do this with an onSoundComplete function:

```
myMusic1.onSoundComplete = function() {
  status.text="NOT PLAYING";
  playing = false;
}
```

This code says that once the new sound object, myMusic, is finished playing, the sound attached to it then it should tell the variable status to display NOT PLAYING. The variable status is actually the variable name of one of the text boxes that we've added to the stage. This text box will display the message NOT PLAYING once the sound has finished playing. The purpose of this simple example is to illustrate that you can add any event to this onSoundComplete function.

6. The next variable, playing, is set to false. This variable is essentially a toggle that is set after the events happen, so you can check to see if the music track is playing or not before another event occurs.

Interactivity with Buttons

With Flash MX 2004 you can now give movie clips many of the capabilities of standard buttons. In earlier versions of Flash, the codes that referenced a user's mouse actions such as onPress, onRelease, or onReleaseOutside had to always be attached to a button. With Flash MX 2004 (as with Flash MX) you can use movie clips to act as buttons. This new method is very beneficial because you can add much interactivity to those movie clips that you couldn't normally add to buttons, such as extending animation throughout the timeline of that movie clip. With the new method, your code will look something like this:

Old way:

```
onRelease(){
  gotoAndPlay(20);
}
```

New way:

```
someMovieClip.onRelease = function(){
  gotoAndPlay(20);
}
```

The old and new code look very similar, but they're each performing the same action in a totally different way. The "old way" code is placed on the button itself and directs it to do something; the "new way" code is located in the main timeline *referencing* the movie clip and tells it to perform some actions.

Let's look at the button code in detail.

7. The movie clip labeled startButton for an onRelease function is initialized:

```
startButton.onRelease = function(){
```

8. If the variable playing isn't true, process the following:

```
if (!playing) {
```

9. Start playing sound object myMusic1 and play it from the beginning only one time. The other part of the start code (0,1) represents SecondOffset and the number of times the sounds loop. So for this example, the music track will play from the very beginning and loop only one time. If your start() command was (10, 999), then the music track would start 10 seconds into the track and loop 999 times.

```
myMusic1.start(0, 1);
```

10. Set the variable myMusic1Volume to 100%:

```
myMusic1Volume = 100;
```

11. Display the volume level in the dynamic text box with the instance name volstatus:

```
volStatus.text="Volume Level "+myMusic1Volume;
```

12. Set myMusic1's volume to 100%:

```
myMusic1.setVolume(myMusic1Volume);
```

13. Display the playing status in the status dynamic text box:

```
status.text="PLAYING";
```

14. Set the variable playing to true. If the button is clicked, the sound should play, no problem. But if the button is clicked again, the sound will play again, right over the top of the current sound already playing. This may be all right for sound effects, but not for music tracks. The ideal situation is to click the button and have the music track play once. For a more practical situation, you may want that track to play during a certain point in the game. So instead of the button triggering the sound, maybe it's an event in the game: an asteroid exploding, an enemy ship being destroyed, or simply victory in the game. But for the purpose of demonstrating how to prevent sounds from playing over one another, you'll use the button again.

```
        playing = true;
    }
};
```

15. The movie clip labeled startButton for an onRollOver function is initialized:

```
    startButton.onRollOver = function(){
```

16. Tell the movie clip startButton go to and stop on frame 2, displaying the "over" state:

```
        startButton.gotoAndStop(2);
    };
```

17. The movie clip labeled startButton for an onRollOut function is initialized:

```
    startButton.onRollOut = function(){
```

18. Tell the movie clip startButton go to and stop on frame 1, displaying the "off" state:

```
        startButton.gotoAndStop(1);
    };
```

19. The next two buttons have similar code, except you're asking a different movie clip to perform a different task:

```
    stopButton.onRelease = function(){
```

20. Stop playing the sound object myMusic1. It's important to note that if the identifier, music1, isn't used in the stop() command, then all the sounds will stop (if there are multiple sounds).

```
    myMusic1.stop("music1");
```

21. Display the volume level in the dynamic text box:

```
    volStatus.text="Volume Level "+myMusic1Volume;
```

22. Display the playing status in the other dynamic text box:

```
    status.text="NOT PLAYING";
```

23. Sets the variable playing to false, and sets up the stop button with onRollOver and onRollOut functions, as we did for the start button.

```
    playing = false;
  };
  stopButton.onRollOver = function(){
    stopButton.gotoAndStop(2);
  };
  stopButton.onRollOut = function(){
    stopButton.gotoAndStop(1);
  };
```

24. The volume button sets myMusic1 to 25% of full volume. For this situation, it's best to place this code on a button to simulate the music getting quiet at a certain point in a game. Keep in mind, though, that if the sound is stopped and then started again, it will be played at 100% because the start button sets it to 100%.

```
  volButton.onRelease = function(){
```

25. Set the variable myMusic1Volume to 25:

```
    myMusic1Volume=25;
```

26. Set the volume of myMusic1 to 25%:

```
    myMusic1.setVolume(myMusic1Volume);
```

27. Display the volume level in the appropriate dynamic text box:

```
    volStatus.text="Volume Level "+myMusic1Volume;
  };
  volButton.onRollOver = function(){
    volButton.gotoAndStop(2);
  };
  volButton.onRollOut = function(){
    volButton.gotoAndStop(1);
  };
```

That's it for the ActionScript—you just need to finish off some of the graphical elements now.

28. In the Text Boxes layer, place two **dynamic** text fields on the stage. Select the first text field and give it the instance name status in the Property inspector:

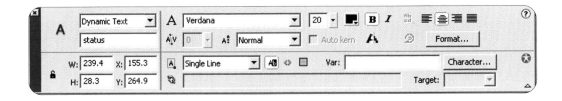

29. Select the second box and name that instance volStatus:

30. In the Button layer, drag out the three movie clips in the Library: button start, button stop, and button 25% volume. Place them on the stage in that order. You can center everything to the stage as we did if you want:

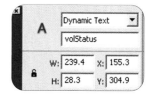

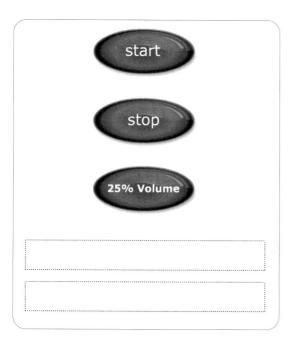

31. Select the start button and give it an instance name of startButton in the Property inspector.

32. Select the stop button and label it stopButton. Then select the 25% Volume button and label it volButton.

That's it! Export the movie and test it. When you click the start button, the song should begin playing and the first text field should say PLAYING and the second text field should say Volume Level 100. If you click the 25% Volume button, the music should be significantly reduced and the text fields should say PLAYING and Volume Level 25, respectively. Now click the stop button and the sound should stop—the text field will say NOT PLAYING and the volume should be left at the last state it was in.

OK, this is fine and dandy, but what if you have multiple sounds that affect each other in a more complex situation such as a game? Well, that's where the next exercise comes in.

Playing with Sounds

I have never really considered myself a "coder." I always thought of myself as the guy who likes to create cool visuals or interesting sound. I realized a while back that in order to create cool things in Flash these days, you have to be something of a coder. The best part about needing to code in Flash is that I don't mind! Flash code is so cool when it all comes together. I've always been the guy talking about graphics or sound. I now find myself having discussions about code in Flash, and that's OK.

Because I'm still in the process of refining the code curve, I felt like I needed to get some help wiring together my Sound Box. So before I begin this section, I'd like to thank Daniel Dura (www.danieldura.com) and Josh Dura (www.joshdura.com and www.duramedia.com) for helping me put this code together. I knew what I wanted to do, I knew my logic, but I needed some outside assistance to provide the best advice on how to code it. I'd also like to thank Bill Cutshall (www.tocquigny.com and www.wherearemypants.com) for teaching me coding ethics and structure. I wouldn't be where I am professionally if it wasn't for Bill. Thanks so much, my friends! Anyway, on with the show. . . .

The Logic

The logic behind this next reconstruction is that the Sound Box (original name, huh?) is a mechanism to play dynamically loaded sounds with triggers. The triggers are the buttons on the box. You can think of these buttons as events in Flash games. For example, where a spaceship might fire a weapon, you can re-create that event via the buttons on the box; the logic is the same. The same goes for music tracks being played. When the mood of the game changes, an event is triggered that changes the music, and you can also re-create this through the use of buttons in this exercise.

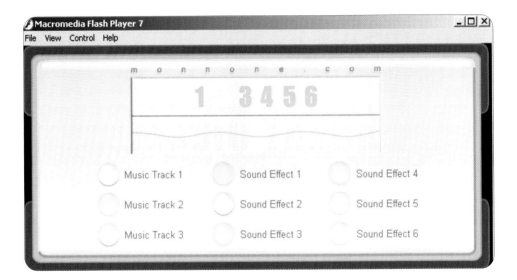

To get a better idea of how dynamic sounds play a part in Flash games, we provide an empty FLA once again. This FLA will have all the elements of the final Sound Box. The reason for this is so you can concentrate on the sounds rather than on the construction of the box itself. As an analogy, think of the shell of a car on a car manufacturer's assembly line. The shell of the car is already made, but the wiring needs to be placed. In our case, the sound and the code behind it is the wiring.

The functional idea behind the box is this:

> You want to create a sound box that plays the appropriate sound when the buttons are clicked. There will be nine buttons: the first three are for music, and the last six are for sound effects. The music tracks shouldn't play on top of each other, meaning that if a button is clicked it plays the music for that button, and if another music button is clicked any other music and graphics related to the original music are stopped and the new music and graphics are played. You have two graphics that need to be affected by the music playing. These are the buttons lighting up and the wave lines that display when the music is playing. The other six buttons are for sound effects. They too have two graphical elements affected by the sound they're playing: the button lights up and the number for that sound effect shows in the main window.

To help you sort out the code, we'll break things down into logical steps. Our logic goes like this:

Music

When a music button is clicked,

1. The music plays.
2. The button lights up.
3. The wave line plays.
4. Any other music is turned off.
5. Any other music graphics are turned off.
6. Sound effects are *not* affected.

When the music is finished playing,

1. The music needs to stop.
2. The button turns off.
3. The wave line turns off.

When the same music button is clicked while that music track is playing,

1. The music needs to stop.
2. The button turns off.
3. The wave line turns off.

Sound Effects

When a sound effects button is clicked,

1. The sound effect plays.
2. The button lights up.
3. The sound effect number displays.
4. All sound effects can be played over the top of each other.
5. The music is *not* affected.

When the sound effect is finished playing,

1. The button turns off.
2. The button number turns off.

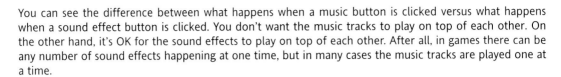

You can see the difference between what happens when a music button is clicked versus what happens when a sound effect button is clicked. You don't want the music tracks to play on top of each other. On the other hand, it's OK for the sound effects to play on top of each other. After all, in games there can be any number of sound effects happening at one time, but in many cases the music tracks are played one at a time.

Note that Flash can play only eight sounds simultaneously. This can cause problems, but if you're aware of this drawback, you can plan your game sound effects accordingly.

Creating the Sound Box

We decided that the best way to accomplish our task was to make the button controlling the music or sound effects a component. **Components** are basically movie clips that contain elements (graphics and code) that have defined parameters typically set during authoring. Usually, components are used to make authoring in Flash much easier. You can create a component and have it show up in your Components panel every time you open Flash, so it's available to be dragged onto the stage for use. A component can really be anything you decide it should be: a list box, a scrollbar, a radio button, or even a custom button. Adding a component to the Components panel in the Flash MX 2004 interface is a different task altogether. If you'd like to read more about components, please visit this site for a great tutorial: `www.flashcomponents.net/tutorials/triangle/triangle.html`.

In this section you'll actually make two different components. One component will handle the music and the other will handle the sound effects. The reason you'll want to do this is that the sound effects will have different enough properties to warrant a different component; for example, they'll have the capability to play sounds over the top of each other.

1. Open `empty_sound_box.fla` to follow along. This empty FLA has all of the graphical elements already in it. Your main focus here is to create the wiring for this Sound Box, not necessarily to learn how each graphic was made. This being the case, you'll notice when you open the FLA that most of the graphics are already in place, which makes re-creating the code much easier to follow. The one thing *not* in the FLA is the components, so you'll create them. First, if you haven't already looked at the final Sound Box, `sound_box.swf`, please do so now so you can get an idea of how the Sound Box is supposed to work. Play all of the sounds in different orders to get a feel for how the events react while other buttons are being clicked.

2. With the FLA open, you'll see four layers in the timeline: Components, Labels, Viewport, and Background. Components is empty because that's where you'll add all of your component buttons. You first need to name the appropriate movie clips so the component will be able to address them properly. Let's focus on the contents of the layer Viewport. You need to name this movie clip so your future component can reference it.

3. Select the movie clip on the stage in the Viewport layer and give it the instance name window in the Property inspector, as you've done in earlier examples.

4. You need to add some code and names to some of the graphical elements inside the viewport, so you'll edit the window movie clip. Open it and select the first blue wave line on the stage inside the Wave Lines layer. You'll see that we've named this instance musicBox1 in the Property inspector. Now select the second wave line and name it musicBox2. Then select the third wave line and name it musicBox3.

5. Under the Sf/x layer, you'll need to name the sound effect numbers as well. Select the number 1 and name it sfx_number1, and name the other five numbers similarly: 2 is named sfx_number2, 3 is named sfx_number3, and so on.

6. In the Actions layer, add this code:

```
musicBox1._visible=false;
musicBox2._visible=false;
musicBox3._visible=false;
sfx_number1._visible=false;
sfx_number2._visible=false;
sfx_number3._visible=false;
sfx_number4._visible=false;
sfx_number5._visible=false;
sfx_number6._visible=false;
```

This code initializes the wave lines and the sound effects numbers to be hidden when the movie first plays. Notice that this code references the movie clips that you've just named.

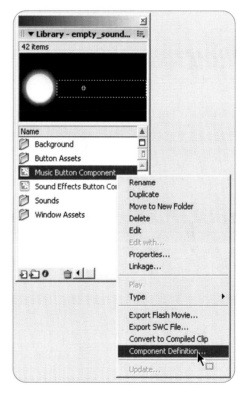

7. Next, you'll create the components, so head back to the root timeline of the movie by using the navigation bar. Creating components is actually quite painless—the component must be initialized as a component and given some properties to function as one. In the Library you'll see the movie clips Music Button Component and Sound Effects Button Component. Let's start by creating the music component first.

Right-click (CMD+click on a Mac) Music Button Component and select Component Definition.

The Component Definition window will then appear:

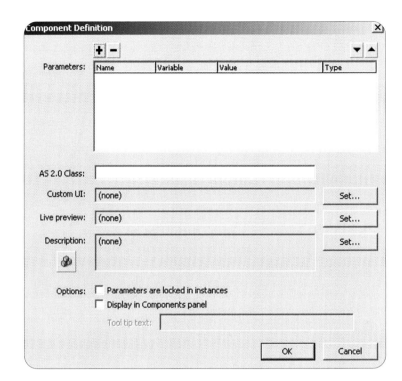

Because you're creating a component that you'll use only in this FLA, it's not really necessary to fill everything out in the Component Definition dialog box. At the top of the box you'll find a plus sign (+) and a minus sign (–). The plus sign adds parameters to the component, and the minus sign removes the selected parameters.

All you're concerned about for your component is the Parameters section (and one other option at the bottom of this box, which we discuss shortly). The Parameters section has four areas to enter information:

- The Name field is the descriptive title that you want to see in the component property box for the variable.

- The Variable field is where you insert the property name used in the component.

- The Value field contains the default value for the defined variable. In this case, you should simply put a question mark here so you can answer this question when you finally drop the variable onto the stage.

- The Type field tells the component the type of the variable—for example, Default, Boolean, Array, Object, String, etc.

8. Click the plus sign three times to add three new parameters, and enter their details as outlined in the following screenshot:

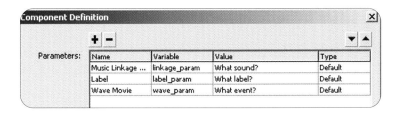

9. The final section of concern is the Options section. Check the option Parameters are locked in instances.

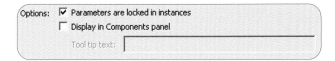

Checking this option prevents other parameters from being entered in the component's Property inspector, which you can access after the component is dropped onto the stage. It looks like this (more on this soon):

10. Now click OK, and you should notice that the icon on the Music Button Component movie clip changed. This default icon tells you at a glance that this movie clip is now a component. You still need to do one last thing to this component in the Library.

11. Right-click Music Button Component again and select Linkage. You need to identify this component with the Object class you'll create inside the component in a moment. Check Export for ActionScript and Export in first frame, and name the component FMusicButton. Export for ActionScript means that you want to use this linkage identifier name within your ActionScript code. Export in first frame means that the linkage and code will be ready for use in the first frame of your movie. Click OK to finish this part.

12. You now need to add the main part of the code to the component itself. From the Library, edit your new component Music Button Component. Here's the relevant code, which you add to the Actions layer. Note that the code is heavily commented—be sure to read through all the comments to ensure you understand what each portion of the ActionScript is for.

```
////INITIALIZE MUSIC COMPONENT
#initclip

////SET CLASS
function MusicButtonClass() {

  //Call the initialize function when a Button is added
  this.init();
}
////SET MAIN MUSIC MOVIECLIP
MusicButtonClass.prototype = new MovieClip();

////SET COMPONENT PARAMETERS
MusicButtonClass.prototype.init = function() {

  //Set setTextLabel to label_param, which is initialized in the
  //properties of the component in the Library - this is the
  //label next to each button (defined in Property inspector)
  this.setTextLabel(this.label_param);

  //Set waveMovie to wave_param, which is initialized in the
  //properties of the component in the Library
  //(defined in component Property inspector)
  this.waveMovie = eval(this.wave_param);

  //Initialize the createMusicObject() function
  this.createMusicObject();

  //Set the variable 'playing' as a toggle switch to
  //determine a state of the music playing or not
  //-- here it is set to false or NOT playing
  this.playing = false;

  //Run the setButtonOff() function, making sure the button is
  //OFF when SWF is first opened
  this.setButtonOff();

  //We want to be able to store a globally available list
  //of MusicButtons so we can access them from anywhere in the
  //movie. If this is the first instance of the button, we need
  //to create the Array and then add the current instance of the
  //button to it.
  if (_global.MusicButtonList == undefined) {
    _global.MusicButtonList = new Array();
  }
  MusicButtonList.push(this);
};

////SET MAIN SOUND OBJECT
MusicButtonClass.prototype.createMusicObject = function() {
```

```
  //Create new sound object
  this.musicObject = new Sound(this);

  //Attach sound object from above to proper music
  //(user defines in component Property inspector)
  this.musicObject.attachSound(this.linkage_param);

  //Give the music object a 'path' back to this class to notify
  //us of certain events - i.e., when the sound stops.
  this.musicObject.CallBack = this;

  //Need to determine what to do when sound has finished
  //playing(onSoundComplete)
  this.musicObject.onSoundComplete = function() {

    //Call the function stopMusic, using the path back to the
    //main button object, when the SWF is first opened so the
    //sound and visual effects do not play
    this.CallBack.stopMusic();
  };
};
////SET BUTTON GLOW OFF AND ON
MusicButtonClass.prototype.setButtonOn = function() {

  //Set the glow button to 'show'
  this.button_lit._visible = true;
};
MusicButtonClass.prototype.setButtonOff = function() {

  //Set the glow button to 'hide'
  this.button_lit._visible = false;
};
////SET TEXT LABEL FOR EACH MUSIC TRACK
MusicButtonClass.prototype.setTextLabel = function(labeltext) {

  //Set the text label for each button
  //(user defines this for component)
  this.label_txt.text = labeltext;
};
////SET MAIN PLAY EVENT
MusicButtonClass.prototype.playMusic = function() {

  //Because only one music clip can play at a time, we need to
  //make sure that any other instances of the MusicButton are
  //stopped. We access the global array that we created in the
  //'init' method of this class
  for (var i=0; i<MusicButtonList.length; i++) {
    MusicButtonList[i].stopMusic();
  }
```

```
//Tell the sound object to play from the very beginning of
//the track (0) and loop only one time(1)
this.musicObject.start(0, 1);

//Run the setButtonOn() function to turn button ON
this.setButtonOn();

//Set the 'playing' variable to true because
//the music IS playing
this.playing = true;

//'Show' the 'wave' in the MUSIC TRACK window
this.waveMovie._visible = true;
};
////SET MAIN STOP EVENT
MusicButtonClass.prototype.stopMusic = function() {

//Tell the sound object to STOP playing
this.musicObject.stop();

//Run the setButtonOff() function to turn the button OFF
this.setButtonOff();

//Set the 'playing' variable to false because the music IS NOT playing
this.playing = false;

//'Hide' the 'wave' in the MUSIC TRACK window
this.waveMovie._visible = false;
};
////SET BUTTON RELEASE ACTION
MusicButtonClass.prototype.onRelease = function() {

//Asks the question: If the defined variable 'playing' is TRUE
//then stop the music with the function 'stopMusic', otherwise
//run the function 'playMusic' to play the music and event.
//This is written so that the music TOGGLES and does not play
//multiple instances on top each other
if (this.playing) {
  this.stopMusic();
} else {
  this.playMusic();
}
};
////SET IDENTIFIER TO THE COMPONENT TO THE LIBRARY
Object.registerClass("FMusicButton", MusicButtonClass);
////ENDS MUSIC COMPONENT DEFINITION
#endinitclip
```

13. The last thing you need to do inside this component is add an instance name to the dynamic text box in the Label layer, so just select the dynamic text box (it's a dotted-line rectangle on the stage when unselected), and in the Property inspector name it label_txt.

14. You now need to create the sound effects component, which is almost identical to the music one. As before, you need to define the component parameters, so right-click the Sound Effects Button Component movie clip in the Library. In the Parameters box of the Component Definition window, add the following parameters:

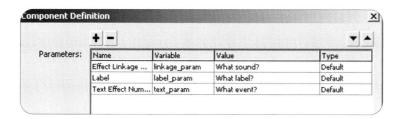

Again, be sure to check the Parameters are locked in instances option in the Options section at the bottom of the Component Definition dialog box. Finally, click OK.

15. Right-click Sound Effects Button Component again and select Linkage. As you did with the music component, check Export for ActionScript and Export in first frame, and give it the name FSoundEffectButton. Click OK.

16. You now need to add the main part of the code to the sound component itself. From the Library, edit your new Sound Effects Button Component component. You'll add the following ActionScript to the Actions layer. This looks very similar to the code for your previous component at first glance, so again we've decided to list all the code here with detailed comments so that it's easy for you to understand how it all works together. Let's see what going on:

```
//--INITIALIZE SOUND EFFECT COMPONENT
#initclip
//--SET CLASS
function SoundEffectButtonClass() {

   ///Call the initialize function when a Button is added
   this.init();
}

//--SET MAIN SOUND EFFECT MOVIECLIP
SoundEffectButtonClass.prototype = new MovieClip();
//--SET COMPONENT PARAMETERS
SoundEffectButtonClass.prototype.init = function() {

   //Set setTextLabel to label_param, which is defined in the
   //properties of the component in the Library - this is the
   //label next to each button (defined in Property inspector)
   this.setTextLabel(this.label_param);
```

```
                //Set textMovie to text_param, which is defined in the
                //properties of the component in the Library - this is the
                //number label in the effect section
                this.textMovie = eval(this.text_param);

                //Initialize the createMusicObject() function
                this.createMusicObject();

                //Run the setButtonOff() function, making sure the button is
                //OFF when SWF is first opened
                this.setButtonOff();
        };
        //--SET MAIN SOUND OBJECT
        SoundEffectButtonClass.prototype.createMusicObject = function() {

                //Create new sound object
                this.musicObject = new Sound(this);

                //Attach sound object from above to proper sound effect
                //(user defines in component)
                this.musicObject.attachSound(this.linkage_param);

                //Give the music object a 'path' back to this class to notify
                //us of certain events - i.e., when the sound stops.
                this.musicObject.CallBack = this;

                //Need to determine what to do when sound had finished
                //playing(onSoundComplete)
                this.musicObject.onSoundComplete = function() {

                        //Call the function stopEffect, using the path back to the
                        //main button object, when the SWF is first opened so the
                        //sound and visual effects do not play
                        this.CallBack.stopEffect();
                };
        };
        //--SET BUTTON GLOW OFF AND ON
        SoundEffectButtonClass.prototype.setButtonOn = function() {

                //Set the glow button to 'show'
                this.button_lit._visible = true;
        };
        SoundEffectButtonClass.prototype.setButtonOff = function() {

                //Set the glow button to 'hide'
                this.button_lit._visible = false;
        };
        //--SET TEXT LABEL FOR EACH SOUND EFFECT
        SoundEffectButtonClass.prototype.setTextLabel = function(labeltext) {
```

```
    //Set the text label for each button
    //(defined in Property inspector)
    this.label_txt.text = labeltext;
};
//--SET MAIN PLAY EVENTS
SoundEffectButtonClass.prototype.playEffect = function() {

    //Tell the sound object to play from the very beginning of
    //the track (0) and loop only one time(1)
    this.musicObject.start(0, 1);

    //Run the setButtonOn() function to turn button ON
    this.setButtonOn();

    //'Show' the text effect number in the SOUND EFFECTS window
    this.textMovie._visible = true;
};
//--SET MAIN STOP EVENTS
SoundEffectButtonClass.prototype.stopEffect = function() {

    //Tell the sound object to STOP playing
    this.musicObject.stop();

    //Run the setButtonOff() function to turn the button OFF
    this.setButtonOff();

    //'Hide' the text effect number in the SOUND EFFECTS window
    this.textMovie._visible = false;
};
//--SET BUTTON RELEASE ACTION
SoundEffectButtonClass.prototype.onRelease = function() {

    //Run the function playEffect() (The sfx needs to play as many
    // times as the user clicks the button)
    this.playEffect();
};
//--SET IDENTIFIER TO THE COMPONENT TO THE LIBRARY
Object.registerClass("FSoundEffectButton", SoundEffectButtonClass);
//--ENDS SOUND EFFECT COMPONENT DEFINITION
#endinitclip
```

17. As with the previous component, there's one last thing to do—you need to add an instance name for the dynamic text box in the Label layer. Select the dynamic text box and in the Property inspector give it an instance name of label_txt (just like with the music component).

18. Now you must drop the components onto the stage in the correct locations and fill in some details in the Property inspector. If you want them lined up just right, we've provided guides on the stage. With the Library open, simply drag the Music Button Component component out and drop it on the stage, aligning the left side to the leftmost guide. Drag out two more instances of music button components and line them up underneath the first.

19. Now drag out six Sound Effects Button Component components and line them up in the remaining space on the right, using the other two vertical guides if you like. Once they're all on the stage it should look something like this:

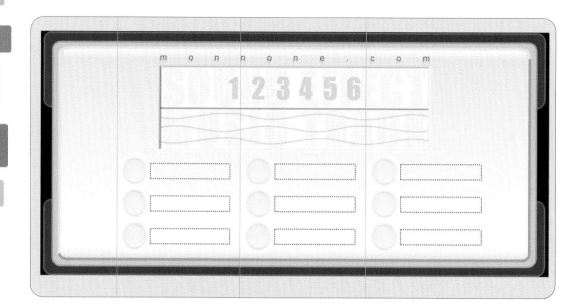

20. Next, you need to fill in the relevant parameters in each component's Property inspector. Select the top-left component, which is one of music ones, and refer to your Property inspector. Here you'll see that it's now the Component Property inspector. Fill in the three music components with the parameters indicated in the following table (alternatively, just refer to the finished example file, sound_box.fla).

Music Component	Linkage Name	Label	Wave Movie
Music Component 1	music1	Music Track 1	_root.window.musicBox1
Music Component 2	music2	Music Track 2	_root.window.musicBox2
Music Component 3	music3	Music Track 3	_root.window.musicBox3

21. Moving on to the sound component, starting with the top-middle component, fill in these six components with their required parameters:

Sound Component	Effect Linkage Name	Label	Text Effect Number
Sound Component 1	sfx1	Sound Effect 1	_root.window.sfx_number1
Sound Component 2	sfx2	Sound Effect 2	_root.window.sfx_number2
Sound Component 3	sfx3	Sound Effect 3	_root.window.sfx_number3
Sound Component 4	sfx4	Sound Effect 4	_root.window.sfx_number 4
Sound Component 5	sfx5	Sound Effect 5	_root.window.sfx_number5
Sound Component 6	sfx6	Sound Effect 6	_root.window.sfx_number

22. The very last thing you need to do is give linkage IDs to the music and sound effects in the Library. In the Library open the folder called Sounds. Right-click the first sound called mus_1.mp3 and choose Linkage. As usual, check Export for ActionScript and Export in first frame, and then give this sound the linkage ID music1. Likewise, give the other two MP3s the linkage IDs music2 and music3, respectively. Do the same with Soundfx1.wav, but call it sfx1. The other sound effects will of course be sfx2, sfx3, sfx4, sfx5, and sfx6, respectively.

That's it! The only thing to do at this point is test this thing out. So press *CTRL/CMD+ENTER* (or just open sound_box.swf) to play around with the Sound Box. You can apply the principles you've learned here to many other ways of triggering sound events, such as the event entering a frame or a variable hitting the right number. In this case, you simply used buttons to trigger the sounds to get a handle on what the sound object is capable of.

ActionScript 2.0

With the release of Flash MX 2004, developers now have a new way to code their Flash games and applications: *ActionScript 2.0*. We're sure that when many Flash developers heard this, quite a few gave off a little shudder of fear (ourselves included) at having to relearn what we've become so comfortable with. However, there are a couple of important points to consider:

1. "In with the new" doesn't necessarily mean "out with the old"—ActionScript 1.0 is still here and is an extremely strong and flexible way of coding your movies.

2. ActionScript 2.0 is pretty easy to grasp if you have a firm knowledge of ActionScript 1.0.

ActionScript 2.0 (AS 2.0) is really just a different way to write what you already know, using a structure that should be very familiar to anyone coming from another object-oriented programming language. This scripting style features a number of new concepts and benefits, including keywords such as class, interface, and implements, and concepts such as *packages* and *strict data typing*. AS 2.0 helps developers most in Flash in the testing and debugging phase, as the stricter coding structure keeps coders "honest" and will return much more useful and informative error and debugging information as a result.

Because instructions on coding in a new form could a fill a whole book (or at least a few healthy chapters), a book specifically on Flash games isn't the best place to explore this new style. However, to get your feet wet with AS 2.0, and possibly to get you hungry to learn more, we thought it might be helpful to take the code you used throughout this tutorial and recast it as AS 2.0. Because you already know what the code does, seeing it in a new form hopefully won't be too daunting.

If you open sound_box_AS2.fla, you'll see that it looks the same as your previous movie. In fact, all we did with this movie was *remove* code, instead of adding anything. Double-click the Music Button Component symbol in your Library and notice that all the code is gone from inside the clip. If you look at Sound Effects Button Component you'll see that its code is gone as well.

Now right-click the Sound Effects Button Component symbol and open the Linkage dialog box. The AS 2 Class text box has been filled in with the value SoundEffectButtonClass. What we've done here is associate this clip with an external class that contains all of its code. Open the file SoundEffectButtonClass.as to see what's become of it.

We've removed all the comments so you can see how very little code is needed for this to work. If you're using Flash MX Professional 2004, you can just double-click SoundEffectButtonClass.as to open the file within the Flash ActionScript editor (alternatively, Flash MX 2004 users can open and edit this .as file from any text editor). Here's a snippet:

```
class SoundEffectButtonClass extends MovieClip {

    public var label_param:String;
    public var text_param:String;
    public var linkage_param:String;
    private var textMovie:MovieClip;
    private var musicObject:Object;

    private function SoundEffectButtonClass() {
        this.setTextLabel(this.label_param);
        this.textMovie = eval(this.text_param);
        this.createMusicObject();
        this.setButton(false);
        this.onRelease = function() {
            this.playEffect();
        };
    }

    private function createMusicObject():Void {
        this.musicObject = new Sound(this);
        this.musicObject.attachSound(this.linkage_param);
        this.musicObject.callBack = this;
        this.musicObject.onSoundComplete = function() {
            this.callBack.stopEffect();
        };
    }
```

Just a few extra keywords, but nothing too overwhelming, right? You create a class in AS 2.0 with the `class` keyword. Because this class will inherit properties and methods from the `MovieClip` object, you use extends. Next, you declare the variables you'll use with the var keyword, and you specify whether a variable can be accessed by outside objects (public) or not (private). Notice the strict data typing of each variable as well (`label_param:String`). This is extremely helpful in the debugging stages, as Flash will tell you if you're putting the wrong type of value into a variable (no automatic data conversion like in AS 1.0).

After you declare the variables, you have your constructor function, which takes the same name as the class itself. You can make a function both public and private. If you want to be able to create a new instance of `SoundEffectButtonClass` through code elsewhere in your movie, you could make this public instead of private.

Finally, to conclude your small taste of AS 2.0, you can specify the type of value a function should return, or you can specify Void if nothing is returned (which is what we use here). Not all of these keywords are necessary, such as setting variables or functions as public or private, or specifying the data type, but they all can prove useful.

To use AS 2.0 in a movie, make sure to specify this in the publish settings. Test the movie to see the same results as in your previous work. Again, the greatest benefit for coding in such a form is the help during development, which we skipped right over!

Optimizing Sounds in Flash

Our final thoughts relate to a topic relating to sound that's probably just as important as loading the sounds themselves: **optimization**. After spending many hours of blood, sweat, and tears over your Flash game, you should spend a moment or two looking at how to get the most out of your sounds by reducing the files to more manageable sizes.

Although Flash can't create sounds as such, it has a nice way to compress them, and that's MP3. The MP3 compressor in Flash is quite efficient. In fact, we strongly recommend importing WAV or AIF files with high quality and bit rates and letting Flash do the hard work. Let's take a quick look at some of the compression options within Flash MX 2004.

Compression Options

Which compression option is right for your particular sound depends one thing: your ear! People have tried to nail down a technique on this subject in the past, but we're here to say that it simply comes down to putting headphones on and listening to the sound under each compression type and setting. Many people use the MP3 setting the most, with good cause. Under most circumstances, this compression type yields the best quality in comparison to file size. In this section, we examine the sound compression process for Flash MX 2004.

Select Soundfx1.wav in the Library and right-click (*CMD*+click) Properties to bring up the Sound Properties dialog box:

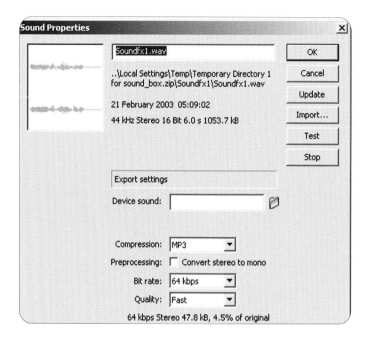

In the Sound Properties dialog box are several settings to look at and compare. The top of the box shows the location of the original file, the date, and settings for its kHz or Kbps. The bottom of the box has the options for compression. (In Flash MX 2004, you can also specify using a device sound for your projects, but this has much more common use in application development than in game development.)

So, for example, in the case of Soundfx1.wav we chose MP3 with no preprocessing, 64 kbps, and Fast quality. The very bottom of the Property inspector tells you how compressed the sound is and its size. Again, determining which compression type to use mainly depends on the type of sound you're using and how you're using it. Here's an overview of the compression options:

■ Default: This method uses the settings in the Publish Settings dialog box during publishing. There are no addition settings for this type. This type isn't recommended.

■ ADPCM: This method is good for small sounds such as pops or clicks. It's best when working with sound files that are 8 and 16 bit. This setting is also good for using the small sounds as events sounds. This file type supports 5, 11, 22, and 44 kHz.

■ MP3: This is the most commonly used method because of its ability to compress and maintain good-sounding files. Flash can import MP3s within the range of 8 through 160 Kbps constant bit rate (CBR). It can also export with those settings. Flash can't increase the quality of the imported file by selecting a higher bit rate. This will only produced overinflated file sizes.

■ Raw: This option exports sound with no compression at all. This method isn't advised, not even for high bandwidth productions or CD-ROMs. The "fatter" your sound files, the more memory and processor power you'll need to accommodate those files.

■ Speech: This compression type is specially adapted for sound files that are speech-only. It supports 5, 11, 22, and 44 kHz. The recommended setting is 11 if you need really compressed speech files.

Another thing to consider is that even if you chose MP3 as your compression type, you may still want to go through each sound independently and adjust the bit rate for each one to squeeze every last drop out of its file size and maintain acceptable sound. For the Sound Box project, we went through each sound separately to determine the proper settings. We suggest you do the same with your own Flash games projects.

Summary

Sound is a very important part of any multimedia presentation, but it's even more important for games. The best way to use sound for games in Flash is with sound objects. These objects give you the freedom to start, stop, pause, and replay loops, sound effects, and music tracks. It's important to remember, though, that sound in your Flash games can be one of the biggest file size expanders. Although Flash handles sound very elegantly, it still requires that you carefully consider when to incorporate sounds. Try to reuse your sounds wherever possible. With the envelope tools and start and stop points, you can create different sounds from the ones already in the Library without an increase in file size.

Even though your game may kick butt and have great sounds, amazing graphics, and addictive game play, large file sizes will bring the game to its knees for many web users. So just remember to use, reuse, and optimize—your 56K users will really appreciate you for it!

Sham Bhangal

Sham Bhangal has written about new media topics for 3 years, in which time he has authored and coauthored numerous friends of ED books, including critically acclaimed, award-winning, best-selling titles such as *Foundation Flash 5*, *New Masters of Flash*, *Macromedia Flash MX Upgrade Essentials*, *Flash MX Most Wanted: Effects & Movies*, and *Macromedia Flash MX Designer's ActionScript Reference*. He has considerable working experience with Macromedia and Adobe products, as well as other general web design technologies (such as HTML, CSS, JavaScript, and so on). In addition to making speaking appearances at Flashforward, the biggest Macromedia Flash developers' conference, Sham has been a Beta tester for Macromedia and Discreet products for a number of years.

RETRO FLASH GAMING

INSERT COIN TO PLAY! ! !

Computer games today are closer to simulations than games. You'll invariably find yourself battling in World War II airplanes that closely model the attributes of the original machines or leading a battalion of soldiers whose actions are modified by how well the team is doing.

It never used to be like that. You used to have to make do with a simple dot-star field to model deep space (rather than a fully working planetary economic and social model), and cars were little more than rectangles viewed from above (rather than full 3D texture-mapped objects with damage modeling and performance curves taken from the manufacturer's specification sheets).

WHY GO RETRO ?

Why? Well, two words: performance and memory. Early computers were very slow in today's terms, and there were no graphics cards or other dedicated hardware to help things. The most memory you got was about 64KB, which limited the amount of moving graphics, and you couldn't even have pretty *static* graphics to spice it all up! Sounds like an unimaginable development nightmare for early game programmers, right? Well, not quite unimaginable. What they had to put up with is *very* close to the web today.

Early game programmers had slow processors. Today we have fast processors, but we can only access that power through virtual interfaces and software layers that dissipate it in other tasks, so the Flash player doesn't see all that much. We might have gigabytes of memory, but we're limited by how much data we can get to the end user through a web connection. We're also limited to how much game data we can save by the Flash Shared object, which is designed to allow a few tens of kilobytes rather than megabytes.

> *Of course, you can get around some of these limitations by using a multimedia heavyweight such as Macromedia Director, but not as many people have the Shockwave for Director plug-in as have the Shockwave for Flash plug-in, so you reduce your audience significantly. You can also use Java to create your games, but you have the same problem—not as many browsers have Java support turned on as have the Flash plug-in.*

So, nothing has really changed. Early game developers had the same problems current motion graphics developers have. It's not all bad, though.

GET READY ! ! !

One thing the early developers had was the learned ability (through necessity) to create games with very few resources. They didn't need motion-capture suites and three CD-ROMs for the game code and data. They didn't need a Hollywood film tie-in, and they certainly didn't need a $2 million budget. In most cases, they just needed a good, simple game concept, the target computer, and a development environment that ran on it. That's also all *we* need: a bright idea, a computer, and Flash.

Retrospective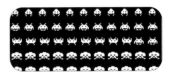

Many of the defining game genres were created in the early 1980s. Many of them fell into a small number of often-copied genres, including

- The shooter game (e.g., Space Invaders, Robotron, and Galaga)
- The scrolling shooter game (e.g., Defender, Scramble, and 1942)
- The maze game (e.g., Pac-Man)
- The platform game (e.g., Mario Brothers and Shinobi)
- The vector simulation game (e.g., Tempest and Battle Zone)
- The adventure game (e.g., MUD)
- The beat-'em-up game (e.g., Double Dragon and Mortal Kombat)
- The racing game (e.g., Super Sprint)
- The sports game (e.g., Super Basketball and 10-Yard Fight)
- The puzzle game (e.g., Tetris)

For a reminder of what some of these games looked like, check out a good emulator website such as www.mame.net:

Many of these games and associated graphics are almost as widely recognized as many global trademarks, which is no small feat and is indicative of the sublime influence retro games have had on a generation.

So why would you ever want to base a game written in the early part of the twenty-first century on something that was hacked together in 1980? Well, good question. There's an equally good answer though.

Although gaming has, of course, moved on since those early days, with other genres such as the God game, complex flight simulators, and the ubiquitous first-person shoot-'em-up (FPS—for example, Quake and Unreal Tournament), these later games all have one important feature in common: *they came about because of hardware advances.*

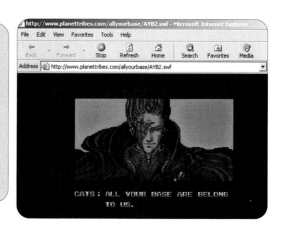

So what? Well, the sorts of things that these hardware advances provided (such as 3D hardware support and large amounts of memory and hard drive space) aren't available to Flash, whereas the general features of early- to mid-1980s hardware closely match the sorts of resources that Flash does have available to it (up to around 300KB of application resources, a few tens of kilobytes for local file storage, and fairly slow graphics redrawing capabilities). That is, of course, the crux of it: retro games will work well on Flash because the environment they were developed for is very similar to the Flash web environment. That also means that *the tricks and shortcuts that the early games used are extremely useful as a base for Flash games.*

Another feature of retro games is that they have a style all their own. The simple graphics aren't even trying to represent the real world but are instead nothing more than animated icons. Not only are the graphics simplistic, but so is the game itself, as it consists of simple rules and immediate gameplay. Although it may be argued that early games were addictive (and hid their underlying crass simplicity) by being structured such that a typical game wouldn't last long enough for the player to get bored, there's a lot to be learned from their structure.

So creating a Flash game based on the retro feel and mindset in terms of graphics, programming techniques, and game play should give you a great game. Of course, to do that, you have to first deconstruct the three areas and see how each applies to retro gaming. Accordingly, in the following sections we'll be looking at these topics:

- Graphics and sound
- Programming techniques
- Game play

Graphics and Sound

Retro games are primarily defined by their graphics. Most of the time, retro games used bitmap-based graphics on very low screen resolutions (typically on the order of 300x200), so you could easily make out the individual pixels:

That's the first problem—Flash is a *vector* render engine and doesn't like working with bitmaps. Although that's cool if you want to emulate a vector-based game such as Meteors, Flash loses the retro feel for bitmap-based games. Given the green alien shape in the following image (on the left), Flash will prefer a vector-based version (see the middle red alien). Further, Flash will also try to smooth the edges of the vector alien via antialiasing (see the red alien on the right), giv-ing you a cool effect, but one you don't want in this case.

When you write games in Flash, it's always a good idea to make the game shapes as angular as possible, with few curves, and to turn off antialiasing. Not only does this give the look of "retro-ness" to your graphics, but it also enables Flash to render them faster. If you must have smooth grad-uations, do what the early programmers did: *use noncon-trasting colors rather than aliasing.*

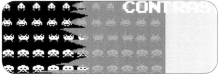

Black on white is high contrast, and without antialiasing, you'll see the pixilation. If that's what you want, then fine, but if you want smooth-looking *and* fast graph-ics, you can simply make both colors closer to each other, such as making black and white two intensities of gray. You can emulate the effect of smaller pixels in the preceding image by squinting at it. Notice that you have to squint far less to make the rightmost aliens appear smooth.

Another less used way of hiding pixilation and simple graphics is to make them move quickly. You can't see details as well on a rapidly moving object as we can when it's at rest, and early game coders used this to great effect in fast-paced games such as Robotron, in which the graphics were full of very quick and noisy explosions. The objects might have consisted of only raw lines of pixels, but you couldn't tell in the actual game—it was just a blur of color and noise!

- If you have fast-moving graphics, don't bother making them detailed. Examples of simplification might be to remove all strokes around shapes and use Modify ➤ Optimize to see how much you can simplify your graphic before you notice a significant change in appearance when it's moving.

- If you want to reduce the graphic complexity of a game, make everything smaller. Doubling the size of something makes the pixel area four times bigger (and therefore increases the redraw time four times), whereas halving the size gives you the reverse—it's four times faster.

- If you can't make things small, there are other ways to reduce the number of screen pixels that have to be drawn to represent a graphic, such as making the graphic big *but hollow*.

- Don't give the user time to think about what you've done. As anyone who has ever played Robotron will tell you, the frenetic pace of the game soon puts any thoughts about the simple graphics to the back of your mind!

> *Robotron is a game from Williams, a manufacturer well known for its loud games, Robotron and Defender being two real room-shakers. The graphics may have only filled a small, low-resolution screen, but the sound filled the room!*

For that real retro feel, you can use the same color schemes that the older hardware had to use. Due to memory limitations, many of the earlier games had to stick to a basic palette of eight colors:

Using these colors will guarantee the same feel of the early games. Exactly the same colors appear in the first column of the Flash color picker:

There's one more trick that retro games tended to use (and this has more to do with coding than with appearance): simplifying collision detection.

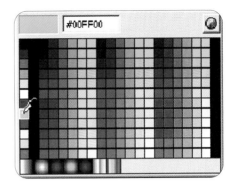

One of the biggest performance hits in early hardware (and also in Flash today) is creating accurate collision detection. You can't easily create collision detection between two shapes (see the left area of the following image) because it's processor intensive. What you *are* able to do quickly is check for collisions between two bounding boxes (see the middle area) or between a shape and a single point (see the right area).

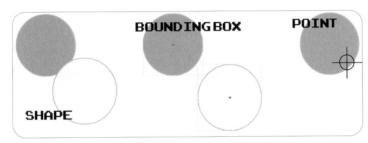

Although shape collision is ideal, few games use it (not even modern games!). Most games use a series of point collisions to detect the most likely collisions. For example, in a platform game, you might use three point collisions: one at feet height (floor collision detection), one at waist height, and one at head height (to detect collisions to the character with other objects).

If you select this method, ensure that there's no shape within the game that can pass between the points.

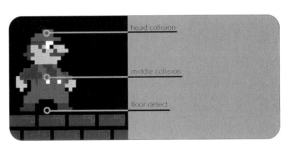

The second way to make fast collision detections is the one we like the best because it's (a) quicker and (b) one of the things that defined the way most early game graphics looked. *Make the graphics fill their bounding boxes.* If you do this, bounding-box collisions look like shape collisions because the shape of the graphics is similar to the shape of the bounding box. So now you're thinking "Uhh, hey, get a grip. I don't want a game with only rectangular-shaped graphics." Yeah, we know, but there's one more trick: you only have to fill the bounding box in the direction you expect a collision. Let's take a look.

Both of the following two graphics will move in a way that means they're likely to be hit from very few directions. The spaceship moves from left to right, which means it tends to get hit from the front. Bullets will have to cross the black line in front of it. The space invader gets hit from the player's ship directly below it, so it will only get hit from its lower edge. Both graphics have filled their bounding box along the line of likely collision, so it's near impossible for anything to cross the line and not appear to hit the graphic. That's a subtle point until you see it, but one to remember. When designing early games, the graphics designers were aware that they had to fill the "direction of likely collision" with pixels. As soon as you do that when designing your game graphics, collision detection becomes less problematic because you can simplify many (if not all) of your collisions by using bounding boxes rather than shapes.

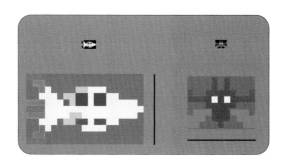

Programming Techniques

In addition to their simplified graphics, retro games had the problem of slow processors and graphic hardware. Many of the speed enhancements older games use have to do with the fact that they could access hardware directly, something that isn't an option with Flash. Some techniques, however, are still relevant, the most pressing being the concept of a "time budget." Essentially, you assume an overall processor time budget of 100%, and as you design your game, you have to assign each of the major features of your game a slice of this budget. The magic of writing games is in reducing this budget for the most time-consuming bits. Much of this paring down comes from the programming.

Area of Focus

One of the best ways to make a game (or for that matter, any application) *appear* faster is to identify the **area of focus** and give more of the processor budget to that. When you do that, the whole game appears to be faster, because the player sees a more responsive game.

Sounds a bit complex and esoteric, right? Well, it isn't really—the practical issue is always the same. The area of focus is what the player is interacting with directly, and it's invariably the player's sprite. In the following game, the area of focus is the player's ship. The enemy also needs to move quickly, but because the enemy isn't directly controlled by the player, it can afford to be moved less often. Finally, the background stars aren't within the area of focus at all. The player would notice if they stopped animating, but he or she won't really notice if the stars are a little sluggish.

In Flash, actually implementing this sort of processor sharing based on user focus was problematic until Flash MX, in which we got the setInterval time-based event. We cover more on this later, but for now have a look at the example files starField01.fla and starfield02.fla. These files show the ubiquitous "spaceship moving along a scrolling star field" effect. In starField01.fla, both the ship and stars are animated every frame. To keep up smoothness, notice that the frame rate in this FLA is 18 fps. In starfield02.fla, the frame rate is set to 12 fps, making for a slower movie. The extra time budget that this gives is all taken up by the player's ship, which uses a setInterval event to animate it every 15 milliseconds (approximately 60 fps, or the closest the Flash player can get to this).

> *Why don't we simply crank up the frame rate to 60? Well, that's actually cheating by increasing your time budget so the processor overheads aren't such a problem. This sort of trick only really starts to shine when you're hitting the performance ceiling.*

This results in a more responsive and smoother player's ship. Once you're playing the completed game and there's lots going on other than the star field, you'll be concentrating on the player's ship, and the game will appear more responsive.

> *A rather ingenious trick is to fool the user into thinking that out-of-focus stuff is moving slower because it's far away (rather than because you're budgeting processor time), thus creating motion parallax effects (things appear to move less often the farther away they are) at the same time as saving processor time.*

Don't Do Anything You Don't Have To

This is an obvious statement, but the implementation isn't always so obvious until you start deconstructing some of the old gaming classics. For example, was Defender really a side-scrolling shooter? Well, not really, because only the line representing the terrain, the aliens, and the background star field actually scrolled. Most of the pixels on the screen never scrolled at all! Not only did this free up lots of processor time, but it also ensured that the game didn't need any fancy hardware scroll feature.

Cheat As Much As You Can!

OK, we're not really suggesting that you all become con artists and grifters. We're suggesting that if you need any complicated events in a game, work out the answers beforehand. Trigonometry and rotational dynamics, for example, are computationally intensive, so the best way to work things like this out quickly is to create a lookup table of answers beforehand. You can see this graphically in the game Galaga. The aliens are able to rotate as they swirl around, but the rotation doesn't occur computationally; it's created by the game designers by using separate graphics, one per available rotated view.

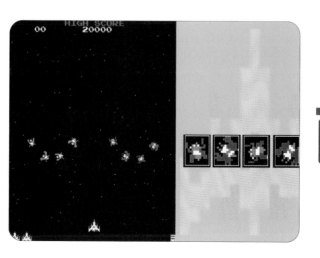

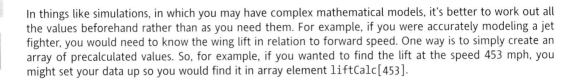

In things like simulations, in which you may have complex mathematical models, it's better to work out all the values beforehand rather than as you need them. For example, if you were accurately modeling a jet fighter, you would need to know the wing lift in relation to forward speed. One way is to simply create an array of precalculated values. So, for example, if you wanted to find the lift at the speed 453 mph, you might set your data up so you would find it in array element liftCalc[453].

> *It's also worth noting that Flash has optimized trigonometry functions (Math.sin, Math.cos, and so on), so you may find that calculating them on the fly is faster than using a precalculated lookup. When you decide between real-time calculations and precalculation, it's always a good idea to test which one is faster first.*

Realize That the Terrain Can Be an Artificial Intelligence Element

This is fundamental. When we talk about artificial intelligence (AI), we always assume that the intelligence is in the sprites (aliens, enemy helicopters, or whatever), but there's one slight problem: none of the characters (or "agents") in your game can actually *see*. An alien can't see your ship, but it has to act as if it can. The way to do achieve this is to effectively make the terrain (or "game world"—the area in which the game takes place) an agent as well. The terrain will say things like "this is where you go when you are in formation," "this is a good place to duck for cover," or "you can't see the player from your current position." As soon as you realize that this decision making isn't being made by the agent itself, but by the terrain, your code becomes much more efficient. Rather than many agents running around trying to work out how to "see," you have one game-world AI going around telling them what's happening. Think of it as the kids' party game in which you have one person blindfolded and someone else telling them where to go. The blindfolded child doesn't know he is about to hit a wall unless he's told so.

> *Although an intelligent environment isn't as obvious in retro games (but it's still important as part of your view of the problem), it's a major issue in current 3D games. An agent in Unreal Tournament 2003 can't actually see you (it knows your position in relation to itself, but it can't tell if there's a wall between it and you, for example). In fact, what holds all the important information is the game world—the terrain itself is the birthday boy telling all the other blindfolded guests where they can move (the individual enemy character then uses this information to decide where it wants to move), and it's sometimes by far the most complex AI entity in a game.*

If you want to go down this route, you may also find that you have to stop controlling graphics directly (such as when you tell where an alien is by looking directly at the individual alien graphics and their _x and _y properties), and instead start using a database that keeps track of where everything is. This database is a major part of your game world, and it's what the game-world AI will query when it looks at what's happening. Optimizations can occur because you can have different versions (or linked sections) of the same database configured to perform particular functions quickly (e.g., a path-finding database, a line-of-sight database, etc.), and also because using such an approach makes it easy to use an object-oriented approach. You'll use a game world in the example coming up later, but you'll keep away from object-oriented programming for now.

Create a Simplified Trigger Propagation Model

Early retro games worked on an event model that was based on the low-level hardware. This event model used a system called *interrupts*, which caused the processor to jump to a new code section when other hardware detected something worth looking into (such as a collision) via a *trigger* signal that entered the processor via one of a number of interrupt pins. Hardware interrupts are functionally similar to Flash events, except that you have less control of the trigger in Flash (which is heavily tied to the frame rate). If you could make some of your animations work faster or slower than the frame rate such that they update only when other game elements require it, rather than being slaves to the frame rate, you would end up with more efficient animation code.

> You can also use listeners to create the triggers, something that we won't cover here because we're just interested in the basics for now.

Suppose you want a ball to move around the perimeter of the screen.

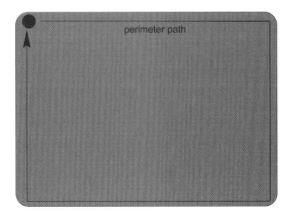

perimeter path

You might have one big event routine, but you then have to continuously consider both the x and y positions of the ball, and that will give you one big, inefficient code section. Consider instead the following breakdown of the animation:

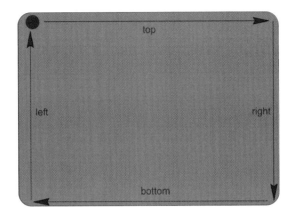

Doesn't seem much different, does it? Well, one thing you've done is to break down the animation into four separate and *simpler* phases of motion. If you could somehow set simple triggers to switch between these four motion sections, you would end up with four shorter code sections. Have a look at this code:

```
top = function () {
  this._x += speed;
  if (this._x>500) {
    this.onEnterFrame = right;
  }
};
right = function () {
  this._y += speed;
  if (this._y>350) {
    this.onEnterFrame = bottom;
  }
};
bottom = function () {
  this._x -= speed;
  if (this._x<50) {
    this.onEnterFrame = left;
  }
};
left = function () {
  this._y -= speed;
  if (this._y<50) {
    this.onEnterFrame = top;
  }
};
//
speed=10;
ball.onEnterFrame = top;
```

If you create an instance ball and run this (or use `ball.fla`), you'll see that this does indeed create the "ball moving around the screen perimeter" animation. It's also *optimized,* because each code section (i.e., each event function) performs a simple subanimation and checks for a simple trigger point to switch to the next phase.

Not only does this create cleaner code, but also it allows you to do something else *much* more cool: it allows you to propagate events between agents. Suppose you want something else to happen when the ball reaches a corner. You could start something else going on this trigger point very easily:

```
bottom = function () {
  this._x -= speed;
  if (this._x<50) {
    this.onEnterFrame = left;
    ball2.onEnterFrame = doSomething;
  }
};
```

By applying an event to `ball2`, you're using a trigger in the ball animation cycle to affect something in `ball2`.

> A more scalable approach is to have methods that broadcast events such as bottomComplete, topComplete, *and so on, but the code used here is a precursor to this style of code and a good introduction to the concept when you're ready to move over to object-oriented programming and user-defined events.*

This method of coding can be very powerful for the following reasons:

- It allows you to create complex, event-driven code, in which you are not only creating animation via events, but also using event-driven triggers to control the events themselves. For example, when the player's ship explodes, you could make all the aliens switch from an *attack* animation to a *victory* one. Using listeners also lends itself to this process.

- It allows you to create modular event code.

- It allows you to conditionally delete (or "cull") unneeded events. Rather than having lots of free-running events working all the time, using a trigger-based approach allows you to remove events with `delete (myEvent)`, so that all your events work *conditionally* on the question "Am I needed?"

Game Play

As mentioned earlier, there are two schools of thought with retro games. One group thinks that they contain the essence of all video games since, and that the only things that have really changed are the hardware and the graphic appearance of games. The other group thinks that retro games don't stand up to close scrutiny, and the only thing that made them addictive in the first place was that they were just too darn *hard.* Well, we'll stay out of that argument, but there are a couple of things you can copy from the video games of yesterday:

- **Simplify by using prior knowledge:** Donkey Kong. What's that all about, then? A big red gorilla kidnaps the girl and stands at the top of the screen throwing barrels at you—where did that slip in from? The game assumes you've seen King Kong, and therefore it doesn't have to explain anything. A lot of game rules are like that in retro games—you take one look at it and say, "Ah, that's taken from such-and-such, so I must have to do *this*," in the case of Donkey Kong, *this* is rescue the girl by getting to the top of the screen. Simple. (If anyone out there who knows what Tempest is all about, though, please e-mail us!)

- **Know your genres:** Video games look different, but there are only so many different fundamental types. Knowing the rules of each puts you in a good place to know what will and won't work, and it also gives you insight into the basic game mechanics. Good excuse for playing Mame as well!

OK, that's our history and background covered—let's continue now with a working example.

Defender

OK, so now we have to pick a game. My favorite retro game by far is the Williams classic, Defender. I love the remake of Tempest they did for the Atari Jaguar, called Tempest 2000—the former is still a classic because of its graphical simplicity and compelling game play. Tempest 2000 isn't really a retro game (rather, it's a remake of one), but one of the things Williams added that inspired me was an interactive soundtrack. Every noise that the game created was in time to a cool pumping techno track.

I have a theory that the stripped-down sound of techno dance music goes well with the stripped-down graphical feel of retro games, so for this game, you'll have both a techno sound engine and a retro game engine.

> One of the biggest issues with retro games was, of course, the slow speed of the processor. To create efficient code, retro programmers worked close to the hardware, writing directly to internal processor registers and timers. This is something that modern programmers used to high-level languages won't be familiar with. This game has been developed using the same hardware-centric philosophy—there are a few niceties such as local variables and object-oriented programming (while still keeping it structured, of course), but there's also total mindfulness of the performance budget. All we're interested in is speed!

As far as the code goes, you'll develop a game engine loosely based on the old-school real-time concept of *interrupts* rather than standard Flash events. The two are very closely linked; both essentially run from a trigger. The interrupt trigger was usually generated from an event (making it identical to Flash event–event handler pairs), but old-school programmers will tell you that interrupts could also run from one of a number of timers (or clock pulses). Flash has one main clock pulse, the frame rate, but for efficient coding, you really need to go back to the retro way of doing things and define *separate* clocks that trigger at the rates *you* want different things to happen. To do this, you'll use setInterval, an addition in Flash MX that game programmers don't really seem to have taken to (because the system-clock event onEnterFrame is so ingrained in motion graphics, it's hard to shake!).

> Most game hardware has separate sets of interrupts for the different func-
> tions; the graphics hardware interrupts would be served more often than the
> input/output hardware interrupts in something like an Xbox. This leads to
> efficient use of the system time, but it doesn't readily occur in Flash if you're
> a slave to the frame rate. You typically want some animations to be updated
> more quickly than others. setInterval *allows you to do this because it isn't*
> *closely tied to the frame rate.*

Anyway, for those of you who want to have an early look at the finished game, take a peek at
FlashDefender.swf. After a few games, turn your attention to FlashDefender.fla. In the following sections you'll first look at this game's all-important sound engine, and then you'll learn about the main devel-
opmental stages.

Bass (How Low Can You Go?)

Not only do we have an efficient retro-style event to play with in terms of animation, but also we have
something that isn't tied to the frame rate when it comes to sound: onSoundComplete. The problem with
Flash 5 (and previous Flash versions) is that you can only start a new sound on the start of a new frame (the
frame-based system clock rears its ugly head again). Unfortunately, the human ear is more sensitive to
breaks in sound than it is to visual breaks, so it was very difficult to sequence sounds together in old versions of Flash. The onSoundComplete sound event fires off at a resolution of around ten times the frame
rate, allowing you to splice sounds together much more accurately. Have a look at soundEngine.fla. This
shows the music code used in the final game:

```
function soundtrack() {
  soundtrack_snd.attachSound(nextLoop);
  soundtrack_snd.start(0, 1);
}
captureKeys = function () {
  if (Key.isDown(NUM1)) {
    nextLoop = "track1";
  } else if (Key.isDown(NUM2)) {
    nextLoop = "track2";
  } else if (Key.isDown(NUM3)) {
    nextLoop = "track3";
  } else if (Key.isDown(NUM4)) {
    nextLoop = "track4";
  }
  loop_txt.text = nextLoop;
};
/*
Sound track control initialization
*/
```

```
// set up variables
nextLoop = "track1";
NUM1 = 97;
NUM2 = 98;
NUM3 = 99;
NUM4 = 100;
// Set up sound object and event handling...
soundtrack_snd = new Sound(this);
soundtrack();
soundtrack_snd.onSoundComplete = soundtrack;
this.onEnterFrame = captureKeys;
// color text box..
loop_txt.backgroundColor = 0xFFCC00;
loop_txt.border = false;
```

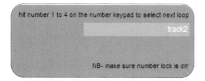

All you have here is four sounds that are attached to the sound object soundtrack_snd depending on which key was last pressed (number pad keys 1 to 4). The function soundtrack does the switching (it runs every time the current sound loop has completed), and captureKeys takes input in from the four keys, setting up the next loop to play. A couple of things to notice/be aware of here are as follows:

■ You don't need four separate sound objects. Reattaching a sound seems to be a very fast process, so you instead have one sound object that's attached to one of four sounds. This is cool because it saves you from having to set up four events for each of your four sound objects, assuming you took the textbook approach.

■ As any deejay will tell you, you can only properly mix beats in musical time. Put simply, for your samples this means you must wait for the current sample to complete before you change over to a new sound loop. The music sometimes changes well after you first tell it to, but this is part of engine's advantage: it keeps musical time and creates an interactive composition, rather than simply changing sounds with no regard to the rhythm (that is, the samples keep 4:4 time whatever happens).

> We've imported CD-quality sound samples into soundEngine.fla. *This is always a good idea, because it gives you the best quality output, and it allows you to change the exported sound quality later. We've also set the MP3 export quality to best, so on slower computers, SWF compilation may take a while. A final thing to bear in mind is that you're using only one of the eight available channels for the music—just think what you can achieve with a few more!*

Back to Basics

Many designers who remake old games try to update the graphics. That's a good idea in many cases, but you'll be sticking closely to source here with simple icons and solid colors. The following images show the two protagonists in your game: the players' ship and the ubiquitous evil alien.

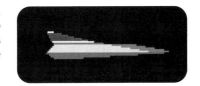

To get the rough pixilated effect, we selected an Auto Low quality in the Publish Settings window (File ➤ Publish Settings and then select the HTML tab):

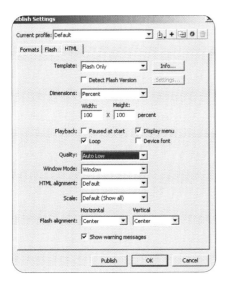

We've also made full use of the garish primary and secondary colors we looked at earlier, and we didn't use gradients and alpha at all. Not only do these colors have an authentic retro feel to them, but also Flash will be able to display them quickly, making for a responsive game.

As a finishing touch, we've used a suitably retro font, ArcadeClassic by PizzaDude (which you should install if you want to replicate the screenshots you see in this chapter).

Overview of the Game Design

The game consists of several different characters, and we'll look at them in order.

With reference to the preceding screenshot, the main elements of the game are as follows:

- The score-
- The radar blips
- The player's ship
- The player's cursor
- The aliens (note that, unlike in the original game, the aliens have to be hit three times before they die in this version)
- The plasma bullets fired by the player
- The scrolling terrain
- The scrolling stars

There is, of course, also one other thing that you can't see (or rather, that you don't notice): the game world itself. Flash has to know all about what's going on in the game, and the data you use to tell it defines your game world.

> There's one very good reason why you can't simply use the position properties (_x and _y) in this game: you have two representations of the game world, the lower play area and the upper radar. One of the reasons we picked this game to reproduce is that it's one of the more difficult ones. Classic Space Invaders should be easy after this one!

Before you look at each of the preceding properties, you'll take a quick peek at the timeline of the game. We've created most of the game within an embedded movie clip called `mc.world`. You'll find it in the folder world within the Library:

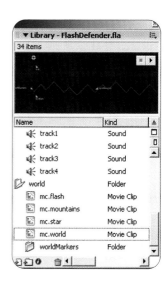

If you look inside mc.world, you'll see the following timeline:

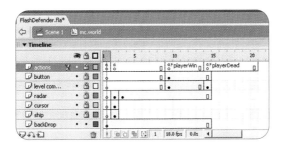

Frame 1 initializes the current game, but it's otherwise blank. Frame 2 is the start of the game, and the main guts of the game. You'll look closely at these two frames later in the chapter, because between them they drive the core game.

Frames 9 (playerWin) and 10 (playerDead) are the frames at which the game will end, depending on whether you clear the level or die trying:

The movie clip world is embedded on the main (_root) timeline, so let's also take a quick look at that:

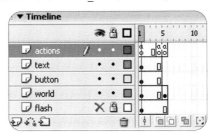

Although it would have been more Flash-fashionable to use a single timeline (_root) for all the code, rather than having the embedded clip world, it makes more sense to do it the way we have when you're thinking about streaming the game over the web. The main game needs to preload rather than stream, and the way to do this is to place it in a movie clip. At the same time, frames within _root will stream, so you don't also leave the user looking at a blank screen for ages.

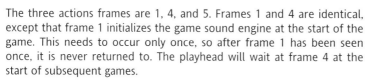
The three actions frames are 1, 4, and 5. Frames 1 and 4 are identical, except that frame 1 initializes the game sound engine at the start of the game. This needs to occur only once, so after frame 1 has been seen once, it is never returned to. The playhead will wait at frame 4 at the start of subsequent games.

Frame 5 contains the movie clip with the game itself inside it (which you looked at earlier), and this frame is reached when the user clicks the Click Here To Go!! text.

The Root Timeline

The root timeline does two things:

1. It contains the soundtrack code.

2. It contains the game start screen, as shown previously.

> In the following code listings, we've left in all trace actions. We used these to test each critical part of the code, so if you don't quite understand any major part of the code, try running the FLA with each trace uncommented in turn.

Sound Engine Initialization

The sound engine is functionally identical to the basic soundEngine.fla you looked at earlier, as you can see by looking at the code for frame 1 of _root. The only real difference is that your controlling variable, nextLoop, is changed by the game logic rather than the via user interaction.

The color object definition some of you may notice at the end is what creates the dull flash every time you hit something. There's a big rectangle at the back of the game area that is made to flash quickly from black to a gray (via the color object) every time an alien is hit.

```
start_btn.onRelease = function() {
  play();
};
function soundtrack() {
  // sound engine logic
  //trace(nextLoop);
  soundtrack_snd.attachSound(nextLoop);
  soundtrack_snd.start(0, 1);
}
/*
Sound track control initialization
*/
// Set up a mute and volume sound control object...
```

```
soundtrack_snd = new Sound(this);
nextLoop = "track1";
soundtrack();
soundtrack_snd.onSoundComplete = soundtrack;
//
gameScore = 0;
flash = new Color(back);
stop();
```

Frame 4 is almost exactly the same, except that this time you don't need to reinitialize the sound engine, which is why frame 4 exists at all—it's simply the onRelease event for your Click Here To Go!! button:

```
start_btn.onRelease = function() {
  play();
};
gameScore = 0;
```

On frame 5, the game movie clip is seen, and to signify this, you change the soundtrack to the next loop, track02:

```
nextLoop = "track2";
stop();
```

The Game Code

The game clip mc.world contains the guts of the game.

Initialization and Setup

On frame 1 of the actions layer of mc.world you define your game's world via two objects, world and database. The former creates world constants and game limits (that is, properties that define the size of the world), and the latter is a more structured and dynamic set of data used to control the inhabitants of the world:

```
// Define world parameters...
world = new Object();
//
// Limits and constants...
world.LEFTSCREEN = leftScreen._x;
world.RIGHTSCREEN = rightScreen._x;
world.BIGLEFT = -1500;
world.BIGRIGHT = 2000;
world.BOTTOM = bottom._y;
world.TOP = top._y;
world.OUTLEFT = world.LEFTSCREEN-50;
world.OUTRIGHT = world.RIGHTSCREEN+50;
world.INERTIA = 3;
world.ACCELERATION = 0.5;
world.MAXSPEED = 15;
world.MAXALIENS = 20;
// Define game databases...
database = new Object();
```

211

```
database.shipX = new Array();
database.shipY = new Array();
database.shipDead = new Array();
database.score = new Array();
database.index = 1;
// game
score = 0;
// Hide...
leftScreen._visible = false;
rightScreen._visible = false;
bottom._visible = false;
top._visible = false;
```

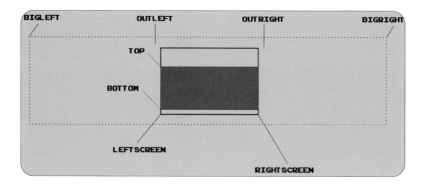

Your game requires eight limits, and these are defined as properties of world:

■ LEFTSCREEN and RIGHTSCREEN are the leftmost and rightmost extents of the viewable screen.

■ TOP and BOTTOM are the topmost and bottommost points that the game graphics can move in the main game area. These are *not* the same as the top and bottom of the viewable screen, because there also has to be room for the radar area.

■ OUTLEFT and OUTRIGHT are the points at which an object has to be before it is no longer viewable.

■ BIGLEFT and BIGRIGHT define the extents of the world. The world extends beyond the screen area—it's several screens longer. You can see this by looking at the radar screen. Aliens that are offscreen still have a position, and this is because they're somewhere between BIGLEFT and BIGRIGHT, but outside the viewable area.

Notice that we haven't given these limits literal values; we've instead placed "marker" clips onto the screen itself and used the properties of the markers to set values. This may seem longwinded to some, but it stops us from having to think in pixels. It also allows us to quickly change our limits if we ever change the game screen size or decide to put a border around the game area. The markers are set invisible by the last few lines of this code listing, which is why you never see them.

There are three other constants that aren't related to the game-world sizing:

- INERTIA defines the inertia/acceleration effect you see when the ship changes direction.
- ACCELERATION defines the acceleration/deceleration of the game scrolling.
- maxSpeed and MAXALIENS set the maximum speed of the game world and the maximum number of aliens, respectively.

The database object is an object whose properties are each an array. These properties describe the player's ship and the aliens. For all arrays, element[0] represents the player's ship, and the other elements are for the aliens. This makes it easier to handle the game world, because the player's graphic and the computer-controlled aliens can essentially be treated as the same thing, apart from the functions that are controlling them. Where an array element isn't relevant for the current graphic, it's simply ignored.

- shipX and shipY contain the x and y position.
- shipDead contains a Boolean specifying whether the current graphic is "dead."
- score is the score you get for killing the current graphic. This is only relevant for aliens. Although this is the same for all aliens in this game, you could, of course, change it per alien type if you decided to extend this game demo.
- index is a single property that is used by code accessing the database to point to the last updated database entry.

Game Logic

Frame 2 contains the game logic. Although this listing is long, almost all of it is simple if and if else chains that are performing the animation. Because of the length of the code, it's probably better to first look at what each function is doing in general, rather than poring over each line.

The first part of the code lists the *controller* functions. These control each of the game elements:

- Player's ship (shipController)
- Cursor (cursorController)
- Background stars (starController)
- Scrolling terrain (terrainController)
- Radar (radarController)
- Aliens (alienController)
- Player's bullets (fireController)
- Score update (scoreController)

These functions are fired off at regular intervals to drive all the graphics in the game. Not all of them fire at the same rate, however, so they're assigned via a mixture of setIntervals and onEnterFrames.

The remaining functions (that is, those from approximately line 190 onward) are additional functions that help run the game without directly controlling the main graphics. They include alienspawn, which creates the aliens, and fireUp, fireDown, and autofiretimer, all of which have to do with capturing the player's fire button and the bullet delay.

The final section of this listing (from around line 240 onward) initializes the graphics, sets up various local variables, and attaches movie clips and events. OK, let's have a closer look.

Setting Up the Event Triggers

As mentioned earlier, for an efficient game, you need to update different parts of the game at different rates.

The final SWF runs at 18 fps, which gives you a system clock of 1/18 seconds or 55 milliseconds. The elements that animate at this rate are the cursor, the aliens, the blue terrain line, and the player's bullets (given that to kill something running at 18 fps, the player's weapon should also run at 18 fps to make things fair!).

The player's ship runs almost twice as fast at 30 milliseconds. You set this up as follows:

```
shipControl = setInterval(shipController, 30);
```

shipControl is a named setInterval event that will call shipcontroller every 30 milliseconds. (This is set up in the MAIN PROGRAM segment of code, around line 240 onward.)

The radar is run on an onEnterFrame, but there's only one event for the whole radar, rather than one for every blip. The radar updates one blip every frame. This not only saves on the performance budget, but also seems to look a more like real radar, with different parts of the screen updating over time. Faster is not always better!

The stars are updated at a *much* lower rate than the other graphics—every 250 milliseconds to 500 milliseconds (or a frame rate of 2 to 4 fps). This is, of course, our area of focus tip at work: you don't interact with the stars, and pretty soon you stop noticing them, so why bother wasting lots of that precious performance budget on them?

The score is also updated slowly, every 1 second or at 1 fps. The reason for this is that updating text in Flash is *very* processor intensive. There are games in which updating the text at 24 fps takes up *half of the total performance budget*. This is because fonts can be mathematically very complex, and if there's a lot of text, it takes Flash ages to redraw it, especially if aliasing is enabled.

> *Like all interrupt-driven code, the timings aren't guaranteed. Depending on how large you view the game (or your computer's performance), the rate at which the setIntervals are processed may be less than advertised. This isn't a function of Flash, but more a function of interrupt/event-driven code—stuff can only be handled at the rate data can be processed, and not necessarily at any given rate you specify. As always, it's about balancing your performance budget effectively, not simply trying to make your code run everything quickly.*

Cursor Control

The cursor controls both the player's ship and the screen scrolling. As you'll see later, the ship controller picks up the cursor position and uses it as its "this is where I need to be" position. If the cursor is at one of the extreme ends of the screen (that is, in one of the red areas shown in the following image), then the screen will scroll in that direction. The red areas are defined by cursor.leftPos and cursor.rightPos (and the player may also see that these areas are also somewhat subtly defined for her as well—the line above these areas is red rather than yellow).

The cursor follows the mouse because it's set up as a startDrag here. Note that the reason the player's ship doesn't just follow the mouse directly is that the cursor is range limited, so it stays within the main game area (the following line is in the MAIN PROGRAM section).

```
cursor.startDrag(true, world.LEFTSCREEN, world.TOP, world.RIGHTSCREEN, world.BOTTOM);
cursor.onEnterFrame = cursorController;
```

The onEnterFrame for the cursor looks like this:

```
function cursorController() {
  // control viewport scroll speed via
  // current cursor x position...
  if (this._x<this.leftPos) {
    if (-viewSpeed<world.MAXSPEED) {
      viewSpeed -= world.ACCELERATION;
    }
  } else if (this._x>this.rightPos) {
    if (viewSpeed<world.MAXSPEED) {
      viewSpeed += world.ACCELERATION;
    }
  } else {
    viewSpeed = viewSpeed*0.9;
  }
}
```

This code sets the variable viewSpeed, which is picked up by all the other graphics to create scrolling, and it defines the speed of the scroll. Notice that if the cursor is *not* within the red areas marked up in the previous image, the following line creates your deceleration:

```
viewSpeed = viewSpeed*0.9;
```

This reduces viewSpeed by 0.9 every frame you're not trying to scroll in any direction.

Ship Control

Although the ship code looks long, it's doing only two very simple things:

- If the database tells you that the ship is dead, the ship movie clip will play, thus initiating the ship death sequence.

- Otherwise, the ship will move to keep at the same y position as the cursor, and it will move to the opposite side of the screen to the cursor but always remain facing it.

If the ship is found to be dead, it's stripped of its controlling events and the plasma ammunition, and it plays out its death via the if (database.shipDead[0]) branch at the top of this function. If it's not dead, it will do the following:

- Move to the left or right of the screen based on which side of the screen the cursor is on (checked via the if chain if (ship.myTarget.x<ship.centerPos)).
- Move to the same height as the cursor.
- Scale itself by either 100 or -100 (that is, variable ship.orient) to flip itself so that it's always pointing toward the cursor.

The relevant function looks like this:

```
function shipController() {
  // Am I dead?
  if (database.shipDead[0]) {
    ship.play();
    clearInterval(shipControl);
    delete plasma.onEnterFrame;
    // If not...
  } else {
    // Get current cursor position...
    ship.myTarget.x = cursor._x;
    ship.myTarget.y = cursor._y;
    // trace (ship.myTarget.x);
    // trace (ship.myTarget.y);
    // Decide which orientation I am facing in...
    if (ship.myTarget.x<ship.centerPos) {
      ship.myTarget.x = ship.rightPos;
      ship.orient = -100;
    } else {
      ship.myTarget.x = ship.leftPos;
      ship.orient = 100;
    }
    // trace (ship.orient);
    // Move toward cursor position...
    ship.myPos.x -= (ship.myPos.x-
ship.myTarget.x)/ship.inertiaTurn;
    ship.myPos.y -= (ship.myPos.y-ship.myTarget.y)/world.INERTIA;
    // trace (ship.myPos.x);
    // trace (ship.myPos.y);
    ship._x = ship.myPos.x;
    ship._y = ship.myPos.y;
    ship._xscale = ship.orient;
    database.shipX[0] = ship.myPos.x;
    database.shipY[0] = ship.myPos.y;
    orient = ship.orient;
  }
  updateAfterEvent();
}
```

An important thing to notice is that because this is a setInterval rather than an onEnterFrame, the this path doesn't refer to the ship clip; rather, it refers to the current timeline, so you have to refer to ship explicitly in your paths. Also, because the update rate of this event is faster than the frame rate of the movie, you need to force Flash to update the screen at the faster rate. You do this via the last line of this function:

```
updateAfterEvent();
```

Note that updateAfterEvent() must always be the last line; otherwise, it may not work.

Stars

The star code also uses a setInterval event, but it has more than one of them. Because you can't refer to all the star clips via this (for the reasons noted in the last section), you have to work around this restriction by always making sure you know the current star explicitly. You do this via an argument, star, that refers to the current star clip name.

```
function starController(star) {
  //trace(star);
  //trace(_root.world[star]._x);
  _root.world[star]._x -= viewSpeed/4;
  if (_root.world[star]._x<world.LEFTSCREEN) {
    _root.world[star]._x = world.RIGHTSCREEN;
    _root.world[star]._y = world.top+Math.random()*((world.BOTTOM-world.TOP)/2);
  } else if (_root.world[star]._x>world.RIGHTSCREEN) {
    _root.world[star]._x = world.LEFTSCREEN;
    _root.world[star]._y = world.TOP+Math.random()*((world.BOTTOM-world.TOP)/2);
  }
}
```

So how do you set up this argument? Well, you have set up a separate setInterval for each star and use the star name as an argument (it's in the MAIN PROGRAM section):

```
this[name+"interval"] = setInterval(starController, updateRate, name);
```

There's one additional bit of cleverness at work here. Because you'd rather hide the slow update rate of the stars, it's a good idea that they don't all change position at once. To fix this, each interval is set at a different rate (500 milliseconds +/– 250 milliseconds). If you watch the star field, you'll see that the stars all move at a slightly different speed, and this is a function of their separate update rates.

Terrain

The terrain moves based on the current viewSpeed value, as noted in the discussion for the cursor. There is one bit of cleverness, though, related to the way you never seem to run out of terrain.

This is related to clever symbol design rather than to code. The terrain repeats itself twice, as shown in the following image (notice that the terrain on the stage area is a repeat of the section of terrain offscreen):

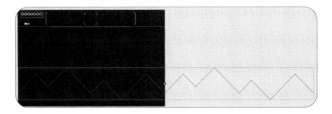

So how does that help you? Well, as soon as the center point of the terrain comes out of the visible area past one of the screen edges, all you have to do is move it so that the center point is now just hitting the other screen edge. Confused? Well, we don't blame you—it took us a while to work it out. Here's a "what-if" scenario to make it clearer.

Suppose the preceding image has the terrain moving right. The center point has just moved past the right screen edge. To make sure you don't run out of terrain, you move the center point so that it's now touching the left edge:

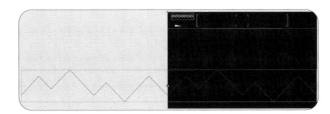

The user won't notice that he's now seeing the other side of the terrain because the two halves are identical. Totally sneaky, and an instance of the "don't do anything you don't have to" rule. There are all sorts of other complicated solutions to this problem, but the one shown here is the fastest by far!

> *If you're still perplexed and want to see this trick at work, view the game in a browser that's much longer than it is high. We haven't hidden the offscreen terrain in the FLA, so you can see what's going on in the parts normally out of view.*

Now that you know the trick, the terrain controller looks easy—all it's doing is adding viewSpeed to the current x position to scroll it and then moving the clip to the left/right edge of the screen as soon as it hits the right/left edge:

```
terrainController = function () {
  // scroll me in opposite direction to ship direction...
  this._x -= viewSpeed;
  // cycle me...
  if (this._x<world.LEFTSCREEN) {
    this._x += this.screenWidth;
  } else if (this._x>world.RIGHTSCREEN) {
    this._x -= this.screenWidth;
  }
};
```

Aliens

The alien code looks long and winding, but again, it's rather simple once you know what the aliens do:

■ **Motion:** The first thing the aliens do is follow a zigzag path through the game world. They essentially bounce on the top and bottom edges (world.TOP and world.BOTTOM) of the main game area. They continue to do this when they're out of the game area (although you can still see the motion on the radar). If they get to the far edge of the game area, they wrap around to the other side.

■ **Collision:** The only other thing the aliens do is check if they've been hit by the player. The collision-detection method is far easier (surprise, surprise!) than you might think, and you can get away with it because of the way you've arranged the graphics.

What you might *think* you're doing is checking for a collision between the alien and the bullet plasma beams. That would be cool, but you'd have to use the rather slow movieClip.hitTest method. What you *actually* do is check for something much simpler. You check to see whether any alien is in line with the player's ship when the laser is fired:

If the alien is in a space that means that it would *eventually* get hit by the beam (between the dotted lines in the preceding image) it's *immediately* marked as hit. You can see this at work if you play the game; sometimes the aliens flash *before* the laser hits them!

219

> *As you've probably already realized, the reason you can get away with this cruel trick is that you've made sure that the alien fills its bounding box in the direction it will most likely be hit (from the side) and you've made the beams so fast that the user is usually fooled into thinking that the aliens flash when the laser hits them. You're also assuming the user will fill in the gaps in the animation via prior knowledge: "The aliens must flash when the beam hits them, right?"*

The first half of `alienController` does the zigzag motion. This motion is hidden somewhat because the scroll speed viewSpeed is also added to the alien x position to make it scroll along with the terrain:

```
alienController = function () {
  // Update my position due to speed and scrolling...
  this.myPos.x -= viewSpeed-this.mySpeed.x;
  this.myPos.y += this.mySpeed.y;
  // wraparound check for radar screen...
  if (this.myPos.x<world.BIGLEFT) {
    this.myPos.x = world.BIGRIGHT;
  } else if (this.myPos.x>world.BIGRIGHT) {
    this.myPos.x = world.BIGLEFT;
  }
  // top/bottom  collision check...
  if (this.myPos.y<world.TOP) {
    this.mySpeed.y = -this.mySpeed.y;
    this.myPos.y = world.TOP;
  } else if (this.myPos.y>world.BOTTOM) {
    this.mySpeed.y = -this.mySpeed.y;
    this.myPos.y = world.BOTTOM;
  }
```

The second half of the function checks for the alien being hit (either by the plasma bullets or by the player's ship itself). Because the collision detection has to be performed against every alien (and can therefore be a rather processor-heavy feature of the game), you try to identify all aliens that *aren't* hit as early as possible, so you can ignore (or cull) them from your collision search and reduce the processor overhead significantly.

The rules applied (in order) are as follows:

1. If the alien isn't on the visible screen, it can't be hit and is ignored:

```
// if I am on the visible screen...
if ((this.myPos.x>world.OUTLEFT) && (this.myPos.x<world.OUTRIGHT)) {
```

2. If the alien is in line with the ship y position +/–10 pixels and in the same x position +/–20 pixels, then the player's ship has collided with this alien:

```
      // Have I hit the player's ship?
      if (Math.abs(database.shipY[0]-this.myPos.y)<10) {
        // trace("hit")
        if (Math.abs(database.shipX[0]-this.myPos.x)<20) {
          // trace("hit")
          database.shipDead[0] = true;
        }
      }
```

3. If the alien is in line with the y position that the ship was in when the beam was fired (killLine), then do a more detailed check that looks at whether the alien is also on the right side of the ship to be shot. If it is, then mark it as hit:

```
      // Might I have been shot?
      // Do rough collision detection...
      if (Math.abs(this.myPos.y-killLine)<6) {
        // Do detailed collision detection...
        // Am I on the right side of the
        // player to be shot?
        if (direction == 100) {
          if (this.myPos.x>database.ship[0]) {
            // Flag me up as hit
            this.play();
          }
        } else if (direction == -100) {
          if (this.myPos.x<database.ship[0]) {
            // Flag me up as hit
            this.play();
          }
        }
      }
```

4. The final section of the alien code moves the alien graphic, but only if it's visible. Notice that the last two lines *always* update the database with the alien's final position. This is so that the alien position is always updated for the radar.

```
      // calculate my movement
      this._x = this.myPos.x;
      this._y = this.myPos.y;
      this._visible = true;
    } else {
      // I am not on screen so don't bother
      // drawing or animating me...
      this._visible = false;
    }
    database.shipX[this.myIndex] = this.myPos.x;
    database.shipY[this.myIndex] = this.myPos.y;
  };
```

Radar

The radar takes the database values that show where each alien is and updates one every frame, assuming that the alien in question is still alive. It also *always* updates the player's position on the radar (the white dot).

> *The player dot is, of course, updated much more often because one of the fundamental rules of retro game programming is that the dot is in the area of focus. The player will look at it often, so it's the one dot you also have to redraw often.*

The function starts by updating a value update between 1 and the maximum number of aliens:

```
function radarController() {
  // Do next enemy ship in database
  this.update++;
  //trace(this.update);
  if (this.update>world.MAXALIENS) {
    this.update = 0;
  }
```

This value is used as an index into the game database. If the database entry for the current alien shows that this alien is dead, then you make the current blip invisible and mark its database entry to "I am dead". You also reduce the number of aliens by one, and if you find there are no more left, this is where you need to end the game. If the alien isn't dead, then you update its radar blip:

```
  // Has this alien just died?
  if (database.shipDead[this.update]) {
    // Remove its blip and update its shipDead
    // flag to "not in game"...
    this["blip"+this.update]._visible = false;
    database.shipDead[this.update] = "";
    // Reduce number of aliens by 1.
    // If I am the last alien, then level complete...
    this.aliensRemaining-;
    // trace(this.aliensRemaining);
    if (this.aliensRemaining == 0) {
      gotoAndPlay("playerWin");
      delete plasma.onMouseDown;
    }
  } else {
    // do this alien's radar blip...
    this["blip"+this.update]._x = database.shipX[this.update]/this.my.xScale;
    this["blip"+this.update]._y = database.shipY[this.update]/this.my.yScale;
  }
```

Finally, you update the player's blip (remembering that the player's database entry is entry[0]) as long as the player is still alive:

```
    // Is the player still alive?
    if (!database.shipDead[0]) {
      // update play ship's radar blip position..
      this.blip._x = database.shipX0]/this.my.xScale;
      this.blip._y = database.shipY[0]/this.my.yScale;
    }
  }
```

And that's all the core code in the game!

Summary

There are a few functions in the main code listing for this game (the way the laser animation works and the way the various graphics are placed on the screen at the start of the game), but they're really just basic Flash scripting, and we'll leave that for you to look at later. The real magic of the game is the way it keeps up performance by doing as little as possible. This comes partly from using stripped-down graphics and partly from using code that only updates elements when absolutely necessary. Of course, there's also the underhanded and tricky cheating in some of the code, such as in the faux collision detection.

OK, so now that you have the basic Defender game engine, let's see if you can create the full game with it.

Anthony Eden

From an early age, Anthony developed a love of interaction with mathematics and computational languages, along the way gaining an appreciation of any given natural environment and the ability to transform his environment into a digital construct. Inspiration for his latest project, www.arseiam.com (essentially an ActionScript anthology of his Flash work), is testament to this philosophy. The last decade has included commercial roles with Microsoft, Disney, Toyota, and Adobe, providing a sound framework in which to explore and diversify his project development life cycle skills. Spare time? If he's not thinking about it, he's doing it!

RACING CARS

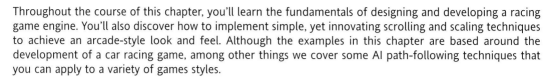

Throughout the course of this chapter, you'll learn the fundamentals of designing and developing a racing game engine. You'll also discover how to implement simple, yet innovating scrolling and scaling techniques to achieve an arcade-style look and feel. Although the examples in this chapter are based around the development of a car racing game, among other things we cover some AI path-following techniques that you can apply to a variety of games styles.

The racing game that we develop is a top-view game in which the car is positioned in the middle of the play area and the track moves and scales relative to the car's angle and velocity. We cover user control creation, collision detection, and computer-controlled opponents.

Open the file `race_final.swf` and familiarize yourself with the game play, the car physics, and the different types of objects used to build the track.

Getting Started

Before you start building the game you should establish the structure and details of the Flash file. If you're feeling lazy, then you can just open `race_structure.fla` and skip to the following instructions:

1. Create a new Flash document with the dimensions 550x400, a background of dark gray (#333333 should suffice), and a frame rate of 21.

> *Science has proven that humans need a frame rate between 21 and 23 to convince the eye that the motion is fluid and not made up of frames. Thus, a frame rate of 21 is the lowest frame rate required to give the feel of fluid, not frame-based, motion.*

2. Create five new layers (you need six layers in total) and name them as, gui, mask, overhead, car, and track from top to bottom.

3. On layer mask, create a square (any fill color, but without a line) 350x350 pixels and place it at the coordinates 10,10. Convert layer mask into a mask and make all layers beneath it masked.

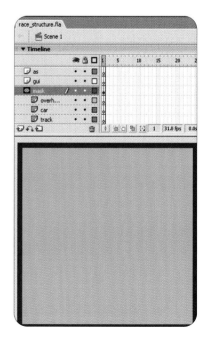

When you first create the mask, only the layer immediately beneath the mask turns into a masked layer. To turn the other layers into masked layers, double-click the layer icon to open the Layer Properties dialog box, and then choose Masked from the options. Alternatively, you can drag each layer to the bottom of the stack of masked layers. A small rectangle appearing below the icon of the previous masked layer should indicate that dropping the dragged layer will also make it masked.

Once you've completed these steps, your final layer structure should look like this:

Now that we've covered the file structure, let's take a quick look at the steps required to build the game. We'll take a more detailed look at each of these steps in the subsequent sections of this chapter.

- **Building the racetrack:** Here we'll look at ways to create and detail the track and its elements.

- **Creating the race car:** Once the track is built, you'll be ready to put the wheels into motion by creating a race car and adding some user controls.

- **Moving the track:** As the car is stationary, you need to use the user controls to move the track beneath the car. If you do so, the user is able to move around the track.

- **Handling the vehicle when it leaves the track:** Well, there's no point having a racetrack on which you can drive off the road and into buildings unscathed. This section explains how to make sure the right things happen when the driver does the wrong things.

- **Scaling the racetrack:** To achieve an arcade look and feel, we establish an easy-to-learn method for scaling the track while keeping the center of scale beneath the vehicle.

- **Moving the computer-controlled cars:** AI made easy. This section covers a simple, yet effective path-following technique.

- **Creating the graphical user interface (GUI):** Here we look at adding detail to the user experience by creating a user interface that gives real-time feedback on laps and velocity.

- **Adding audio:** Here we look at adding sound to your game. Music tracks, event effects, and ambient sound can add great depth to the game play.

- **Adding customization and enhancements:** Once you have the game up and running, we discuss some of the endless possibilities for increasing the game functionality and user experience.

Building the Racetrack

The track is essentially broken down into four main sections:

1. **The track:** The area you drive on (or are supposed to).

2. **The track edges:** The corner burns and grass/dirt areas that slow the car down if you fail to keep it on the track.

3. **Obstacles:** Buildings, walls, spectator stands, and trees will all cause you to crash the car if you're unfortunate enough to drive into them.

4. **Overhead objects:** The tops of bridges and shadows cast by obstacles in general have no effect on your vehicle and only serve an aesthetic purpose.

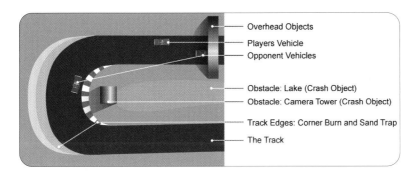

- Overhead Objects
- Players Vehicle
- Opponent Vehicles
- Obstacle: Lake (Crash Object)
- Obstacle: Camera Tower (Crash Object)
- Track Edges: Corner Burn and Sand Trap
- The Track

Initially you'll focus on creating the container movie clip that contains (nested within) the track elements required for collision detection and opponent vehicles. The container movie clip is structured to optimize the way in which you manage collision detection and scale the track. Here's an outline of the movie clip structure that we describe throughout this section:

- **Container:** This movie clip holds all track layers.
- **Crash zone:** This movie clip contains the elements that cause the player's car to crash.
- **Track:** This movie clip contains the track data, opponent vehicles, and the movie clip track inner.
- **Track/track inner:** This movie clip is used by the opponent vehicles to ensure they stay on the track.

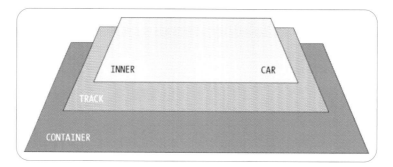

The Track

1. Open the FLA file you created earlier (or refer to the downloaded file race_structure.fla). On layer track create a rectangle 1000 pixels wide and 1000 pixels high anywhere on the stage. Convert it to a movie clip named container—this will be the base of your track, so there's no need for an outline. It should be an earthy solid green.

2. Edit container and, using the Pencil tool in Smooth pencil mode, create a dark gray line color with a thickness of 10. Draw the shape of the racetrack on top of the green base, so you have a track that looks something like this image:

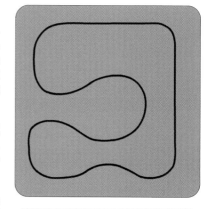

3. Next, using Modify ➤ Shape ➤ Smooth and Modify ➤ Shape ➤ Optimize, reduce the line to the minimum number of points possible while retaining the basic shape of your track.

4. Once you're happy with the shape of your track, convert the lines to fills (Modify ➤ Shape ➤ Convert Lines to Fills) and expand (Modify ➤ Shape ➤ Expand Fill) to a distance of 75 pixels. You've now built your basic track:

5. Fill out the track by adding burns and sand traps at the corners. It's easiest to draw a line across the track from the start of the corner to the end of the corner and then adjust the curve of the line to create the outline of traps and burns. You can then add detail for a more realistic effect. We recommend that you widen the track on corners to make cornering and overtaking easier:

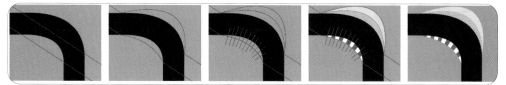

6. This process can be a little tedious and time consuming, but the more effort you put into creating these elements, the better the track will look. Continue to process all corners in this way until the entire track is complete:

7. Now select the area of the track that the cars drive on and delete it. You're deleting the track because you're going to use the shape of everything else for your collision detection. Finally, select all your shapes and convert them into an movie clip named `track inner`, and then convert that movie clip into another and name it `track` so that you now have three levels of nested movie clips: `container/track/inner`.

8. Make sure to name the instances of each of these movie clips `container`, `track`, and `inner`, respectively, and place the container movie clip on the `track` layer.

Open the file `race1.fla` to load the track used in this chapter.

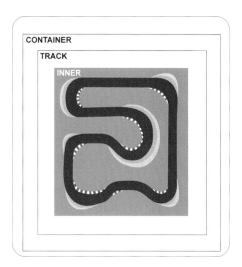

Building the Crash Zone

A crash zone is needed for when the user drives the car off the track and collides with something that would normally make the vehicle crash. Stadiums, trees, lakes, and so on are all types of objects that could cause a nasty crash. The crash zone is also handy in terms of preventing players from cheating and taking shortcuts through nontrack areas. Open the file race_2.fla to view a sample track with a crash zone included.

1. To begin making your crash cone layer, edit the container movie clip. If you haven't already done so, rename the layer containing the track movie clip to Race Track and create a new layer above called Crash Zone.

2. Make a copy of the instance of track and place it at the exactly the same coordinates (Edit ➤ Paste in Place) on layer Crash Zone. You should now have two instances of track on two separate layers with the top instance directly over the top of the bottom instance. If you're starting to get a little lost, just refer to race_2.fla.

3. You're now going to use this new instance of track as your guide for creating a crash zone. To start, name the new instance of the track movie clip crash, and while it's still selected choose Swap from the Property inspector. You should have track selected. Now make a duplicate of track (click the Duplicate Symbol button in the Swap Symbol dialog box), call it crash zone, and select it to replace the current selected instance. Now edit crash zone in place, and create a new layer above any layers you may have in there. On this layer you can start drawing the areas that you want to have as your crash zone.

    Start by roughly tracing out the area you want to use (in this case, the areas are indicated in yellow):

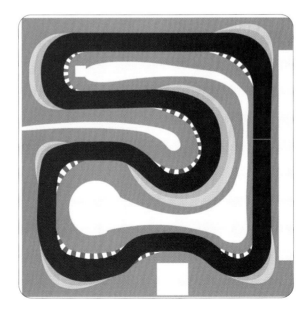

4. Now gradually color and detail the area to look like water, trees, buildings, or whatever you want:

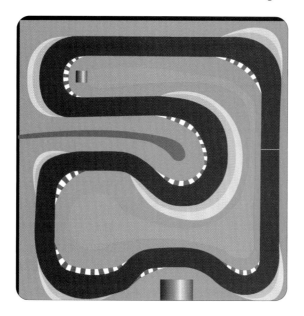

> *Notice the thin black outline around the bounding box of the crash zone in the preceding image? This prevents players from leaving the track completely. In a commercial release of this game, I left a gap in the outside of the track to allow the player to drive off and explore the game production credits—these kind of Easter egg features can be real bonuses!*

5. Once you're happy with the design and rendering of the crash zone, you can delete any layers that belong to the track, leaving just your crash zone details:

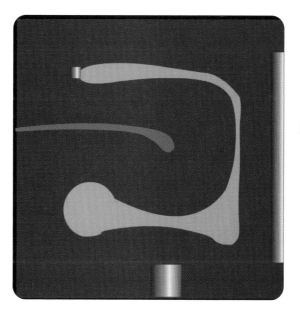

6. Check how the crash zone looks with the track by viewing the container movie clip, which should look exactly the same as it did two steps ago:

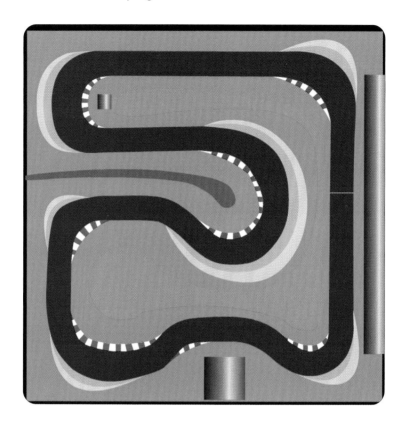

Adding Track Overheads

You're probably itching to get down and dirty with some ActionScript by now. Well, if you really want to you can skip this section and come back to it later (alternatively, you can just take a glance at the file race_3.fla), as it only affects the game's aesthetics and doesn't involve any actual functionality. However, paying attention here will make your game look even cooler.

The overhead layer allows you to add shadows, bridges, and any other object that the cars can drive under safely. It works in a very similar way to the track layer, except there's no hit detection required (you'll learn about this shortly).

1. To begin with, go to your root timeline, copy the container movie clip, and paste (Edit ➤ Paste in Place) another copy of it into your overhead layer. In a similar process to the construction of the crash zone, you're going to use previously created movie clips as a guide to creating your overhead layer. This also needs to be nested inside a container movie clip in the same way as the track movie clip.

2. Now that you have a new instance of container, go to the Property inspector and select Swap. Make a duplicate of container, name it container over, and select it for use. Name this instance container_over.

3. Edit in place container over, select all (*CTRL/CMD+A*), and convert both selected layers into a movie clip called overhead inner. Name its instance inner. You've just made a copy of container and prepared it for use in the overhead layer by adding overhead inner as a nested movie clip that contains all the track/crash details.

4. Now edit overhead inner and create a new layer above the layer containing your track and crash movie clips. On this layer, create shadows falling from the buildings and add a little bridge to one of the straights on your track.

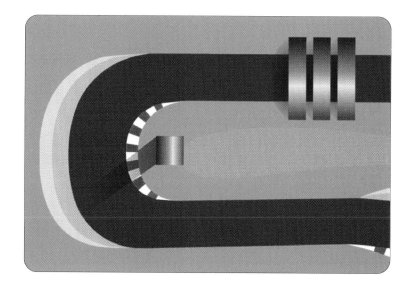

5. The preceding image illustrates the addition of a bridge with shadows as well as a shadow for the camera tower on the hairpin turn that we've added. Once you're happy with the details, delete the track and crash movie clips, which leaves you with only the overhead details, like this (admittedly, this isn't such an exciting image!):

Creating the Race Car

Create a car using your preferred techniques—either draw something in Flash or import a bitmap and manually trace the car details (or use the movie clip in the file race_4.fla). For the best results, make sure your car is made completely of optimized shapes (using bitmaps causes undesirable effects when they're scaled and is more processor intensive). Make sure that the car is facing downward, convert it into a movie clip (named car), and also name the instance car. Place car on layer car and align it to the center of the mask.

> *Important note: When you design the car, keep in mind that the car must point downward and have a width of approximately 15 pixels and a height of approximately 35 pixels.*

User Controls

Now that you've set up your track, its various components, and the car, you can start to define the way in which the different objects react to user input and Flash player events.

1. To start, you need to set some basic variables that will be used to control the velocity and rotation of the vehicle. You're going to consolidate all of the core code into one central point to make changes easier. Place the following script on the first frame of the layer as:

```
// this is optional but the game will be more
// responsive on lower speed processors.
_quality = "low";
// the maximum velocity of the vehicle (pixels per frame)
max_vel = 10;
// the maximum velocity of opponent vehicles (pixels per frame)
opponent_max_vel = 10;
// the minimum velocity of the vehicle (pixels per frame)
min_vel = 0;
// the acceleration of the vehicle (pixels per frame per frame)
acceleration = 0.4;
// the acceleration of opponent vehicles
// (pixels per frame per frame)
opponent_acceleration = 0.4;
// the deceleration of the vehicle when not accelerating
// (pixels per frame per frame)
deceleration = 0.98;
// the deceleration of the vehicle when braking
// (pixels per frame)
brake = -1;
// the acceleration of the vehicle when in reverse
// (pixels per frame)
reverse = -0.1;
```

```
// the maximum speed of the vehicle when in reverse
// (pixels per frame)
max_rev_vel = -3;
// the amount the car turns (_rotation per frame)
turn = 4;
// the amount the opponent car turns (_rotation per frame)
opponent_turn = 10;
// the rate at which the car slows down if it leaves the track
slow = 0.85;
// the rate at which the opponent car slows down
// when it detects the track
opponent_slow = 0.85;
// the starting lap number
lap = 1;
// the number of laps per race
totallaps = 5;
// rate at which car is moving
vel = 0;
// a function that starts the race
startRace();
```

2. Let's tidy all that up a little bit by adding a stop() function and making an init (short for "initialize") function like so:

```
stop();
function init() {
  _quality = "low";
  max_vel = 10;
  opponent_max_vel = 10;
  min_vel = 0;
  acceleration = 0.4;
  opponent_acceleration = 0.4;
  deceleration = 0.98;
  brake = -1;
  reverse = -0.1;
  max_rev_vel = -3;
  turn = 4;
  opponent_turn = 10;
  slow = 0.85;
  opponent_slow = 0.85;
  lap = 1;
  totallaps = 5;
  vel = 0;
  startRace();
}
init();
```

3. Now that you have an init function, you should create a function for the race start and race end. Most of your action happens during the race and needs to be updated every frame. To do this, you need to define what the movie is going to do at the onEnterFrame event handler, and in this case, you're going to define the onEnterFrame event handler for the car movie clip. After your init function, write this:

```
function startRace() {
  car.onEnterFrame = function(){
    // code goes here
  };
}
```

4. And, for the case of ending the race, you need to remove that onEnterFrame event handler:

```
function endRace() {
  delete car.onEnterFrame;
}
```

5. For the moment you don't need to do anything further with the endRace function, so let's focus on startRace. First, you need to capture some keyboard interaction by adding code to the event handlers for the spacebar and cursor keys:

```
function startRace() {
  car.onEnterFrame = function(){
    if (Key.isDown(39)){
    } else if (Key.isDown(37)){
    }
    if (Key.isDown(38)){
    } else if (Key.isDown(40)){
    }
    if (Key.isDown(32)){
    }
  };
}
```

Note the use of ASCII characters for the right cursor (39), left cursor (37), up cursor (38), down cursor (40), and spacebar (32). You could create a new object and use Key.addListener, though this method is somewhat simpler and in most cases at least one of the keys will be used during every frame.

6. Now you'll give those keypresses some functionality. The right and left cursor keys are used to rotate the car right and left, respectively. To do this you simply increase the car's _rotation by the amount defined by the variable turn:

```
function startRace() {
  car.onEnterFrame = function(){
    if (Key.isDown(39)){
      this._rotation += turn;
    }
    if (Key.isDown(37)){
      this._rotation -= turn;
    } else if (Key.isDown(38)){
    }
    if (Key.isDown(40)){
    } else if (Key.isDown(32)){
    }
    if (Key.isDown(32)){
    }
  };
}
```

7. The up cursor key is used to increase the velocity of the car (this is bit of a misnomer as the car is stationary and turns on the spot—velocity is actually used to define the speed that the track moves underneath the car and not the movement of the car itself):

```
function startRace() {
  car.onEnterFrame = function(){
    if (Key.isDown(39)){
      this._rotation += turn;
    } else if (Key.isDown(37)) {
      this._rotation -= turn;
    }
    if (Key.isDown(38)){
      if (vel < max_vel){
        vel += acceleration;
      }
    } else if (Key.isDown(40)){
    } else {
      vel*=deceleration;
    }
    if (Key.isDown(32)){
    }
  };
}
```

In this case, the car accelerates whenever the up arrow key is pressed, and the car decelerates when the key isn't pressed. Note that you only allow the car to continue accelerating so long as its velocity is less than the maximum velocity you allowed earlier.

8. The reverse functions in a similar manner, but you're making sure that the car's velocity only changes if it's greater than the maximum reverse speed:

```
function startRace() {
  car.onEnterFrame = function(){
    if (Key.isDown(39)){
      this._rotation += turn;
    } else if (Key.isDown(37)){
      this._rotation -= turn;
    }
    if (Key.isDown(38)){
      if (vel < max_vel){
        vel += acceleration;
      }
    } else if (Key.isDown(40)){
      if (vel > max_rev_vel){
        vel += reverse;
      }
    } else {
      vel*=deceleration;
    }
    if (Key.isDown(32)){
    }
  };
}
```

9. The brake follows the same process as the acceleration and reverse, except you ensure that on the last iteration of slowing down if the velocity is less than the minimum speed you force it to be equal to the minimum velocity. Generally, the minimum velocity is 0, and if you allow even the slightest negative velocity, the car will continue to roll backward.

```
function startRace() {
  car.onEnterFrame = function(){
    if (Key.isDown(39)){
      this._rotation += turn;
    } else if (Key.isDown(37)){
      this._rotation -= turn;
    }
    if (Key.isDown(38)){
      if (vel < max_vel){
        vel += acceleration;
      }
    } else if (Key.isDown(40)){
      if (vel > max_rev_vel){
        vel += reverse;
      }
    } else {
      vel*=deceleration;
    }
    if (Key.isDown(32)){
      if (vel>min_vel){
        vel += brake;
      } else {
        vel = 0;
      }
    }
  }
};
}
```

Moving the Track

Let's put things into motion now:

1. First of all, you need to make sure that everything is aligned properly. Ensure that the center of container, container_over, and the car is aligned to the center of the mask. It's essential that all these elements be aligned correctly. Refer to the file race5a.fla if you're unsure.

2. Having established the car's velocity and rotation, you can use a little trigonometry to control the way in which the track actually moves. Fortunately, the trigonometry required in this race engine is fairly simple, so the following crash course on the basics should cover things nicely.

    As the car rotates, you need to calculate the _x and _y components of its trajectory. The following illustration shows the angles involved when the car is rotated relative to the stage:

If you aren't familiar with the basics of trigonometry, then I suggest you check out some of the excellent online tutorials. In any case, I like to use the old trigonometry rule I learned in the early days of school: **SOH CAH TOA** (sounds like a famous extinct volcano!).

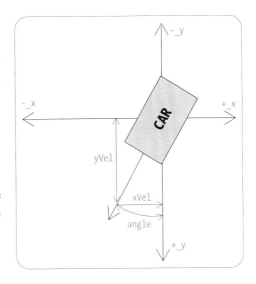

SOH: Sine (angle) = opposite / hypotenuse

CAH: Cosine (angle) = adjacent / hypotenuse

TOA: Tan (angle) = opposite / adjacent

3. In this case, in order to calculate the x component of velocity (xVel), you have the angle and hypotenuse (vel), so you need to use this:

    Sin(angle) = xVel/vel

    or, more usefully, this:

    XVel = vel * Sin(angle)

4. Before you get ahead of yourself, you need to convert the angle (this._rotation, where this refers to the car movie clip) from degrees to radians (because Flash likes it that way):

    xVel = vel * Math.sin(this._rotation * (Math.PI/180))

    As xVel is the _x component that you need to move the track (which is located inside of container), you can remove the use of xVel and use the track position directly. Put this line into the car's onEnterFrame handler in the startRace function, right after the key code you entered in the last step:

    ```
    container.track._x += vel * Math.sin(this._rotation * (Math.PI/180))
    ```

5. Finally, you use the same process to calculate the _y component (only this time, you use Cosine(angle) = Opposite / Hypotenuse), and you simplify the code a little by setting a variable (toRadians) equal to your degrees-to-radians conversion (Math.Pi/180), leaving you with the following:

    ```
    toRadians = Math.PI/180;
    container.track._x += vel*Math.sin(this._rotation * toRadians);
    container.track._y -= vel*Math.cos(this._rotation * toRadians);
    ```

6. Don't forget that you're using multiple layers of movie clips: track, crash zone, and container over. All three need to be moved in the same way as the track; therefore, you add a little more code to ensure this happens, referencing the clips by their instance names:

    ```
    toRadians = Math.PI/180;
    container.track._x += vel*Math.sin(this._rotation * toRadians);
    container.track._y -= vel*Math.cos(this._rotation * toRadians);
    container.crash._x = container_over.inner._x = container.track._x;
    container.crash._y = container_over.inner._y = container.track._y;
    ```

Because you need to move these layers every frame while the game is playing, you place this code within the onEnterFrame event handler inside the startRace function. Your code should now look like this:

```
function startRace() {
  car.onEnterFrame = function() {
    // user controls code described in the previous section...

    // move
    toRadians = Math.PI/180;
    container.track._x += vel*Math.sin(this._rotation*toRadians);
    container.track._y -= vel*Math.cos(this._rotation*toRadians);
    container.crash._x = container_over.inner._x=container.track._x;
    container.crash._y = container_over.inner._y=container.track._y;
  };
}
```

You can now test the movie. You should be able to drive the car around and have the track move relatively beneath it. If you're having trouble getting this far, refer to the file race_5b.fla. (You might consider moving the toRadians variable up into your init function. It really needs to be calculated only once, not every frame, but we've included it here to make this section more understandable.)

Handling the Vehicle When It Leaves the Track

Up until now, you've been able to drive the vehicle in any direction and over anything—you could take a quick spin over the lake, for instance.

Because you want the car to slow down whenever it leaves the track, you're going to use a simple hitTest to determine if the center of the car is over the track. But first let us remind you of the variable slow that defines how much the car will slow down:

```
slow = 0.85;
```

slow is the multiplication factor that the track has on the car's velocity. Set it to 0 and the car will come to a dead stop; set it to 1 and the track has no effect. Keep in mind that if it's set too low, then the car may not be able to get back onto the track.

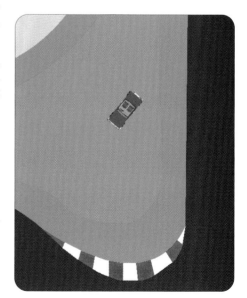

1. Let's see what the hitTest looks like within the startRace function:

```
function startRace() {
  car.onEnterFrame = function(){
    // user controls code
    // track move code
```

```
      // is the car off the track?
      if (container.hitTest(this._x, this._y, true)) {
        vel *= slow;
      }
    };
  }
```

Here you're detecting if the center of the car (_x and _y) is over any of the elements inside of the track movie clip. Remember earlier when you removed the actual track? Had you not removed it, the car would always be on top of the track and would never be able to accelerate properly. Setting the shapeflag argument to true in the hitTest call, you can test whether the car is over any actual movie clip inside of container (as opposed to using container's bounding box).

2. Similarly, you can use your crash clip to see if the car has crashed into anything (and ended the race). The crash movie clip hitTest is used in the same way (see also race_6.fla):

```
    function startRace() {
      car.onEnterFrame = function(){
        // user controls code
        // track move code
        // is car over the track?
        if (container.hitTest(this._x, this._y, true)) {
          vel *= slow;
        }
        // is car over the crash area?
        if (container.crash.hitTest(this._x, this._y, true)) {
          endRace();
          attachMovie("game_over", "game_over", 1);
          game_over.onRelease = function() {
            this.removeMovieClip();
            gotoAndStop(1);
          };
          game_over._x = 180;
          game_over._y = 200;
        }
      };
    }
```

Here you're testing to see if the car is over the crash movie clip and, if so, you execute the function endRace, which removes the onEnterFrame event handler used to control the car and track motion. You also add an onRelease event handler to the movie clip so that if the user wants to play again, she can simply click the game over movie clip. There are a number of ways you can end the game—in this case you're attaching a movie clip to the main timeline that states the game is over.

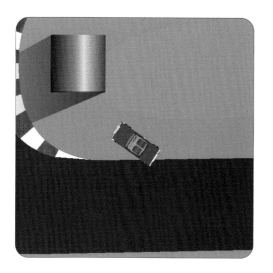

For the game over movie clip, we simply created a rectangle (200x100) with the words Game Over – click to start again in it and converted it into a movie clip named game over. Next, we set its linkage properties to Export for ActionScript, Export in first frame, and gave it a linkage identifier of game_over. Later in the chapter you'll look at ways of improving the end-of-game experience through the implementation of high scores and play-again functionality.

You now have the basic elements that allow the user to drive a car around a track and to have the off-track areas slow the vehicle or cause it to crash.

Scaling the Racetrack

As the car moves throughout the course, the track and the car itself scale according to the velocity of the car. For the track to scale properly, the center of container needs to be aligned to the center of the mask (where the car should currently be). This ensures that the center of scale is always in the center of the game screen and underneath the player's car.

> *To place your car at its starting point on the track, you'll have to realign the track movie clip rather than the container clip. You can do this by editing container and making sure that the point at which you want your car to start is also aligned to the center of container.*

1. To get the track scaling, you need to add the following code to the onEnterFrame defined in the first frame of layer as:

```
function startRace() {
  car.onEnterFrame = function(){
    // user controls code
    // track move code
    // is car over the track?
    // is car over the crash area?

    // scale track code
    scale_factor = 200-vel*10;
    container._yscale = container._xscale = scale_factor;
    container_over._yscale = container_over._xscale = scale_factor;
    this._yscale = this._xscale = scale_factor;
  };
}
```

The first new line of ActionScript here defines the way in which the track and car scale relative to the velocity of the car, and it's better represented by this:

```
scale_factor = Maximum Scale - Car Velocity * Scale Factor;
```

In the case of your script, you have a maximum scale of 200% and a scale factor of 10. When the car is stationary (vel = 0), the track scales at 200%. When the car is at maximum velocity (vel = 10 as defined by the variable max_vel), the track scales at 200 - 10*10 or 100%. You can change these values to suit the amount of track scaling you desire (consider making a variable out of the maximum scale value as well to make things even easier to update).

The remaining three lines of script scale the track container, the overhead container, and the car to the amount of scale_factor. Test the movie and experiment with different scale values. The following image shows the effect of scale on the track, ranging from 200% through 50%:

2. You may have found that the scaling is a little jerky. To resolve this, you can implement a simple ease algorithm. **Easing** is the process by which you set a target, establish how far away the target is, and then move a percentage toward that target, constantly reducing the distance between your current position and your target position. Think of a frog trying to jump out of a well—every time it jumps it covers half of the remaining distance. As it gets closer to the top of the well, its movements become shorter and it eases toward jumps of infinitely smaller length (and therefore it never actually manages to escape).

```
position = position + (target position - current position) * factor;
current position = position;
```

Or in the case of the scale_factor (see race_7.fla):

```
function startRace() {
    car.onEnterFrame = function(){
        // user controls code
        // track move code
        // is car over the track?
        // is car over the crash area?

        // scale track code
        rate = 0.1;
        scale_factor = 200-_root.vel*10;
        scaleSmooth = scaleSmooth+(scale_factor-container._yscale)*rate;
        container._yscale = container._xscale=scaleSmooth;
        container_over._yscale = container_over._xscale=scaleSmooth;
        this._yscale = this._xscale=scaleSmooth;
    };
}
```

Of course, to get this to work, you need to declare an initial value for scaleSmooth when the game begins (this is a new concern with coding in Flash MX 2004). So jump back up to the init function and add this line:

```
scaleSmooth = 0;
```

Test the movie to see the effect. Experiment with different values of rate to get the desired speed of scale.

Moving the Computer-Controlled Cars

The following method for computer-controlled opponents is surprisingly straightforward. This technique is a simple form of artificial intelligence (AI), which breaks the stigma that all AI involves lots of nasty code and high-level mathematics. It also offers a wide scope for modification and inclusion into all sorts of motion and game development techniques.

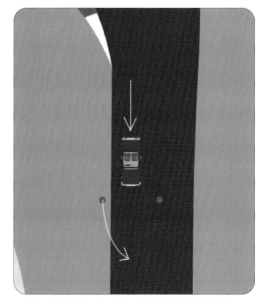

Imagine that each of the opponent cars has two points ahead of it: one forward and to the left, and one forward and to the right. If the point on the left hits the track, then the car turns to the right. If the point to the right hits the track, then the car turns to the left. The following illustration shows a car traveling downward, and the red point on the car's right has hit the grass area off the track. When this hit is detected, the car is rotated a negative amount, forcing it to steer away from the detected grass area.

Easy enough! It would also be possible to add a third point directly in front of the car. Then, if the car was to hit the point directly in front of it, it would turn to the direction in which it turned last (that is, if it last turned right, then when the forward point hits the track it will continue to turn right). In other words, the three points detect the track and turn the car away to avoid running over it and thus stay on the track course. Note that the forward point isn't necessary for curved tracks because it's mostly used to avoid colliding with objects when approaching them at a perpendicular angle, so we omit it from this exercise.

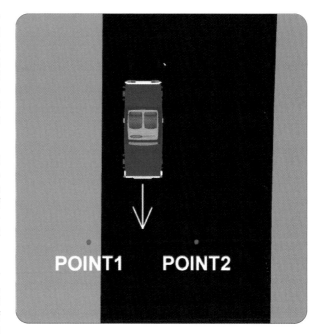

POINT1   POINT2

1. Make a duplicate of the user's car and change its color or design to visually differentiate it from the user's car. Call this duplicate opponent and place a copy of it inside the track movie clip at a position on the track from which you want the computer-controlled car to start.

2. Edit track, select your opponent vehicle, and name its instance opponent1. Edit opponent1 and place a small red circle (about 2 pixels wide) in front of the car, convert it into a movie clip named point, and name its instance point1. Make a copy of point1 and name this second instance point2. Open your Info panel and move point1 to coordinates –20, 40 and move point2 to coordinates 20, 40.

3. You're now ready to start adding the computer AI code. The car needs to move, so let's define an onEnterFrame event handler. Add the following script to your startRace function after the car's onEnterFrame handler (alternatively, check out our version in race_8.fla):

```
container.track.opponent1.vel = 0;
container.track.opponent1.onEnterFrame = function() {
  if (this.vel <= opponent_max_vel) {
    this.vel += opponent_acceleration;
  }
};
```

Take note that you're defining the onEnterFrame handler for the opponent1 vehicle, so on each frame the variable vel (which you initialize at 0) will increase at a rate of opponent_acceleration until it reaches a maximum value, in this case opponent_max_vel (that is, the car accelerates to its top speed).

4. Now to put this acceleration to use, you need to add a few more lines of ActionScript:

```
container.track.opponent1.onEnterFrame = function() {
  var rot = this._rotation;
  if (this.vel <= opponent_max_vel) {
    this.vel += opponent_acceleration;
  }
  this._x -= Math.sin(rot*toRadians)*this.vel;
  this._y += Math.cos(rot*toRadians)*this.vel;
};
```

You're now establishing a variable rot and making it equal to the _rotation of your opponent vehicle. Using a combination of this rotational value and velocity you can then use some trigonometry similar to what you used earlier when moving the track:

```
this._x -= Math.sin(rot*toRadians)*this.vel;
this._y += Math.cos(rot*toRadians)*this.vel;
```

Notice how you now subtract the _x component and add the _y component, whereas with the track you did the opposite? Previously, you were moving the track in the opposite direction of the car. Now you're moving the car itself, thus the _x and _y component values need to change accordingly.

Test the movie and the car should drive down the bottom of your screen. Try rotating opponent1 and then testing the movie. Your car should now drive off in whatever direction it is pointing.

5. Back to those two points you created in opponent1 earlier. Place the following code after the previous chunk:

```
container.track.opponent1.point1.onEnterFrame = function() {
  var myPoint = new Object();
  myPoint.x = this._x;
  myPoint.y = this._y;
  this._parent.localToGlobal(myPoint);
  if (this._parent._parent.inner.hitTest(myPoint.x, myPoint.y, true)) {
    this._parent._rotation -= opponent_turn;
    this._parent.vel *= opponent_slow;
  }
};
```

Here you're using new Object to convert the _x and _y coordinates of point1 from local space (relative to its parent movie clip) to global space (relative to the stage). This code makes good use of the localToGlobal() coordinate-conversion method by testing to see if myPoint is over inner (your track) and, if so, it makes the car rotate away from it. The car is also partially slowed down (_parent.vel is decreased proportionally) to simulate the vehicle slowing down for corners.

6. The next batch of script is required for point2 and is exactly the same, with the exception of the direction in which the car is rotated:

```
container.track.opponent1.point2.onEnterFrame = function() {
  var myPoint = new Object();
  myPoint.x = this._x;
  myPoint.y = this._y;
  this._parent.localToGlobal(myPoint);
  if (this._parent._parent.inner.hitTest(myPoint.x, myPoint.y, true)) {
    this._parent._rotation += opponent_turn;
    this._parent.vel *= opponent_slow;
  }
};
```

By testing the movie, you should now see the car driving along the track, avoiding the edges and slowing for corners. If your car has a tendency to drive off the track or zigzag along it, then experiment with the _root.opponent_turn value or the distance in which point1 and point2 lay relative to the car. Generally, the farther away the points are from the car along the x axis, the more the car will zigzag, and the closer the points are to the car on the y axis, the less likely it is that the car will turn in time to avoid running off the track. Also be aware that the car's capability to stick to the track will be affected by its maximum velocity and rate of turn. Should you continue to have trouble, please refer to the file race_8a.fla.

Note that because the previous two onEnterFrame handlers refer to almost identical functions, you may want to consolidate your code by making a single function that both points may reference. For instance, you could replace the two previous sections of code with the following lines:

```
function checkTurn() {
  var myPoint = new Object();
  myPoint.x = this._x;
  myPoint.y = this._y;
  this._parent.localToGlobal(myPoint);
  if (this._parent._parent.inner.hitTest(myPoint.x, myPoint.y, true)) {
    this._parent._rotation += (opponent_turn*this.direction);
    this._parent.vel *= opponent_slow;
  }
};
container.track.opponent1.point1.direction = -1;
container.track.opponent1.point2.direction = 1;
container.track.opponent1.point1.onEnterFrame = checkTurn;
container.track.opponent1.point2.onEnterFrame = checkTurn;
```

Generally, it's a good idea to abstract functionality, when you can, to keep your code more modular and easier to debug.

7. Finally, a little bit of housekeeping. When the game ends, you should turn off the event handlers used to control the opponent vehicle, so add the following script to your endRace function:

```
function endRace() {
  delete car.onEnterFrame;
  delete container.track.opponent1.point2.onEnterFrame;
  delete container.track.opponent1.point1.onEnterFrame;
  delete container.track.opponent1.onEnterFrame;
}
```

Creating the GUI

Ultimately, it's up to you as to how you'd like to lay out the different GUI items. The following is the layout that we've chosen for this demonstration:

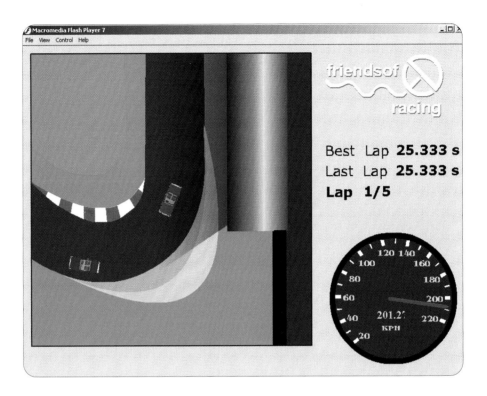

Before we demonstrate the addition of the game play elements that are tracked through the user interface, you'll need to add some further functionality to the game engine itself.

Splash Screen

You need to make room for the splash screen on the main timeline, so move all frame 1 layers to frame 2. Place a stop() function in the first frame on the as layer. On frame 1 of the gui layer, place any designs and instructions that you require for your game.

The only element that you need is a button to start the race. It requires that you place the following code on frame 1 of the as layer (refer to race_final.fla):

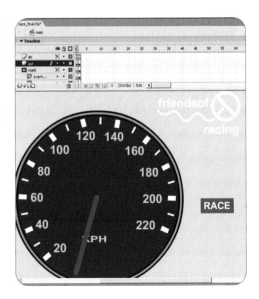

```
start_btn.onRelease = function() {
  play();
};
stop();
```

Laps

To calculate laps, you need to determine whether the starting line has been crossed and, if so, whether the player managed to go all the way around the course (rather than starting and then reversing back over the lap line). To do this, you need to add two new movie clips to the overhead layer (you add them here because you don't want them to be treated as track components).

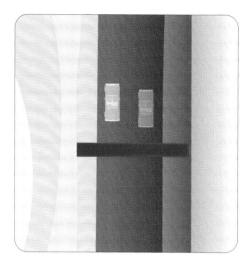

1. On the main timeline, edit the `container_over` movie clip in place and then edit `overheads_inner` in place. On the place where you want your cars to start the race, create a small rectangle that crosses the track and is approximately 10 pixels tall (don't worry about its color—you're going to make it invisible):

2. Turn your rectangle into a movie clip named `lapstart`, name its instance `lapstart`, and place a second instance of it across the course approximately halfway down the track (and name its instance `laphalf`):

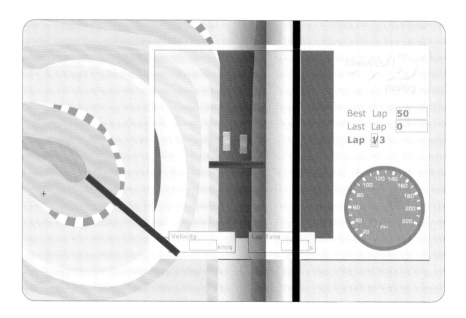

3. You've now created locations for your starting line and halfway point. So, in your `startRace` function, add the following code, which defines `onEnterFrame` for the starting line:

```
// finish line
container_over.inner.lapstart.onEnterFrame = function() {
  if (this.hitTest(car._x, car._y)) {
    if (halfway) {
      gui_lastlap = (getTimer()-startTime)/1000 + " s";
      if (gui_lastlap < gui_bestlap) {
        gui_bestlap = gui_lastlap;
      }
      if (lap == totallaps) {
        endRace();
        attachMovie("congratulations", "congrats", 100);
        congrats.onRelease = function() {
          this.removeMovieClip();
          gotoAndStop(1);
        };
        congrats._x = 180;
        congrats._y = 200;
        delete car.onEnterFrame;
      } else {
        startTime = getTimer();
        lap++;
        halfway = false;
      }
    }
  }
};
```

Let's take a moment to break this code down and ensure that it's perfectly clear. First, you determine if the player's car has hit the lap movie clip:

```
if (this.hitTest(car._x, car._y)) {
```

You then determine if the player has made it to the halfway mark (more on that in a moment):

```
if (halfway) {
```

So the player has made it to the halfway mark and back to the start again (that is, the player has finished a lap). Using the getTimer() function, you can determine how long it has taken the player to complete the lap, and using an if statement, you can determine if it was the player's fastest lap (we cover the use of the startTime variable shortly):

```
gui_lastlap = (getTimer()-startTime)/1000 + " s";
if (gui_lastlap < gui_bestlap) {
  gui_bestlap = gui_lastlap;
}
```

Now you test to see if the current lap is equal to the total number of laps (that is, is this lap the last one?):

```
if (lap == totallaps) {
```

If this is the last lap, you execute the endRace function, display the race congratulations movie clip, and position it accordingly:

```
if (lap ==totallaps) {
  endRace();
  attachMovie("congratulations", "congrats", 100);
  congrats.onRelease = function() {
    this.removeMovieClip();
    gotoAndStop(1);
  };
  congrats._x = 180;
  congrats._y = 200;
  delete car.onEnterFrame;
}
```

For the congratulations movie clip, create a rectangle (200x100) with the words You've finished the race in it, convert it into a movie clip named congratulations, and set its linkage properties to Export for ActionScript, Export in first frame, and its linkage ID to congratulations.

If this isn't the last lap, you increment the lap count and switch the halfway lap flag off:

```
} else {
  startTime = getTimer();
  lap++;
  halfway = false;
}
```

Notice that you also set (or in the case of lap 2 and onward, reset) the variable you're using to determine the starting time of the lap:

```
startTime = getTimer();
```

4. Of course, in Flash MX 2004, you need to initialize startTime so that when you evaluate it at the first lap, the mathematical operation doesn't return NaN (an undefined variable in previous versions of Flash defaulted to 0, but in Flash MX 2004 it defaults to undefined). Add the following line to your init function:

```
startTime = getTimer();
```

5. For your second movie clip, laphalf (the one placed halfway around the track), you need to add the following code:

```
// halfway line
container_over.inner.laphalf.onEnterFrame = function() {
  if (this.hitTest(car._x, car._y)) {
    halfway = true;
  }
};
```

This one is much simpler in that you determine if the car has hit the halfway movie clip. If so, you set the halfway flag to true.

6. You can now set the _alpha for both movie clips to 0 (via the Color options in the Property inspector's color list menu), thus making them invisible to the user but still available for lap counting. You're now

successfully counting laps (so that there are no cheaters!) and triggering a congratulations event when the finish line is reached.

7. Once again, you need to finish by turning off your handlers used for lap counting at the end, so add the following lines of script to the endRace function:

```
function endRace() {
   delete car.onEnterFrame;
   delete container.track.opponent1.point2.onEnterFrame;
   delete container.track.opponent1.point1.onEnterFrame;
   delete container.track.opponent1.onEnterFrame;
   delete container_over.inner.lapstart.onEnterFrame;
   delete container_over.inner.laphalf.onEnterFrame;
}
```

Displaying Variables

Displaying game variables is a simple process and adds greatly to the overall game experience. You can display variables such as current lap (lap), total laps (totallaps), last lap (gui_lastlap), and best lap (gui_bestlap) by placing dynamic text fields onto the stage and in their var field by placing the name (or path) of the variable you want to display.

1. In the case of adding the car's speed to the GUI, place the following code in the onEnterFrame portion of the startRace function:

```
// gui calculations
gui_vel = vel*20;
gui_needle._rotation = gui_vel*1.3;
```

This code calculates the display velocity and rotates a needle on a tachometer. The multiplication factor is up to you—it relates to how fast you think the cars are going in terms of a real-world value.

2. To display these values, design a tachometer that looks something like this:

3. Turn the needle into a movie clip and name its instance gui_needle. Adjust it so that the needle's center of rotation is centered to the movie clip. Somewhere on the tachometer (in this case, above the KPH label), place a dynamic text field and name its instance gui_vel. Test the game and adjust the gui_vel and gui_needle._rotation multiplication factors to your satisfaction.

You can find all of these GUI additions in the file race_final.fla.

Adding Audio

Music tracks and event effects add great depth to the game play, as does ambient sound. There are so many options to consider that it's not possible to cover them all in this chapter. Therefore we focus on a method to add audio dynamically from your Library, as well as a nice little trick that allows you to alter the pitch of a sound.

Sound is best controlled through the sound object as opposed to attaching sounds to frames. You can do this by importing a sound and giving it a linkage name—preparing sound assets is very much the same as preparing movie clip assets. Once you've prepared your sound, you attach and play it by creating an instance of the sound object, attaching a sound to it, and telling it to play, just like this:

```
mySound = new Sound();
mySound.attachSound("mySoundAsset");
mySound.start();
```

In the context of this game, you can create multiple instances of the sound object (with names such as mySound, mySound2, carSound, and so on) by placing the first two lines of script in the init function. You then trigger them by placing them throughout the rest of the ActionScript. For example, you could make the sound of the car crashing like this:

```
crashSound = new Sound();
crashSound.attachSound("crash");
```

And then you could trigger this sound, for example, as part of the relevant crash script:

```
if (container.crash.hitTest(this._x, this._y, true)) {
  endRace();
  attachMovie("game_over", "game_over", 1);
  game_over.onRelease = function() {
    removeMovieClip(this);
    gotoAndStop(1);
  };
  game_over._x = 180;
  game_over._y = 200;
  crashSound.start();
}
```

So far we've been looking at sound at a high level. For more details on using sound in games, see the "Sound for Games" chapter. Let's move on to a neat little trick that demonstrates how you can use the sound object. For this example, we created the sound of an engine revving increasingly faster. If you can't source or create a similar sound, then just use the audio samples supplied within race_final.fla.

1. Once you have your audio file imported into your Library, edit its linkage properties, select Export for ActionScript, and make engine its identifier. Make an instance of the sound object by placing the following script inside the init function of your racing car game:

```
engineSnd = new Sound();
engineSnd.attachSound("engine");
```

2. You're now going to add a function that plays the audio but does it in a way that is probably very different from how you've thought about the sound object so far. Place this function at the end of your code:

```
function engine() {
  var enginePercent = vel/max_vel;
  engineSnd.stop();
  engineSnd.start((engineSnd.duration)*enginePercent/1300);
}
engineInt = setInterval(engine, 100);
```

This function combined with setInterval makes the audio file play from different spots (depending on the car's velocity) in intervals of a hundredth of a second. The result is the sound of an engine that changes pitch relative to the car's speed and its change in speed. Let's walk through it and have a look at what's going on:

```
var enginePercent = vel/max_vel;
```

This line determines the current velocity as a fraction of the maximum velocity (resulting in a number between 0 and 1).

```
engineSnd.stop();
```

This line is fairly obvious—it makes the engine sound stop.

```
engineSnd.start((engineSnd.duration)*enginePercent/1300);
```

This line makes the sound play again, only this time from a different starting point. At first you discovered the percentage of maximum velocity that the car was traveling out; now you want to play the sound at that percentage value. You determine this starting point by multiplying the duration of the sound (which is in milliseconds) by the percentage. Your starting point needs to be in seconds, so you should divide by 1,000. But you don't want the audio to start right at the end (because there would be nothing left to play), so you divide by a number greater than 1,000 (in this case, 1,300. Although there's a mathematical rule of thumb here, we suggest trial and error, as slight changes can have significant effects on the sound of the engine at maximum velocity).

```
engineInt = setInterval(engine, 100);
```

Finally, you use setInterval to run the function independent of the timeline. In this case, you're playing (well, replaying) the audio file every hundredth of a second. You can change this value to get different results. You set the interval ID to enginInt, which allows you to clear the interval when the game is completed.

> Note that Flash doesn't handle audio all that well, so this technique can result in undesirable audio artifacts depending on your sound card and machine setup. If you encounter undesirable sound, try changing the audio or setInterval *rate, or increasing the division value used in* engineSnd.start().

3. When the game is finished (whether through completion of the laps or by running into an obstacle), you need to stop the engine roar by stopping the sound. You do this by simply adding two lines to your endRace function:

```
function endRace() {
    delete car.onEnterFrame;
    delete container.track.opponent1.point2.onEnterFrame;
    delete container.track.opponent1.point1.onEnterFrame;
```

```
        delete container.track.opponent1.onEnterFrame;
        delete container_over.inner.lapstart.onEnterFrame;
        delete container_over.inner.laphalf.onEnterFrame;
        clearInterval(engineInt);
        stopAllSounds();
    }
```

These lines stop the interval from running and stop all sounds currently playing in the movie. If you had more sounds playing in the game (such as music), you might want to simply stop the engine with engineSnd.stop(), but this method works fine for the current game.

Adding Customization and Enhancements

So far we've discussed the development of a basic car racing game and we've covered the fundamental aspects. You can expand these and create your own game-play enhancements and customized functionality. Here are a few suggestions and samples to get you started on building the best darn racing game ever made in Flash.

Power-Ups, Bonuses, and Special Items

Previously we discussed the creation of track and crash layers. Try adding a third layer just for power-ups. Whenever the user drives over a power-up, the user's maximum velocity is temporarily (or permanently) increased. Using the same detection methods, you could allow the computer-controlled cars to also gain power-ups, making the game a struggle to reach the special items before the opponents.

Different Race Surfaces

So far, you have a slowdown area and a collision area in the game, but you can also add many other areas, such as a speed-up area (oil slicks), an area with an increased rotation angle (ice), and so on, simulating other racing surfaces.

Adding Sound Effects

You can easily add sound effects to the movie and to specific events that occur during the race—we've included a skidding sound clip (skid.wav) in race_final.fla for you to play around with. You can also try adding a background soundtrack and sound effects to the key events to add greater depth to the game play.

Track Selection

Instead of sticking to the same track, why not create multiple tracks and display them by changing the contents of the track and overheads movie clips?

Adding Animation

In this current game version, you start the race as soon as you go to frame 2. By adding a starting lights animation that plays through and then calls startRace, you can offset the time before the player starts the actual race. Keep in mind that unless you add a race-started flag for the opponent vehicles, they'll start before you get the chance to. Why not animate the scenery, such as the water and tree, or better yet, add some parallax effects with clouds, birds, and airships that scroll at a quicker speed compared to the track in order to add a greater feeling of depth?

Collision Detection

The clip that represents the set of collision areas can be dynamic; you can include obstacles (such as randomly rolling barrels, animals, or broken-down race cars). The opponent vehicle is also part of the collision area, but because collision is detected based on a single point, you could add more advanced collision detection such as rectangle or even circular collision.

Finish Line

Using a similar technique to the lap counter mechanism, you can count laps for the opponent cars as well. By implementing this, you can determine the final finishing order for the play and computer-controlled cars.

Damage

Whenever the car leaves the track and collides with something on the crash layer, the car is destroyed and the game is over. Alternatively, if the car leaves the track but doesn't crash, it is, instead, slowed down. You could add a variable that increments whenever the car hits the track layer so that when it hits a certain amount, the car is destroyed and you play the crash sequence.

Difficulty

You can achieve different difficulty levels by adding additional opponent cars, increasing the cars' acceleration and velocity, adding power-ups and power-downs, and increasing the player's damage sensitivity. Increase the difficulty progressively by adding tracks and obstacles that become increasingly tricky, or change the functionality so that the game is time-trial based and the tracks have to be completed in a progressively decreasing amount of time.

Multiuser

Through the use of XML socket technology, or indeed the Flash Communication Server, you're able to re-create the game engine, which allows multiple users to access and play on the same track.

Summary

We explored many different techniques in this chapter that cover a wide range of different purposes. We looked at

- Drawing techniques in the Flash authoring environment
- Using keyboard input with ActionScript
- Using basic trigonometry
- Moving and scaling movie clips
- Detecting collisions
- Implementing path-following AI
- Creating a user interface
- Adding events sound and manipulating sound dynamically

By breaking down these techniques into modules and applying them systematically, you can now see how you can use some simple ActionScript to great effect. This knowledge, combined with what you've learned in the other chapters of this book, will allow you to create high-quality, engaging games.

The most important thing to remember is now that you've learned the basics of racing game development, you're ready to add your own creativity and personal flair to the creation of bigger and better games.

For further information and more code samples, please refer to www.arseiam.com.

Index

Symbols

10-Yard Fight game, 193
1942 game, 193

A

acceleration, 110
  See also gravitational effects
  Brownian motion and, 118
ActionScript
  character animation frames and, 67
  controlling game logic and
    physics, 63
  controlling sounds, 165–187
    ActionScript 2.0, 185–187
    Sound Box example, 171
    sound objects, 165
  editor, Flash MX Professional 2004,
    186
  MovieClipLoader object, 155
  pool game example use, 71
  Ring Puzzle game improvements, 31
  version of logic rules,
    Monstachase game, 22
ActionScript 2.0, 185–187
  class keyword, 187
  Sound Box code recast as, 186
  specifying return values, 187
ADPCM compression option, 188
aesthetics, 232
AI. *See* Artificial Intelligence
AIF sound file format, 161
  Flash MP3 compression of, 187
  QuickTime and, 162
aim function, pool game example,
  77, 78, 80
  adding shadows, 98
alienController function, Defender
  game, 220, 221
alignment on the stage
  aligning components to guides, 183
  racing cars example game, 238
alignment puzzles, Ring Puzzle game,
  26
alpha values
  avoiding in animations, 34
  avoiding in retro games, 207
  fire-fighting game, 122
  invisible objects, 251
  timed fading of images, 143
animation
  See also character animation
  choice between timing and frame
    rate, 143, 149

idle pose as starting point for
  action, 59
linked subanimations, 203
loop animation, 42, 43
Mole Invasion example game, 8
performance optimization in, 34
racing cars game enhancements,
  255
separating characters' body parts,
  52
simplifying, for efficiency, 202
value of Onion skin tool, 48
Wacom tablets, 34
animation examples
  bouncing ball example, 42–46
  jumping character example, 51–55
  jumping slime ball example, 47–51
  running man example, 58–61
  The Game demonstration, 61–67
animation principles, 40–55
  anticipation, reaction and
    overlapping action, 46
  arcs of movement, 46
  bouncing ball examples and, 51
  character animation, 51
  jumping character example and,
    52
  keyframes, 41
  squash and stretch, 41
  timing, 41
antialiasing, 195
anticipation animation principle, 46
  anticipating the anticipation, 48
arcade-style game example, 226
ArcadeClassic font, 207
arcs of movement. *See* paths of
  action
areas of focus, 198
  background stars, 214
  player position, 222
arrays
  dance to the music game
    body parts additions, 139
    dance moves, 151
    storing movie clips, 148
  fire-fighting game flame colors, 122
  pool game ball colors, 90
  temporary variables and, 92
  two-dimensional arrays, 17
arrow keys
  combinations, dance example
    game, 146
  array of corresponding dance
    moves, 151

distinguishing, 22
Arrow tool, selecting multiple lines,
  39
artificial intelligence
  computer-controlled cars, 244
  database support for game world,
    201
  value of terrain as AI, 200
AS 2.0. *See* ActionScript 2.0
ASCII characters and keyboard
  interaction, 236
Asteroids arcade game, 133
attachMovie function as authoring
  environment alternative, 95
audience size for games based on
  Flash, Director or Java, 192
audio. *See* sounds
authoring environment, removing a
  movie clip, 95

B

backgrounds
  multiplane backgrounds, 64
  star updates and areas of focus,
    214, 217
  use of bitmap images, 65
ballbounce.swf download, 42
ballMove function, pool game
  example, 73
  adding shadows, 97
  allowing for friction, 74
  testing for hole collisions, 94
  two-dimensional collisions, 87
Battle Zone game, 193
beginGradientFill function, fire-
  fighting game, 123
Bill's Tomato Game, 104
billiards. *See* pool game example
bit rates
  adjustment, to optimize sound
    files, 189
  Flash problems with high MP3 bit
    rates, 161
bitmap images
  characteristic of historic games,
    195
  performance optimization and, 65
  undesirable effects when scaled,
    234
body parts
  animation, dance to the music
    game, 135, 138, 139
  cleaning up characters, 52
bounce and friction, pool game, 74

259

bouncing ball animation, 42–46
  jumping slime ball development, 47
bounding boxes
  collision detection and, 93, 197
  racing cars example game, 231
bps variable, dance example game, 143
brainstorming, 55
bridges, racing cars game, 232, 233
Brownian motion, 117, 118
Brush tool
  file size and, 40
  jumping character animation example, 51
buttons
  ease of use, 153
  enlarging hit areas, 108
  fire-fighting game, 108
  triggering sounds in Sound Box example, 172
  using movie clips as, 167

C
Calculation and precalculation, 200
center points as animation aids, 43
channel choice, Edit Envelope dialog, 164
character animation, 51–55
  animation hierarchy, 65
  dance to the music game, 135
character development sketches, 55
characters
  See also opponents; players
  animation and personality, 34–67
  ASCII characters, 236
  character animation, 51
  creating heroes, 55-61
  drawing in Flash, 37
checkAlpha function, dance game, 144
checkCollision function, pool game, 82
  multiple collisions, 91
  two-dimensional collisions, 88
checkers, logical rules, 4
checkTurn function, racing cars game, 247
chess and logical rules, 4
choreography, 151
class keyword, ActionScript 2.0, 187
clearInterval function, fire-fighting game, 109
clock pulse, 204
code
  abstracting functionality, 247
  benefits of centralizing, 141
  controlling game physics and logic, 63
  event-driven, 203

Flash MX 2004 programming styles, 70
location of collision detection code, 81
code examples
  See also individual example games
  empty_button_object.fla, 165
  moving ball example, 202
  Sound Box example
    Music Button Component, 177–180
    recast as ActionScript 2.0, 186
    Sound Effects Button Component, 181–183
collision detection
  billiard ball physics, 70
  bounce and friction, 74
  bounding box collisions, 197
  character animation example, 64
  character animation hierarchies and, 66
  code location, 81
  Defender example game, 219
  point and shape collisions, 197
  pool game example
    ball to wall collisions, 73
    colliding balls, 81
    hitting the cue ball, 78
    multiple collisions, 89
    one-dimensional collisions, 83
    two-dimensional collisions, 87
  racing cars game, 229, 256
  retro games, 197
colors
  applying to a moving flame shape, 122
  applying to drawn characters, 38
  choice for drawing, 38
  differentiating opponents with, 245
  gradient color, 122
  making objects invisible, 251
  non-contrasting, and antialiasing, 195
  retro games, 196, 207
combo variable, dance game, 153
Component Definitions window, 176
Component Property inspector, 184
components
  ActionScript 2.0 classes and, 186
  creating, 175, 181
  defined, 174
compression formats, sound
  Flash MX 2004 options, 187
  limitations on Flash MP3 support, 161
  supported for Flash importation, 160
conservation of momentum, 83, 100
constants
  Defender example game, 212, 213

fire-fighting game, 108
  naming, 73
  pool game example, 74
  universal gravitational constant, 113
container movie clip, racing cars game, 228
control
  choice of keyboard or mouse, 133
  Defender example game, 215
  Importance of, in any game's success, 132
  racing cars game, 234
coordinates, local and global space, 246
countdown timer functionality, 145
crash zone, racing cars game, 230
crosshair theory, minimizing vector points, 35, 38
cue stick, pool game example, 76
  adding shadows, 98
cursorController, Defender example game, 215
Cutshall, Bill, 171

D
damage, incrementing in racing cars game, 256
damping factors
  applied to random acceleration, 119
  pool game example, 74
dance to the music game, 134-157
  adding music, 139
  adjustments and enhancements, 153
  arrow generator, 142
  character movement, 135
  code examples
    checkAlpha function, 144
    danceItUp function, 138
    dancin function, 136
    incrementing scores, 149, 150
    matchTheMove function, 138
    onEnterFrame function, 145
    preloader, 153
    stepTemplateInit function, 144
    turnOn and hitMe functions, 147
  dance routine, 151
  pre-MX Flash coding, 141
  scoring system, 152
  timing, 142
dance-mat games, 134
danceItUp function, dance game, 138
dancin function, dance game, 136
data typing in ActionScript 2.0, 185, 187
database support for game world AI, 201

debugging and ActionScript 2.0
features, 185, 187
default compression option, 188
Defender (original) game, 193, 196,
199
Defender example game, 204–223
aliens code, 219
basic graphics, 207
code examples
alienController function, 220,
221
cursorController, 215
flashDefender files, 205
initialization and setup, 211
radarController function, 222
shipController function, 216
soundEngine music code, 205
soundtrack function, 210
starController function, 217
terrainController function, 218
design overview, 208
event trigger setting, 214
game code, 211
game elements and logic, 213
limiting properties, 212
sound engine, 205, 210
degrees, conversion with radians, 78,
239
depth, suggesting with
multiplane backgrounds, 64
out-of-focus effects, 199
scrolling backgrounds, 255
shadows, 98, 99
development process
character development, 55
layouts and props, 57
device sound, 188
difficulty levels, introducing, 24, 26
racing cars game, 256
direction of likely collision, 197
DirectX EXE projector, 67
Donkey Kong game, 204
Double Dragon game, 193
dragging a movie clip, 111
drawing in Flash
drawing a character, 37
minimizing vector points, 35
drop shadows, 46
Dura, Daniel and Josh, 171

E
ease algorithms, 243
Ease In and Ease out features, 45, 50
Easter egg features, 231
Edit Envelope dialog box, 164
Effect option and audio fading, 140
ending the racing cars game, 241
endRace function, racing cars game,
247, 250, 252, 254

enemy. See opponents
energy dissipation in animation, 50
envelope lines and handles
Edit Envelope dialog box, 164
evap function, fire-fighting game,
110
event functions as code sections, 203
event models, 201
event-driven code, 203
Events, sound synchronization as,
163
example games
See also animation examples
dance to the music game,
134–157
Defender game, 204
fire-fighting game, 104–129
Mole Invasion, 5–10
Monstachase, 11–26
pool game, 71–100
racing cars example game,
226–257
Ring Puzzle, 26–31
Space Kid video game, 55
exits and random creations and, 18
Export for ActionScript box, 106

F
facial expressions and animation
speed and, 53
fading out audio
Edit Envelope dialog box, 164
Effect option, 140
timeLeft movie clip, 141
fading out images, timed, 143
figures, choice of, 7
file size
bit rate adjustment for sound files,
189
compression formats, sound, 161
methods of using sounds and, 160
sound file optimization, 187
vector points and, 35, 40
finishing order, racing cars game, 256
fire-fighting game
adding flame effects, 123
code examples
final complete code, 126
flame effects with color, 122
flame effects with damping, 119
flame movie clip, 120
loading an external SWF
file, 124
pusher movie clip, 115
putting out the fire, 125
spraying water, 107
creating a realistic flame,
117–123
magnetic attraction, 111

possible enhancements, 129
putting out the fire, 125
repulsion effects, 115
spraying water, 105
storyline, 104
flame effects
creating a realistic flame, 117–123
fire-fighting game
adding color, 122
adding the flames, 123
appearance of new flames, 126
flame movie clip, 120
limiting motion, 119
Flash
pre-MX coding, dance example
game, 141
resource similarity with historic
games, 194
suitability for online games, 132
trigonometric functions, 29
flash and fade out, 144, 148
Flash Communication Server, 256
Flash document
Mole Invasion example game, 6
Monstachase example game, 14
Ring Puzzle example game, 28
Flash MX
differences from Flash MX 2004,
18, 89
setInterval event, 198
Flash MX 2004
ActionScript 2.0 and, 185–187
declaring variables, 244, 251
differences from Flash MX, 18, 89
MovieClipLoader object, 155
Professional edition, ActionScript
editor, 186
programming styles, 70
undefined variables, 18, 89
fluid motion and frame rates, 226
focus
areas of focus, 198, 214, 222
distant objects, 199
fonts
complexity of redrawing, 214
suiting retro games, 207
for loops
dance to the music game, 144
pool game, testing for ball colors,
90
force and animation priorities, 54
frame rates
animation code efficiency and, 201
animation examples, 42
clock pulse alternative, 204
Defender example game, 214
forcing faster update rates, 217
motion perceived as fluid, 226
pool game example, 71, 73

processor speed and, 142
racing cars example game, 226
Stream sounds synchronization
and, 163
time budgeting and, 198
timing alternative to, 142
Fraunhofer IIS compression, 162
Free transform tool
bouncing ball animation example,
43
jumping slime ball animation
example, 48
freezing, avoiding in animations, 45
friction and stopping, 74, 75
frog character, dance to the music
game, 135
functions, storing movie clips in an
array, 148

G

Galaga game, 193, 199
game logic, 4–31
game types
arcade-style game example, 226
game play and, 204
retrospective review, 193–204
game worlds. See terrain
Game, the, character animation
example, 61–67
animation hierarchy, 65
collision with the ground, 64
gameover movie clip, racing cars
game, 242
games, example. See example games
games, online, importance of
simplicity, 132, 133
genres. See game types
getTimer function, racing cars game,
250
Gifford, Hoss, Spank the Monkey
author, 132
glide equations, dance to the music
game, 138
global space and local space, 246
God game, 194
gradient color, 122
avoiding in animations, 34
avoiding in retro games, 207
matrix parameters, 123
radial gradients, 123
Grand Theft Auto game, 132
graphics
Defender example game, 207
filling bounding boxes, 197
retro games, 195
simplifying for fast moving images,
195
size and redraw times, 196
gravitational constants
fire-fighting game, 108

universal gravitational constant, 113
gravitational effects, 43, 44, 49, 64
dimensionality and distance
effects, 112
fire-fighting game, 110
model for water magnet, 112
slingshot effect, 114
terminal velocity, 110
grids
layout of logical games and, 5
Mole Invasion example game, 9
Monstachase example game, 16
two-dimensional arrays and, 17
GUI (Graphical User Interface)
racing cars example game, 247
displaying variables, 252
guides, aligning components using,
183

H

halls of fame, 153
handleMag function, fire-fighting
game, 116, 117
hang time, 41
bouncing ball animation example,
45
jumping slime ball animation
example, 49
heroes, creating, 55–61
hierarchies of movie clips in
character animation, 65
high-score tables, 153
historic games
Asteroids arcade game, 133
Bill's Tomato Game, 104
classified into genres, 193
Flash resource similarity with, 194
Pong game and physics, 104
Show's Yer Tackle, 132
Spank the Monkey, 132
hitMe function, dance example
game, 147, 148
hits. See collision detection
hitTest function
fire-fighting game, 125
pool game example, 92, 94
racing cars example game
hitting obstacles, 241
lap calculations, 250
leaving the track, 240
simpler alternative for collision
detection, 219
holes
pool game example, 92, 94
hollow graphics, 196

I

icons, 177, 207
idle animation as starting point for
action, 59

Illustrator, producing Ring Puzzle
graphics, 28
images. See graphics, icons
importing sounds and alternatives to,
160
inbetweeners, 41
init function, racing cars game, 235
instructions, keeping simple, 133
interrupts, 201, 204
intervalID value, fire-fighting game,
108
intuitive interfaces
button design, 153
importance of, for online games,
133
invisibility of objects
with zero alpha values, 251
at zero coordinates, 123

J

Java language and audience size,
192
jumping character animation, 51–55
jumping slime ball animation, 47–51

K

key depressions, distinguishing, 22
key listener, Monstachase game, 23
keyboard
choice between mouse and, 133
interaction, racing cars game, 236
standardization of controls, 134
keyframes
animation principles and, 41
avoiding deleting, 55
bouncing ball animation example,
43
keying out animations, 51
Klingemann, Mario, and flame
effects, 117

L

LAME compression, 162
lap calculation, racing cars game, 249
layers
masking different layers, 226
minimizing vector points using, 35
moving multiple layers, 239
pool game example, 71
separating characters' body
parts, 52
as temporary guides, 47
letsDance function, dance example
game, 144
levels of difficulty
Monstachase example game,
24, 26
racing cars example game, 256
libraries of body part symbols, 53, 58
Library, importing sounds into, 160

Line tool use when drawing, 38
linkages
    fire-fighting game use, 106
    Mole Invasion example game, 8
listeners, 201, 203
    ASCII character alternative, 236
loading messages and preloaders, 153
loadMovie function, fire-fighting game, 124
local space and global space, 246
logical games
    Mole Invasion example game, 5
    Monstachase example game, 11
    Ring Puzzle example game, 26
    turn-based logic and, 13
logical rules
    ActionScript version of Monstachase game, 22
    Defender example game, 213
    Mole Invasion example game, 5
    Monstachase example game, 12
    power of, exemplified by checkers, 4
    Ring Puzzle example game, 26
    Sound Box example, 173
lookup tables and avoiding calculation, 199
loop animation, 43
    bouncing ball example, 42
    running man example, 58
loops, music, 142

M
Macromedia Corporation. See Flash
Macromedia Director potential audience, 192
magnetic attraction, fire-fighting game, 111
mainDancerInit function, dance example game, 139
makeboard function, 20
Mame game, 204
Mario Brothers game, 193
marker clips, 212
masking
    Mole Invasion example game, 7
    pool game example, 99
    racing cars example game, 226
mass, definition, 83
matchTheMove function, dance example game, 138
    moving body parts, 139
Math.atan2 method
    pool game example, 77, 86
    Ring Puzzle example game, 29
Math.cos function, 81, 86
    racing cars example game, 239, 245
Math.random function

fire-fighting game, 109
    appearance of new flames, 126
    Brownian motion and, 119
    flame effects and, 117
    Mole Invasion example game, 9
    Monstachase example game, 19
    pool game example, 73
Math.sin function, 81, 86
    fire-fighting game, 109
    racing cars example game, 239, 245
Math.sqrt function, 114
matrix parameters, gradient color, 123
Metal Gear Solid game, 132
Meteors game, 195
modulo operator, 29
Mole Invasion example game, 5–10
    code examples, 8, 10
    making the game, 6
    possible improvements, 10
momentum, definition, 83
Monstachase example game, 11–26
    code examples
        actions layer, 16
        key listener, 23
        moveMonster function, 22, 26
        movePlayer function, 20
    logical rules, 12
    making the game, 14
    possible improvements, 23
Mortal Kombat game, 193
motion tweens
    absent at ends of animations, 54
    bouncing ball animation example, 43
    inbetweener function, 41
    Mole Invasion example game, 8
mouse, choice between keyboard and, 133
mouse operations, pool game example, 78
move function, fire-fighting game, 109, 110
    incorporating both attraction and repulsion, 116
    incorporating the hitTest function, 125
    incorporating repulsion, 115
    with draggable magnet, 112
movement and simplified graphics, 195
movePlayer function, Monstachase example game, 20
movie clips
    character animation hierarchies, 65
    Defender example game, 209
    draggable, 111
    nesting, 124, 228, 229, 232

using as buttons, 167
MovieClipLoader object, 155
moving ball example code, 202
MP3 compression format
    Flash MP3 compressor, 187
    Flash problems with high bit rates, 161
    introduced, 160
    other compression options compared, 188
MUD game, 193
multi-user versions, racing cars game, 256
multiplane backgrounds, 64
music
    adding audio to games, 139
    changing sounds in musical time, 206
    Defender example game soundEngine code, 205
    preventing tracks from playing over one another, 169, 174
    royalties and, 139
    techno dance and retro games, 204
Music Button Component, 177–180
music buttons, Sound Box example, 173

N
NaN (Not a Number) results, 89, 251
nested movie clips, loading external SWF files, 124
numeric values, avoiding coding, 79

O
object-orientation, 201, 203, 204
obstacles, racing cars game, 230, 256
onClipEvent handlers, dance to the music game, 141
onEnterFrame function
    consolidating code, 247
    dance example game, 145
    firing Defender game functions, 214
    starting and stopping races, 235
Onion skin tool
    bouncing ball animation, 44
    jumping character animation, 52
    jumping slime ball animation, 48
    running man example, 58
    value in animation, 48
online games, importance of simplicity, 132, 133
onRelease function, using sound objects, 168
OnReleaseOutside function, significance, 108
onRollOver function, using sound objects, 169

onSoundComplete function
    Defender example game, 205
    using sound objects, 167
OOP (Object Oriented
        Programming), 70
opponents
    animating aliens exploding, 60
    cars, in racing cars game, 244
    value of terrain as AI, 200
optimization. See performance
        optimization
overlapping action as animation
        principle, 46

P

Pac-Man game, 193
Packages, ActionScript 2.0 feature,
        185
Paint Bucket tool, coloring drawn
        characters, 39
parallax, 64, 199
parameters section, Component
        Definitions window, 176, 181
paths of action
    as animation principle, 46
    jumping character animation
        example, 52
    modifying in game contexts, 63
    value of Onion skin tool, 48
Pencil tool, 228
performance optimization, 34–40
    areas of focus, 198
    collision detection and, 197
    Flash animation limitations, 34
    optimizing sounds in Flash,
        187–189
    precalculation, 199
    time budgeting, 198
    use of bitmap images, 65
personalities. See characters
physics
    See also gravitational effects
    billiard ball physics, 70
    Brownian motion, 118
    colliding balls, 82
    controlling with ActionScript, 63
    definition of, 104
pixel fonts, optimizing, 153
pixilation, 195, 207
player interaction
    advantages of mouse controls, 133
    racing cars game, 234
players' scores. See scoring
        information
point collisions, 197
Pong game, 104
pool game example, 71–100
    bounce and friction, 74
    code examples
        adding shadows, 97

allowing for friction, 74, 76
ballMove function, 94
creating the cue stick, 77
defining constants, 72
hitTest function, 94
hitting the cue ball, 78
one-dimensional collisions, 84
two-dimensional collisions, 87
colliding balls, 81
    multiple collisions, 89
    one-dimensional collisions, 83
    two-dimensional collisions, 87
creating a cue stick, 76
hitting the cue ball, 78
introduction, 71
possible improvements, 95, 96, 100
possible visual enhancements, 96
sinking the balls, 92
touching balls, 88
posing and character animation, 51
power-ups, racing cars example
        game, 255
precalculation, 199
preloading
    dance to the music game, 153
    Defender example game, 209
prior knowledge, 204, 220
processor speed
    sounds synchronization and, 163
    Web connection speed and, 192
programming styles, Flash MX 2004,
        70
projector EXE file and screen
        resolution, 67
propagating events, 203
Pythagorean theorem, 75, 79, 80

Q

Quake game, 194
QuickTime and AIF/WAV portability,
        162

R

racing cars example game, 226–257
    adding audio, 252–255
    adding track overhead features,
        232
    building the crash zone, 230
    building the racetrack, 227–233
    cars leaving the track, 240–242
    code examples
        checkTurn function, 247
        endRace function, 236, 247,
            250, 252, 254
        getTimer function, 250
        init function, 235
        players' controls, 234
        sound object, 253
        startRace function, 235, 240,
            242, 245, 246, 249

creating the GUI, 247–252
creating the race car, 234–238
customizing and enhancing,
        255–256
    Easter egg features, 231
development stages outlined, 227
displaying variables, 252
ending the game, 241
getting started, 226–227
lap calculation, 249
moving the opponent cars,
        244–247
moving the track, 238–240
players' controls, 234
scaling the racetrack, 242–244
starting the race, 248
radarController function, Defender
        example game, 222
radial color gradients, 123
radian and degree conversions, 78,
        239
randomization. See Brownian motion;
        Math.random statement
ratio values, coloring flame effects,
        122
raw sound and Flash compression
        options, 188
reaction as an animation principle, 46
realism
    allowable departures from, 84
    suspension of disbelief, 104
redraw times
    fonts, 214
    size of graphics and, 196
repeating terrain trick, 218
retro Flash games, 192–223
    Defender example game,
        204–223
    game play, 203
    graphics and sound, 195
    programming techniques, 198
retro games and music, 204
return values, specifying for an AS
        2.0 function, 187
Ring Puzzle example game, 26–31
    code examples
        actions layer, 28
        checkRot function, 29
        startTurn function, 28
        turnRing function, 30
    logical rules, 26
    making the game, 27
    possible improvements, 31
Robotron game, 193, 195, 196
root timeline, Defender example
        game, 210
rotational dynamics and
        precalculation, 199
rules. See logical rules

running man animation example, 58–61

S

scaling, racing cars game, 242
    ease algorithms, 243
    unsuitability of bitmaps, 234
scoring information
    dance to the music game, 149, 150
        accuracy of response and, 153
        adding sound effects, 155
    displaying, fire-fighting game, 126
    fire-fighting game, 126
    high-score tables, 153
    rewarding success with sound effects, 151
    updating is processor intensive, 214
Scramble game, 193
screen position setting, Monstachase game, 20
screen resolution and projector EXE files, 67
screen size, value of marker clips, 212
scrolling feature
    Defender example game, 215
    Defender original game, 199
    racing cars game enhancements, 255
setInterval function
    fire-fighting game, 108
    firing Defender game functions, 213, 214
        shipController and starController functions, 217
    processor use and, 198
    replaying audio, 254
    setting interrupts, 205
shadows
    creating realistic shadows, 96
    pool game example, 96
    racing cars example game, 232, 233
    suggesting depth with, 98, 99
shape collisions, 197
shapeflag argument
    pool game, 93, 94
    racing cars game, 241
shared object limitation on Web data transfers, 192
Shinobi game, 193
shipController function, Defender example game, 216
shoot function, pool game example, 78
    adding shadows, 98
    refinement, 79
shortcuts, 194
Show's Yer Tackle game, 132

Silhouettes and character animation posing, 51
simplicity
    breaking down animations, 202
    as essence of Flash games, 132
    prior knowledge and game playing, 204
    retro game graphics, 195
simulations and modern games, 192
simultaneous sounds, Flash limits, 174
size of graphics and redraw times, 196
size variations using Math.sin, 109
sketching characters, 55
slime ball animation example, 47–51
slingshot effect, 114
slowing in and slowing out, 41
Snap to Objects tool, 38, 54
SohCahToa mnemonic, 239
Sound Box example, 172-186
    code examples
        Music Button Component, 177–180
        recast as ActionScript 2.0, 186
        Sound Effects Button Component, 181–183
    creating, 174
    functional requirements, 172
    introduced, 172
    logical rules, 173
    music button requirements, 173
    sound effects button requirements, 173
    wave lines, 175
sound containers, 160
sound effects
    dance to the music game, 151, 155
    racing cars example game, 253, 255
sound effects buttons, Sound Box example, 173, 181–183
Sound Forge editor, 162
sound objects, 165
    Defender example game, 206
    defining, 166
    racing cars example game, 253
Sound Properties dialog box, 187
SoundEffectButton class, 186
soundEngine code, Defender example game, 205
    soundtrack function and, 210
sounds
    See also music
    changing pitch, 254
    compression formats, 160, 161, 187
    controlling dynamically, 165
    Defender example game, 205

device sound, 188
dynamic sounds in Flash games, 172
Flash MX 2004 and, 160
    controlling sounds with ActionScript, 165
    editing capabilities, 164
    importing sounds, 160
    main movie or separate SWF, 160
    optimizing sounds, 187–189
    sound types and effects, 162
    importance in games, 160
    racing cars game, 252
    reattaching, 206
    reusing advised, 189
    sequencing, using onSoundComplete, 205
    simultaneous sounds in Flash, 174
    supported formats, 160
    synchronization in dance example game, 140, 143
    synchronization in Flash MX, 162, 163
    triggering methods, 172, 185
    undesirable artifacts, 254
    value of CD quality samples, 206
soundtrack function, Defender example game, 210
Space Invaders game, 193
Space Kid example video game, 55
Spank the Monkey game, 132
speech compression option, 188
splash screens, 153, 248
squash and stretch
    animation principles and, 41
    bouncing ball animation example, 43
    fine tuning animation, 54
squirt function, fire-fighting game, 108
standardization of keyboard controls, 134
starController function, Defender example game, 217
Start sound synchronization, 163
starting positions, setting, 20
startRace function, racing cars example game, 235
    braking, 238
    hitTest function within, 240
    hitting obstacles, 241
    keyboard interaction, 236
    lap calculations, 249
    moving multiple layers, 240
    moving opponents' cars, 245
    reversing, 237
    rotating the car, 236
    scaling the track, 242
    speed, 237

startTurn function, Ring Puzzle example game, 29
status messages, fire-fighting game, 126
stepTemplateInit function, dance example game, 144
Stop sound synchronization, 163
Stop/Start element, Edit Envelope dialog box, 165
stopping objects, 75
stories, creating, 55–61
Stream sound synchronization, 163
streaming games over the Web, 209
stretch and skew example, 48
strict data typing in ActionScript 2.0, 185, 187
subanimations and trigger points, 203
Super Basketball game, 193
Super Sprint game, 193
surface hazards, racing cars game, 255
suspension of disbelief, 104
Swap button in character animation, 54
SWF files
    flame effects, 123
    loadMovie function, 124
swfXXL program, 67
symbols, body part movie clips, 53
synchronization
    dance example game, 140, 143
    sounds, in Flash MX, 162, 163

T
Tempest game, 193, 204
terminal velocity, 110
terrain
    Defender example game, 208, 211
        limiting properties, 212
        terrain movement, 217
    repeating terrain trick, 218
terrainController function, Defender example game, 218
Tetris game, 193
text boxes
    adding a dynamic text box, 180
    fire-fighting game, 126
    sound objects example, 170
    updating, as processor intensive, 214
time budgeting and frame rate, 198
Time In and Time Out, Edit Envelope dialog box, 164
timeLeft movie clip, dance example game, 141

timelines, Defender example game, 208
    root timeline, 210
timing
    alternative to frame rates, 142, 204
    countdown timer functionality, 145
    dance to the music game, 142
    example of animation over time, 149
    motion and performance in animation, 41
trace actions, Defender example game, 210
track layer, racing cars game, 228
    multiple tracks enhancement, 255
    use in crash zone creation, 230
Travolta, John, 138
trigger propagation model, 201, 203
triggering events, Defender example game, 214
trigonometric functions, Flash, 29
    See also Math.* functions
    pool game example, 80, 86
        rotating the cue stick, 77
    precalculation and, 200
    racing cars example game, 238
    radians and degrees conversion, 78, 239
trigonometry
    precalculation candidate, 199
    Pythagorean theorem, 75, 79-80
    SohCahToa mnemonic, 239
turn-based logic, 13
turnOn function, dance example game, 147, 148
two-dimensional arrays, Monstachase game, 17

U
undefined variables
    differences between Flash MX and MX 2004, 18, 89
units, setting in the Edit Envelope dialog, 165
universal gravitational constant, 113
Unreal Tournament game, 132, 194, 200
update rates
    background stars, 217
    player position, 222
user interfaces. See GUI
users. See players

V
variables
    dance to the music bps variable, 143
    declaring in Flash MX 2004, 89, 244, 251
    descriptive naming, 153
    displaying, 252
    fire-fighting game
        adjusting values by trial and error, 111, 117
        damping factor, 119
    local and timeline, 80
    pool game ball colors, 90
    temporary variables and array elements, 92
vector graphics and Flash retro games, 195
vector point minimization, 34
    example, 35, 37, 40
vectors, velocity as, 85
velocity
    colliding balls, 83, 84
    definition, 82
    fire-fighting game move function and, 110
    representing as a vector, 85
    terminal velocity, 110
    varying using Math.random, 109
viral nature of popular games, 132, 133
volume control
    sound object example, 171

W
Wacom tablets, 34, 37
water magnets. See fire-fighting game
WAV sound file format, 161
    Flash MP3 compression of, 187
    QuickTime and, 162
wave lines, Sound Box example, 175
Web connection speeds, 192
Williams, games manufacturer, 196
    Defender game, 204
wireframe mode
    bouncing ball animation example, 44

X
XML socket technology, 256
Zoom In and Zoom Out
    Edit Envelope dialog box, 165